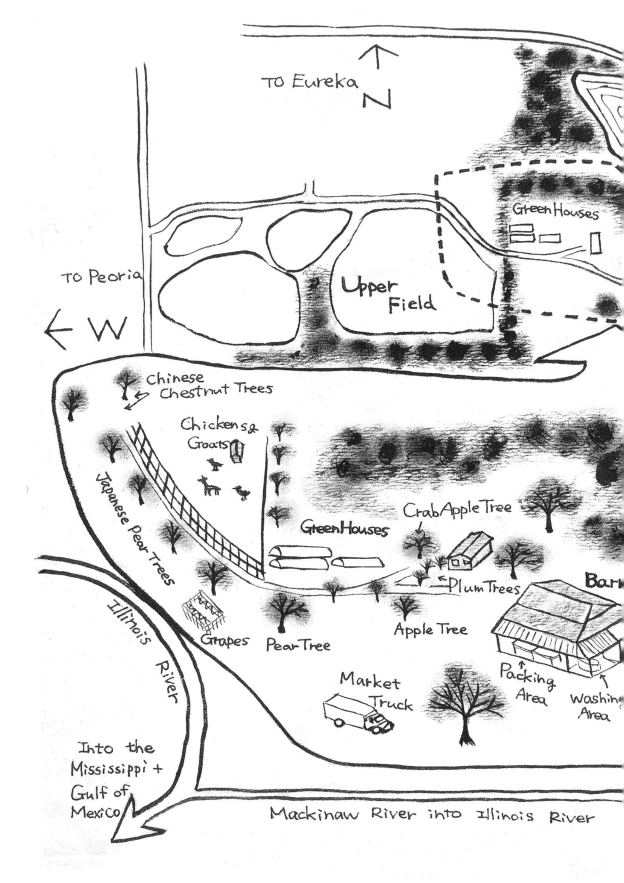

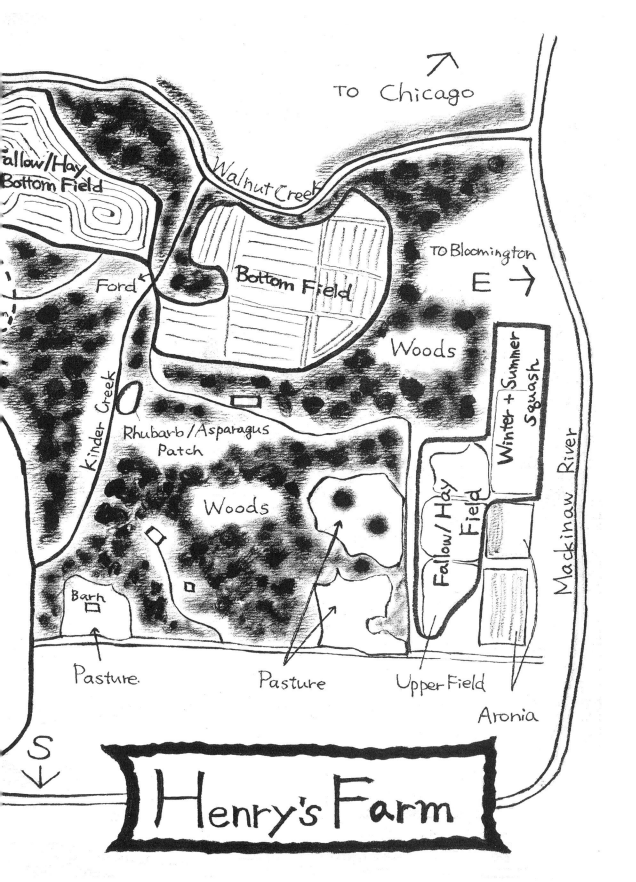

THE SEASONS *ON* HENRY'S FARM

A Year of Food and Life on a Sustainable Farm

THE SEASONS ON
HENRY'S FARM

A Year of Food and Life on a Sustainable Farm

TERRA BROCKMAN

A Surrey Book

AGATE

CHICAGO

Printed in the United States.

Trade paperback edition ISBN-13: 978-1-57284-115-4, ISBN-10: 1-57284-115-X

The Library of Congress has cataloged the hardcover edition of this book as follows:
Library of Congress Cataloging-in-Publication Data

Brockman, Terra, 1958-
 The seasons on Henry's farm : a year of food and life on a sustainable farm / Terra Brockman.
   p. cm.
 Includes index.
 Summary: "Week-by-week chronicle of life on a sustainable farm, with culinary, historical, scientific, and literary reflections and seasonal recipes"--Provided by publisher.
 ISBN-13: 978-1-57284-103-1 (hardcover)
 ISBN-10: 1-57284-103-6 (hardcover)
 1. Organic farming. 2. Organic farming--Illinois. 3. Sustainable agriculture--Illinois. 4. Cookery (Natural foods) 5. Brockman, Terra, 1958- I. Title.
 S605.5.B76 2009
 635'.048409773--dc22
                    2009019432

10 11 12 13   10 9 8 7 6 5 4 3 2 1

Many books, especially this one, flow from the work of others. Throughout the book I've made mention of favorite passages from many writers, including those in my own family. The following are the sources of other authors' works: on page 86, the excerpt from Aldo Leopold's "Goose Music" essay is from *A Sand County Almanac: With Essays on Conservation from Round River*; on page 157, the excerpt is from Chapter 38 of Henry James's *A Little Tour in France*; on page 169, the last two lines of Robert Frost's "Putting in the Seed" is from *Mountain Interval*; on page 173, the passage is from the Moncrieff translation of Marcel Proust's *Swann's Way*; on p. 203, the excerpt from E.B. White's essay "The Pageantry of Peas" is from *One Man's Meat*; on p. 207, the pea soup recipe is adapted from *Vegetable Soups from Deborah Madison's Kitchen*; and on p. 297 the sweet potato recipe is from George Washington Carver's article entitled, "How the Farmer Can Save His Sweet Potatoes and Ways of Preparing Them for the Table."

Photos by:
Terra Brockman: pp. 35, 59, 65, 72, 86, 90, 95, 98, 102, 108, 111, 116, 121, 124, 127, 131, 133, 132, 138, 143, 146, 153, 157, 160, 169, 176, 198, 205, 224, 240, 267, 282, 284, 295
Glenda Kapsalis: pp . 14, 44, 69, 77, 165, 228, 255, 273
Ginny Lee: pp. 18, 24, 48, 182, 200, 232, 262, 277, 290, 300
Renée Mullen: pp. 82, 121, 150, 211, 246
Edible Chicago: p. 188

Map by Hiroko K. Brockman

For Marlene and Herman, who instilled a love of family,
nature, food, farming, thinking, writing, and fighting the good fight to make
this earth a better place for those who will come after us.

And for Henry, without whom there would be no Henry's Farm,
and no The Seasons on Henry's Farm.

And for all my other siblings, nieces, nephews, and in-laws,
who enrich my life in more ways than I can say.

ACKNOWLEDGMENTS

I want to thank the following:

Henry Brockman, Herman Brockman, Zoe Brockman, Teresa Santiago, and Gabriela Santiago, for the use of excerpts of their writings.

Sandra Steingraber, for scientific and writerly rigor, inspiration, and advice, and for Midwestern caring and keeping in touch.

Scott Sanders and all the Sanderlings at Wildbranch who read my early attempts and helped launch this project.

Deborah Madison, for walking the fertile earth of the "flyover states" and writing the foreword.

Yoji Yamaguchi, who reappeared in my life at exactly the right time and was always there with honest words and practical assistance when I needed them most.

Hiroko Kinoshita, for her beautiful endpapers and chapter heading illustrations.

Glenda Kapsalis, for generously donating the cover photograph of Henry's Sungold tomatoes.

Renée Mullen, Ginny Lee, Glenda Kapsalis, and Edible Chicago for providing wonderful photos to illustrate life and work on Henry's Farm.

Doug Seibold and all the good folks at Agate, for putting up with my delays and obsessions, and for recognizing, and in the end accepting, that I am a "putter-inner," not a "taker-outer."

Joel Smith, for feeding me in more ways than one, and making this and so much more possible.

If I got things wrong in here, and I'm sure I did, the fault is wholly my own.

TABLE OF CONTENTS

FOREWORD by Deborah Madison   **13**

INTRODUCTION   **17**

I. **HUNTER'S MOON (November)**   **21**

  Week 1. Garlic Descends   21
    Pockets-Full-of-Garlic Soup   26
  Week 2. One Turkey Gets Lucky   29
  Week 3. Icy Harvest Arrives   37
    Gailan Miracle   52
  Week 4. Wabi-Sabi Prevails   53
    Frost-Sweetened Kale with Garlic   60

II. **LONG NIGHT MOON (December)**   **63**

  Week 5. Garlic Sleeps   63
  Week 6. Seed Catalogs Bloom   67
  Week 7. WINTER SOLSTICE: Time Stretches   71
  Week 8. Goose Music Continues   75
  Week 9. Christmas Guesses   81
    Teresa's Priceless Apple Crisp   87

III. **OLD MOON (January)**   **89**

  Week 10. Plastic Lapses   89
  Week 11. Winter Keepers   94
    Traditional Winter Apple Wassail   96
  Week 12. Digging Deep   97
    Roasted Root Vegetables   100
  Week 13. Calves Birthed   101

IV. SAP MOON (February) — 107

Week 14. Hog Heaven — 107

*Chris Pandel's Grandmother's Lazy Pierogies
with Fresh Italian Sausage* — 112

Week 15. Ice Storm Provides — 115

Sautéed Shiitake Toasts — 117

Week 16. Wood Work — 120

Week 17. Hoophouse Dreams — 123

V. WINDY MOON (March) — 129

Week 18. Invisible Corner Turned — 129

Week 19. Hoophouse Sprouts — 132

Week 20. Ramps Up — 137

Ramp and Goat Cheese Pasta — 140

Week 21. SPRING EQUINOX: Patchwork Emerges — 141

Week 22. New Life Borne — 144

VI. GRASS MOON (April) — 149

Week 23. Wind Sprints — 149

Week 24. A Good Egg — 155

Eggs a la Nabocoque — 158

Week 25. Bees Buzz — 159

Week 26. Drakes Mount — 162

Pan-Fried Duck Cracklings — 166

VII. PLANTING MOON (May) — 167

Week 27. The Enchanted Planting — 167

Week 28. Asparagus Rising — 171

Roasted Asparagus with Olive Oil and Balsamic Vinegar — 174

Week 29. First Harvest 175

Week 30. Floating Love Letters 179

VIII. ROSE MOON (June) **185**

Week 31. Breathing Sweetness 185

Week 32. Stealing Potatoes 190

Boiled Stolen Potatoes 193

Week 33. Allium Hankerings 196

Asian Chive Pancakes 197

Week 34. SUMMER SOLSTICE: Hot Winds Blow 199

Week 35. The Pageantry of Peas 203

"Waste Not, Want Not" Pea Soup 207

IX. THUNDER MOON (July) **209**

Week 36. Garlic Ascends 209

Smashed Garlic Potato Therapy 213

Week 37. Ripe and Rotten 216

Teresa's Simplest Peach Melba 219

Week 38. Fencing Lesson 223

Week 39. Bean by Bean 227

*Joel's Italian Flat Beans with Sweet Onion, Garlic,
and Maple-Glazed Ham* 229

X. GREEN CORN MOON (August) **231**

Week 40. Corn Porn and More 231

Green Corn with Marjoram Butter 236

Week 41. Aronia Comes Home 238

Teresa's Aronia Juice 242

Week 42. Watermelon Heaven   245

X-Melon Salad with Anise Hyssop   251

Week 43. Basil Daze   251

Week 44. Hard Harvest Times   258

Frozen Tomatoes and Frozen Tomato Sauce   264

XI. FRUIT MOON (September)   265

Week 45. Prodigal Fruits   265

Henry's Autumn Pear Salad   269

Week 46. Freeing Roots   270

Mrs. Takayasu's Kimpira Gobo
(Stir-Fried Burdock with Carrots)   274

Week 47. AUTUMN EQUINOX: Three Dog Night   275

Week 48. Blackened Basil   279

Courtney's Fried Green Tomatoes
with Corn Meal and Thyme   280

XII. HARVEST MOON (October)   283

Week 49. Ozark Gold Comfort   283

Grandma Henrietta's Pumpkin–Raisin Bars   286

Week 50. Resurgent Greens   288

Sweet Dressing for Spicy Autumn Salad   292

Week 51. Sweet Potatoes Cure   292

Sweet Potatoes No. 3, Baked in Ashes   297

Week 52. Garlic in the Dark   297

INDEX   302

FOREWORD

by Deborah Madison

WHILE TOURING FOR MY BOOK ON AMERICA'S FARMERS' MARKETS, *Local Flavors*, I returned to the heartland—otherwise known (and sadly so) as the flyover states—where I had visited many fine markets. That's how I found myself at a crossroads in Illinois, with endless cornfields on one side, barren land on the other, and a small sign that read "Henry's Farm" by the side of the road. Nothing about the simple sign hinted at the entanglement of complexity that makes up the fabric of what I've come to think of as the enormous life of a small farm.

When I finally did get to Henry's Farm, the land dipped, the road curved and sloped under overhanging trees, and row upon row of flourishing crops emerged, quietly tended by a crew of family and workers. The flatlands were gone. Texture had appeared, and I can still savor the bright tastes of the simple lunch I enjoyed with two of Henry's sisters, Teresa Santiago, who grows fruits and herbs a few miles away, and Terra Brockman. Since that visit, I have continued to follow the life of Henry's farm through Terra and Teresa's weekly e-newsletter, which has taught me and more than a thousand others not only about the vagaries of farm life and its perennial dance with weather but also about farming itself—about soil, water, varieties, and the multitude of inter-related factors that determine how good food comes to us.

Terra Brockman helps farm the family's land, so her story comes deeply out of her—and the farm's—life. *The Seasons on Henry's Farm*, a book to be reckoned with, lifts you high enough to witness the tremendous possibilities people are capable of expressing in their working lives—in this case, through farming. If you're a fan of Aldo Leopold, or have long suspected that time-honored methods of farming are best for the earth (and our taste buds)

*The land-
scape of
Henry's Farm
is further
revealed in
the things
that grow out
of it—such
as this sturdy
fennel bulb,
full of earthy
sweetness.*

and require intelligence and thoroughness exceeding the levels demanded by most occupations, you will discover here that your suspicions are well founded.

Although Terra Brockman seldom uses the word "sustainability," *The Seasons on Henry's Farm* tells the story of what it looks like when a farm and its family come as close as they can to living a sustainable life. Real sustainability is a complex thing. It's big and minute at the same time. It's hidden but also obvious. It depends on stamina and ingenuity in lieu of fossil fuels. It tests everything and is a tough master. Nothing is concealed in this kind of farming. It's all there—ambitions and hopes, beauty and forgetfulness, and sometimes painful steps to ensure a harvest. (Henry is forever working extra hours at the end of the day, to the point where you want to scream at the pages, "Henry, go have supper!" But it's work that has to be done.)

The Seasons on Henry's Farm is an exhilarating story of observation. It's a humbling one, too, for few of us can imagine mustering the endurance and precision needed to farm this deeply. But that Henry and his familial band of followers can and do, again and again, makes the world of the farm more than a dream or an ideal. It's a great encouraging kick in the pants for all of us, regardless of how we spend our time or what we do, to achieve such excellence in full consciousness of all its complexities and consequences. This book tells a tale as raw and vivid as one could hope for, while gently imparting what we need to know about the soil, plants, and animals that sustain us.

Finally, it is a relief to enter a world where the seasons are not just four of equal duration but are supple times aligned to accommodate one's work and nature's rhythms—say the two-week season for planting garlic in November or the few-days-long season for mulching it over the first icy crust of December. The broad strokes so often used to paint life's portrait have their use perhaps, but they can't capture the fine lines, shadings, and shadows that emerge from the keen knowledge of the whole of our world and all of its seasons.

Terra Brockman has made an enormous painting rendered in the finest detail. *The Seasons on Henry's Farm* hints at what and who we need to be in order to live in concert with the world we wish to know most deeply. The greatest possibilities of human life are expressed not on those flat crossroads where the sign to the farm stands but in the irregular world of slopes and curves—a world of many seasons, and not just four.

—*Deborah Madison*

INTRODUCTION

THIS BOOK, IN THE BAREST TERMS, IS ABOUT 52 WEEKS OF LIFE ON A diverse, sustainable farm in central Illinois. It's the place where I grew up, and the place I couldn't wait to leave.

And leave I did—first to the West Coast and then on to Japan for five years and New York City for ten. But I come from four generations of Illinois farmers on my father's side and untold generations of landless peasants in southern Italy on my mother's side. So the gravitational forces exerted by a patch of fertile earth were hard to resist.

Central Illinois is where my paternal grandparents were born and farmed and where my mother and father and half of my siblings now live. I have three sisters, all younger (Beth, Teresa, and Jill) and two brothers, one older (Fred) and one younger (Henry). Jill lives on the farm where my grandfather and father were born; Teresa raises more than 70 varieties of fruits and dozens of herbs near Walnut Creek in the small town of Eureka; and Henry grows more than 650 varieties of vegetables on 10 acres bordered by Kinder Creek and Walnut Creek, just a few miles downstream from Teresa.

The pull of these people and this land eventually became too intense to ignore, and so, after decades living in major metropolitan areas around the world, I returned to Congerville, Illinois, population 350. That is where this book is centered, in a place that now centers me: my brother Henry's farm.

His farm is nestled in the nation's heartland, midway between the towns of Bloomington and Peoria and midway between the cities of Chicago and St. Louis. It is located in the Mackinaw River Valley, a mecca of diverse organic and sustainable farming hidden in the rolling hills of a small river valley in the middle of the flat, chemical–industrial corn belt that stretches for hundreds

To the west, just behind the treeline in the distance, is Kinder Creek—and hidden beyond that, the fallow field. The fertile bottomland, on both sides of the stream, is an ancient river bed.

of miles in all directions. By contrast, Henry's bottomland fields are nestled in a sheltered bowl surrounded by oak and hickory forests, and his upper fields look out over a panorama of forested bluffs and fertile valleys crisscrossed by waterways.

This book grew out of the weekly *Food & Farm Notes* e-mails I began writing in 1998 to let Henry's customers know what was happening on the farm each week and what was coming to market. Slowly, the *Food & Farm Notes* evolved to include my sister Teresa's "Fruit & Herb Notes," my geneticist father Herman's "Earth-Science Notes," and various contributions from my nieces Zoe and Gabriela. The *Food & Farm Notes* gradually gained an audience beyond Henry's market customers, as people forwarded them to friends and relatives around the world.

Getting immediate feedback from readers at the market week after week made me realize that people were not as interested in what was coming to market as they were in the details of its existence. Where was it grown? By whom? How? I learned that people had a deep longing for earthly details: the quality of light in the fields, the smell of newly mown hay, the sound of frogs in the evening. And they wanted farming details, too. How does Henry manage to get fresh greens to market after the temperature falls below freezing? How do the dogs guard the sweet corn from ravenous raccoons and the lettuce from marauding deer? How did one lucky tom turkey avoid his preordained fate? Slowly, I came to understand that the *Food & Farm Notes* were fulfilling something deeper than the need for food, or even the need for knowledge about how food was raised. They were feeding the hunger for connection—a connection to the source of all sustenance, the earth, and the people who work it.

While most of this book takes place during a single 12-month period, there are a few forays into other years—even other generations—but all are fitted into a single calendar year. Writing the *Food & Farm Notes* year after year let me see the remarkable consistency of the cycles of nature, and that they *are* cycles—circles—without a beginning or end.

The question then became where to start this story. My somewhat arbitrary answer is to begin in November—because it's my favorite month, the month I was born, and most importantly, because it's when we plant the first crop of the season. Instead of calling it November, though, I hearken back to the "moons" of Native American lore, which describe recurring phenomena in the cyclical calendar of nature. We begin with November's Hunter's Moon, move through the summer's Thunder Moon and Green Corn Moon, and end with autumn's Fruit Moon and Harvest Moon. Each "moon" has been beautifully illustrated by Henry's wife, my sister-in-law Hiroko Kinoshita.

This book is tightly focused on one place and one extended family—my own—but it concerns ecology, economy, philosophy, literature, religion, politics, and more. One of my aims is to show how all of these things interrelate, and how each one of us, when we eat, becomes part of the cosmic cycle of life and death via the plants and animals that provide us with our daily sustenance.

This book is also an invitation to eat great food grown by people near you who love the land. That's why I've included recipes featuring produce as it comes into season. These are family favorites, all of them quick and simple: quick because life on the farm is busy, and simple because when you have the very best ingredients, you want to taste them undisguised.

Finally, this book is an invitation to see each week as its own season, and to return to cyclical time, the time of nature and of sustainable agriculture, which mimics nature. It is an invitation to recognize that growing good food does not have to mean destroying soil or polluting air and water, and that we can eat well and live well and still leave this earth a better place than we found it.

White-tailed Deer

I. HUNTER'S MOON

WEEK 1. **Garlic Descends**

NOVEMBER STARTED WITH A WEEK OF FIRSTS. THE FIRST HARD frost. The first glaze of gold hitting the ends of oak branches. The first V of geese leaving an audible wake in the autumn sky. The first deer on the road, fine neck curved back, graceful even in death.

And then, on our way down to the bottomland, I heard Henry muse, "This might be the first year we won't get the garlic in."

Not getting garlic in would be a first. But getting it in is also a first—the first planting for the next season's crops. We plant garlic at the beginning of November, under the Hunter's Moon, when all the other crops are coming out of the ground.

But much of this growing season had been wet and cool, and planting in general had only been accomplished in the nick of time through a combination of luck and preparedness. With most crops, you have a number of windows of opportunity, and you actively space out plantings across the season to have new lettuce (for example) maturing every week. For much of the season, you can just as well plant carrots or beans or lettuce one week as the next. But garlic is an all-or-nothing proposition. You plant it all at once in the fall, and you harvest it all at once in the summer. Or you don't.

This might indeed be the first time in Henry's 16 years of raising garlic that he won't. If the soil remains too wet to plant, we will have no garlic at all for the next season. The garlic we saved back for seed will instead go into sautés and sauces. This is not such a bad fate for garlic in general, but it would mean that a decade and a half of our careful selection of the biggest and best garlic heads—those best suited to our particular patch of earth   would be lost. We would have no green garlic to sell at the market next May and June, and no dry bulbs to sell the rest of the year. Worst of all, we would be back at square one the following fall—purchasing commercial garlic from the seed catalog rather than planting our own stock, which has adapted itself to our soil, our climate, our *terroir*.

The 10 percent of the total garlic harvest that we hold back to use as seed adds up to about 3,000 heads—roughly half each of the soft-neck and hard-neck varieties. This seed garlic has been hanging in long strands from the barn rafters ever since we dug it in early July. We try to hang it out of the way of traffic, but the barn is so well trafficked that it's pretty much impossible. After conking your head a few times on a low-dangling bunch, you learn where you need to duck.

Each strand consists of five bunches, and each bunch has 20 garlic plants. The bunches are tied each one to the next, so they cascade down in vertical sheets of repeating garlic. The plan is to break the 3,000 heads of garlic into some 40,000 individual cloves, and plant them all—except for the very small cloves and any that may have gotten moldy over the humid summer—for next year's crop.

Normally, Henry waits for the first week of November to plant to ensure that a late October warm spell won't encourage the garlic to send up its green shoots early just to be killed off by the winter cold.

This year, however, he decides to plant as soon as a window of dry soil opened and to take his chances with any ensuing unseasonable warmth. So for the last two weeks of October, he follows each day's weather forecast closely. But every time the soil is a few days from being fit for planting, another rain comes. With each passing day, cooler air means less evaporation, and as each day shortens and the angle of the sun's rays fall lower in the southern sky, so do our hopes.

At this point, it seems the field will never dry out enough for the annual garlic planting. But on Friday, as we spend the day harvesting for the Saturday farmers' market in Evanston, a warm wind begins to blow, reviving our dying hopes. Henry judges the soil nearly dry enough, and says that with any luck, we should be ready to start planting immediately after returning from the market Saturday evening.

Our luck doesn't hold. It rains most of Saturday. Not only do we have a meager market day, but we also watch our window of opportunity slide shut once more. On Sunday, the field is far too wet to even contemplate working it. Monday and Tuesday are cloudy, and the weatherman forecasts a cloudy Wednesday as well. So we go to bed with scarcely a glimmer of hope.

Nevertheless, the first thing Henry does on Wednesday morning is go down to the field to check the soil. The verdict is the same: too wet to plant. And so the day fills with other chores—moving the cows to a new pasture and digging some of the last potatoes. Then, without warning, the cloud cover cracks open and the sun pours through. At the same time, a breeze picks up, and so do our spirits. We can almost see the soil getting drier by the minute.

Henry reins in our enthusiasm and waits until noon to check the part of the field set aside for next year's garlic patch. He grabs a harvest knife and jabs three or four inches into the soil near the west side of the field, where the sun has been hitting the longest. He picks up a handful of the loosened earth and crumbles it through his fingers, feeling for stickiness. It falls apart easily, so he moves to the center of the field and uses the knife to loosen more soil. He picks up another handful and rubs the soil between his palms to see if it forms a ribbon or crumbles apart. No ribbon.

So he moves on to the east side of the field, where the sun has just started to warm and dry the soil. He needs to be sure that working the moist soil will not destroy its structure and turn it into lumpy mud, which will turn hard as rock when it dries. So he loosens another patch of earth and rubs it back and forth between his palms. When he opens his palms, he finds a loosely formed ribbon that crumbles apart when he pokes at it with his finger.

Henry swipes his hands along his thighs with satisfaction and calls to the apprentices, "No break today. Just grab a bite to eat, then come back down to plant garlic."

While they eat, Henry rough-tills the beds to open them up and let more moisture escape. Meanwhile, his longtime farmhand Matt and I take the old pickup to the barn. Matt, tall and thin as a beanpole, scrambles gracefully up the rickety ladder. He has been with Henry for eight years, helping tend the vegetables from March through November, and then making art from December through February. The two endeavors are in constant interaction, with ideas and materials from the farm flowing into his art, and with him lending more than a touch of his art to the way he reaches high into the rafters to cut the baling twine holding the long strings of garlic. He is quiet and thoughtful, and he bends low to make sure I have hold of the bottom-most garlic bunch before he lets go.

As the heavy strand of 100 heads travels from heaven to earth, I catch a middle bunch and then carry the swag to the waiting truck, lay it in the bed, and return to the barn for the next one. As I carry each swag to the waiting truck, I think about the garlic's round trip—not ashes to ashes and dust to dust, but from summer to autumn, truck to truck. There is always death involved in the daily life of a farm, and in the daily life of the world, but in general, the movement is from life to life.

With a third of the curtain of garlic dismantled and the truck bed full, Matt and I drive down to the field, where Henry's wife, Hiroko, and the apprentices are waiting as Henry tills the beds three inches deep. He has attached three clamps to the back of the tiller, and the clamps draw straight lines over the smooth bed to guide us as we plant three rows per bed. As soon as Matt kills the engine, everyone grabs a big string of garlic and walks down a row, laying garlic every few feet so one is always within easy reach. We then fall to our knees, breaking apart bulbs and plunging each clove an inch down into the yielding earth.

Head bent to the task, I breathe in the yeasty aromas rising up from the freshly tilled earth and the sweet woodsy smells descending from the forests surrounding the field. The next time I look up, I see that Clare Howard, a local journalist, and her partner, photographer David Zalaznik, have joined us. Agricultural reporting in the Midwest is generally a recitation of statistics and weather, but Clare seeks out the largely untold stories of local sustainable agriculture. In the field, she shadows each person, asking questions as we work. A few weeks later, we read her description: "Farmhands stoop low over the ground as they push thick cloves of garlic into loose loam that has lost all memory of chemical fertilizers, pesticides, and compaction." She calls this cradled field both "a throwback and a prayer" and explains that "it's chemical-free, diverse agriculture more typical of central

Pockets-Full-of-Garlic Soup

Garlic planting signals both an end and a beginning. The sabbath begins at sundown. The phoenix rises from the ashes. Life, some say, begins at death (which is true, at least insofar as fungi and bacteria, those vital decomposers of dead matter without which life would be impossible, are concerned). At the end of one long exhale, the inhale begins. And what better to inhale on a cold dark evening than a bowl of garlic and onion soup to celebrate an ending, a beginning, or both? While planting garlic, we take the tiny cloves too small to grow into big bulbs and put them in our pockets. We end up back in the house with every pocket nearly bursting with garlic cloves.

> **3 tablespoons butter**
>
> **2 cups chopped onions**
>
> **¾ cup cloves garlic (about 30 small ones), peeled**
>
> **2 tablespoons all-purpose flour**
>
> **5 cups chicken or vegetable broth, homemade, from boullion, or canned**
>
> **1 cup half-and-half**
>
> **½ cup dry sherry or white wine**
>
> **1 teaspoon dried thyme**
>
> **1 teaspoon dried sage**
>
> **1 small bay leaf**
>
> **3 slices old-fashioned white bread (or 2 medium-sized cooked potatoes)**
>
> **Salt and pepper, to taste**

Melt the butter in a large pot over medium heat. Add the onions and garlic. Cover; cook until the onions are tender but not brown, stirring occasionally, about 10 minutes. Add the flour; stir 2 minutes.

Add the broth, half-and-half, sherry, thyme, sage, and bay leaf. Bring to a boil, then reduce heat and simmer gently, uncovered, until the garlic is very tender, about 15 minutes. Remove the bay leaf.

If you have one, use an immersion blender to purée the bread into the mixture in the pot, or instead, purée the mixture and the bread together in several batches in a conventional blender until smooth and then return the batches to the pot. Season with salt and pepper.

Rewarm the soup over medium heat and serve. Croutons and/or small pieces of pan-roasted ham make an excellent garnish.

Illinois a century ago. It's also an environmental and economic pro-totype for global survival in an era of accelerating carbon emissions, erratic weather patterns, and commercially raised produce shipped thousands of miles from field to plate."

The repetitive actions soon become automatic—reaching for a head, breaking it apart, and placing each clove into the ground five inches from the previous one, blunt end down, pointy end up. I re-member that when Zoe and Kazami were very young, my dad told them that if they put them in the other way around, then next spring the garlic would emerge not in Congerville, but in China. As the af-ternoon sun warms us, I shed layers of clothing—first my jacket, then my hooded sweatshirt, and then my shirt. I get down to my long un-derwear, an old red union suit, and sweatpants, but I'm still hot. I take off my boots and socks to sink barefoot into the soft earth for the last time this season.

The next time I look up, I see a compact, curly-headed, 13-year-old package of fearless life force hurtling down the hillside on a blur of bicycle. Henry and Hiroko's youngest child, Kazami, has just gotten off the school bus, and he races down to help us. Whenever he or his sister Zoe or brother Asa come into the fields, it's like switching on a light in a dim room. You didn't notice before that the room was dim, but with the light on, everything becomes brighter and clearer, and the work becomes lighter and full of laughter.

In five-inch increments, the augmented team moves down one 200-foot-long bed and up the next. We plant row after row, working our way through the New York White, Russian Red, German Extra Hardy, Inchelium Red, Sicilian Silver, German Red, and Kettle Riv-er Basin. Except for the Sicilian, each of the garlic heads is tightly wrapped, with layers of paper skin strong as packing tape. Every so often, you hear a grunt of effort as yet another head is broken open.

When my dad helped us plant garlic in previous years, he used a screwdriver to help his arthritic hands do the task, wedging the tool into the center of each head to force the cloves apart. This year, he hasn't been in the field as much. After a sickly childhood, he's enjoyed some seven decades of excellent health. Now, as he approaches his seventy-third year with a host of undiagnosed symptoms, he is more frail and weak. I find myself beginning to feel the long, slow slide as well, in my knees and hips and in fingers that aren't as reliable in garlic deconstruction as they once had been. As I break the heads into their constituent cloves, my thumbs begin to feel bruised, and Dad's screwdriver seems like a very good idea.

The sun begins to sink toward the lip of the hill at the western edge of the natural bowl that cradles the bottomland fields. Chill air rolls down the hillside, seeping into the soil and into my soles. I run to the edge of the field to put my socks and boots back on. Back to planting, I realize I'm still cold, and the next time I reach the end of the bed near the stream, I put on my shirt and hooded sweatshirt, saving the jacket for my next return trip.

The team has nearly finished the last tilled bed, but Henry is tilling another, so he sends Matt and me up to the barn to bring another load of garlic down. When we return, it seems like someone has sped up the movie. Everyone is planting faster, racing against the turning clock of the earth, which is like a tide lapping at our heels as we try to outrun it. The weatherman is certain that tomorrow will bring rain, so this afternoon is our one and only chance to plant garlic this year. We have put more than 20,000 individual cloves in the ground, but thousands more await.

Clare has asked her questions and taken her notes, but she lingers like a girl on the sidelines at her first junior high school dance. Finally, she asks if she can help us plant, and we welcome her into our ranks.

The horizon suddenly gulps the sun, but a tangerine glow lingers in the sky. Henry tills yet another bed, which, even if we could complete it, still wouldn't be the end of the garlic we saved back for planting. It feels good to have accomplished what we have over the past six hours, but it seems a pity the task has not been completed.

As we leave the newly planted field, I glance back like Lot's wife—not the one in Genesis, but the one in the poem by Anna Akhmatova. That wife looked back at the place where she was born, where she had sung and worked, and she doesn't mind paying the penalty, if a penalty must be paid for looking back lovingly at one's home. I look back, with just the barest light still hanging in the sky—just enough to make out the white confetti of garlic husks and stems left scattered over the black earth. The first crop of the next season is in the ground, and to celebrate, the earth is decked out in black tuxedo and white tie for the evening.

WEEK 2. **One Turkey Gets Lucky**

I CAN'T QUITE SAY WHY, BUT DURING MY FIRST YEAR BACK IN CEN-tral Illinois, after nearly two decades of living in major metropolitan areas in the U.S. and abroad, I decided to raise turkeys. This was before my life was taken over by the Land Connection—the educational nonprofit I founded in 2001—and the turkey-raising was taken over by my sister Teresa.

Teresa is the fourth of the six Brockman siblings, the one I was jealous of when we were growing up for her beauty and kindness. She is slender and fine-featured, with dark hair and eyes that reflect our mother's roots in southern Italy. Even as a young adult, I was jealous of her and the charmed life she seemed to lead: marrying a doctor, having three beautiful girls, living overseas.

But things are often not what they seem. Many right things are proven wrong in this world, and many wrong things are proven right. Although it now seems abundantly clear that I was, in fact, the petty and insecure older sister, and that Teresa had made a bad match, she and I may never have become close except for the fact that her marriage ended. This "bad thing" led Teresa to find a house surrounded by five acres for herself and her three girls just five miles north of where Henry, our parents, and I live. And that led to a very good thing—her farming career. The very next spring, she started planting fruit trees, berries, and herbs. Within a year, she had established her own business, Teresa's Fruits and Herbs, and began a local CSA in addition to selling at the Evanston Farmers Market.

"CSA" stands for community-supported agriculture, although I have often thought it would be more accurate to call them "ASCs," for "agriculturally supported communities." It is a direct farmer–consumer arrangement in which people "subscribe" to a farm by paying a set amount of money at the beginning of each year, just as they would for a magazine subscription. Instead of receiving reading material each week, they receive eating material. Every CSA arrangement is slightly different: Teresa provides a different type of fruit nearly every week for a total of 18 weeks. Henry provides seven to nine different vegetables each week for 26 weeks, ending the week before Thanksgiving.

Although Teresa's enterprise is primarily a fruit and herb farm, she also raises flowers, goats, hens, and bees—plus about 25 turkeys a year, to help provide fertilizer and pest control. They range freely under her fruit trees by day, fertilizing the ground while feasting on dandelions, grass, rotten fruit, and bugs of every description. Each night, Teresa herds them into moveable pens to keep them safe from predators. After they are fully grown, and their fertilizing and pest-controlling work is done, they become holiday dinners for the extended family and a select few market customers. Similarly, although Henry's farming operation is predominantly vegetable production, he also raises chickens and goats—again, mainly for the fertilizer they churn out—with the side benefits being meat, milk, and eggs.

Because they pair crop-growing and animal husbandry, Teresa's and Henry's farms, as well as many of our neighbors' organic farms, mimic the symbiotic relationships between plants and animals in the natural world. For nearly all of the 10,000 years we humans have been engaged in agriculture, farming has involved a mix of plants and animals for the simple reason that plants feed animals, and animals feed plants. In nature, large herbivorous mammals coevolved with grasslands. The animals' manure fed the plants, while the plants fed the animals. At the same time, the animals' grazing allowed a variety of plant species to maintain viable populations. Some research shows that ungrazed vegetation tends to inhibit the germination and growth of plants by using up most of the available water and mineral resources in the soil and by producing large amounts of thatch.

From the dawn of civilization until the early part of the twentieth century, most U.S. farms integrated both crop and livestock operations because the two were highly complementary, both biologically and economically speaking. Like all their neighbors, my grandparents raised wheat, oats, alfalfa, and corn to feed both animals and humans, along with cows, pigs, horses, chickens, ducks, geese, and sheep to feed the crops with manure, as well as to feed the humans with milk, eggs, and meat.

In contrast to this elegant system with proven long-term sustainability, today's livestock farmers have a manure problem, while grain farmers have a fertility problem. A confined animal feeding operation with, for example, 100,000 pigs, produces as much sewage as a town of 100,000 people, but the farm's sewage is untreated. This means that by doing the right thing, according to the experts, and going to a factory model of efficient meat production, a livestock farmer has a waste problem—animal manure stored in lagoons that foul the water and air. On the other side of the coin, grain farmers who heeded the expert advice of university ag schools and the policy directives of the U.S. government (most notably, Earl Butz's exhortations to "get big or get out" and to plant from "fencerow to fencerow") now have fertility problems. To get their corn to grow, they must purchase fertilizer in the form of anhydrous ammonia made with vast amounts of natural gas. This fertilizer is not just increasingly expensive; it's also a major source of pollution of groundwater, and the major culprit in the pollution of surface waters that have created the enormous dead zone in the Gulf of Mexico. Thus, a mutually beneficial arrangement with complementary solutions, where plants feed animals and animals feed plants, has turned into two intractable problems.

Luckily, here in the hills of the Mackinaw Valley, our "poor" timber soils and rolling terrain meant that it was impossible to "get big." Because it was not possible to farm thousands of acres of row crops, many small, diverse farms continued to have both grains and livestock, which enriched the economic and environmental quality of the farms and the community. Instead of buying commercial fertilizers, our neighbors spread the manure from their livestock over their grain

Since nearly all Broad-Breasted White turkeys are dispatched while young, it is rare to see a fully mature adult tom (male) like this proud, though slightly tattered, fellow we named Lucky Tom.

fields. Henry uses composted manure from Dad's cattle—collected during the winter—to maintain the fertility of his hoophouses, which must produce thousands of seedlings each year without benefit of fallow time or legume cover crops. The manure is always composted at high temperatures, so by the time it is applied, all pathogenic bacteria have been killed. Teresa uses the high-nitrogen fertilizer of composted turkey droppings to keep her fruit trees thriving.

Although many people have commented on how stupid turkeys are—the classic statement is that they are so stupid that when it rains, they look up to see what's happening and drown (which, in defense of turkeys, I must say I have never seen happen)—I suspect they are a lot like people. When they are in a bad environment, they are recalcitrant and appear dull-witted. But when they are in a lush and stimulating environment, they are lively and engaged. You can hear this in the turkey conversations taking place under Teresa's fruit trees, which are full of chirps and whistles, purrs and clucks and cackles, and even gobbles.

Back when I first raised turkeys, I had 50 of the factory farm-standard Broad-Breasted Whites and 50 heritage breeds, consisting of 25 rare Bourbon Red and 25 even rarer Narragansett birds. I got them in the mail (yes, the U.S. Postal Service delivers chicks, or "poults," as baby turkeys are called) and made them comfortable in a big cardboard box in my basement, with a heat lamp hanging overhead in place of the warm breast of a mother, a feeder and waterer, and plenty of wood shavings to absorb their droppings. This would be their home for the next few weeks, until they were big and hardy enough to move into the coop outdoors, and eventually out into the pasture.

Everyone falls in love with the bright-eyed fluff balls that are baby birds. I am hesitant to share them with people who consider any cute animal a pet and recoil at the notion that it will become dinner. But when Brian and Natalie, two chefs from Chicago, came down to visit, they wanted to see the turkeys. So I brought them to the basement and showed them how to hold one—cradling its feet under one hand and cupping the other over the top of the bird, barely touching, so as not to squeeze the life out of the delicate creature. I left them there cooing to the baby birds while I went out to do chores. When I came back, they announced they'd named one of the birds.

"Oh, no, you can't do that," I said. "We don't name birds we're going to eat."

"But that's why we named it Dinner," they said.

And so it was that little Dinner and his cohort led a bucolic life for the next 24 weeks, growing tall and strong on organic feed (grown and mixed by our neighbors, Dennis and Emily Wettstein) and a pasture full of delicious plants and insects. The birds grew quickly and soon became like unruly teenagers, wanting to go where they wanted when they wanted. The fast-growing Broad-Breasted Whites were soon too heavy to jump or fly, but the heritage breeds were leaping over the four-foot fence with a single bound. We clipped their wing feathers so they wouldn't fly off into the trees to roost at night—there, they most certainly would have been eaten by raccoons or other varmints. But even so, their powerful legs, plus a little flap of their ineffectual wings, brought them up to the top of fence posts and other roosts.

Eventually we decided that, for their own good, we'd put them into mobile coops we could drag along the ground to new pasture each day. As Thanksgiving Day grew near, the males began fighting, less from their ability to read the future than from the hormones of puberty. I would often return in the evening to find a number of the males with wounds on their heads and necks after a day spent working out the literal pecking order. There was not much that I could do, except look forward to the day when it would all be over.

There is only one poultry processing plant left in central Illinois, and it's about three hours east of us, in the Amish community of Arthur. Our neighbors Larry and Marilyn Wettstein (Denny and Larry are cousins) raise a lot more poultry than we do, so I had arranged to combine my turkeys with theirs and use the same processing date. Just after dark on the evening before that date, the turkeys had settled into their lethargic nighttime state. Larry came over with the lowboy trailer and backed it up to the moveable coop. That's when I saw that my turkeys' planned date with destiny had come one day too late.

The males had been at each other worse than ever before, and two bloodied birds were down in a sad, feathery heap, unable to get to their feet. I grabbed each of the other birds, one by one, and handed them to Larry, who put them in the trailer. At night, even the most feisty or nervous turkey turns mellow and docile, so we quickly got all of the able-bodied birds into the trailer. Then I turned to the two casualties. Now that the tormentors were gone, one of them seemed to be recovering. I got him to drink some water, and found that he was shaky, but could stand. So I handed him up to Larry, and he, too, went into the trailer for the night.

Then I tried to get the other bird to come around. Although he would eat and drink a little when I coaxed him, he could not stand. Even when I lifted his body up, put his legs right under him, and slowly lowered him onto his feet, his legs collapsed underneath him. I showed Larry, who concluded the turkey had a broken leg, and that the surrounding tissues were probably too damaged to make him a good candidate for anyone's Thanksgiving dinner. We closed up the trailer, and I put the crippled critter into a box and drove it over to my Dad's barn.

I spread some new straw in a stall, and put a waterer and some feed in the corner. I gently placed the turkey there, facing him into the corner where he could easily reach the food and water by stretching his neck a little. Then I went to tell my dad what had happened.

Dad never liked killing anything, but he would grab his gun and run out to the chicken shed whenever we heard a commotion that meant a fox or other predator was nearby. But never once did I hear the gun go off. Although my Dad butchered chickens when we were younger, for the past 15 years or so, the chicken killing has always fallen to Henry. You would think that once you've killed one sort of domesticated fowl, you're pretty much able to kill any of them, but for some reason, this is not quite so in my family. We've never killed a goose since one late fall day when we were teenagers. On that day, Henry and Dad went out to butcher a goose for the family. As they lay its long neck across the stump in preparation for the descent of the hatchet, it looked up at them with, as Dad said, "blue eyes like angels." In an Abrahamic moment, Dad asked Henry what he himself was thinking.

"Do you want to take it back to the barn?"

The geese are good watchdogs, raising a ruckus whenever something disturbs the peace.

Henry nodded, and the goose was spared. Since then, members of the flock of geese my father keeps have fallen to predators, but never to the hatchet.

So our kindhearted father agreed to check in on the damaged turkey, and give it feed and water when he did his morning and evening chores. I told him I didn't expect the bird to survive, but if he could make it comfortable in its final days, that would be good. And if it lived, we'd have to find a time when Henry could kill it, and then decide whether it was fit to eat or not.

Then I was off to meetings and other business, and the next time I dropped by Dad's, weeks after the other birds had met their maker, I saw a big tom turkey trailing after him as he did the chores. The turkey was a little unsteady on his feet, lurching from side to side like a person with a bum leg. But he was purposeful in his movements, following my father just like a farm dog.

"Is that the turkey?" I asked, not believing it could possibly be the lame bird I had brought over.

"Yep," he said. "A miraculous recovery."

That evening I told Teresa the story, breathless with amazement.

"Oh, that's the oldest trick in the book," she scoffed. "The day before going off to slaughter, a turkey suddenly goes 'Oh! My leg, my leg! I can't walk!'"

"No, really," I said. "He couldn't. His legs wouldn't support him at all."

She shook her head in disbelief that I could be so naive. "No, you just got one smart bird. That's one lucky tom."

So I began calling the big bird Lucky Tom. Whenever Dad went out, Lucky Tom would come to greet him with friendly, burbling chirps and purrs. Then he would trail slowly after him as he did his chores. As he got older and heavier, Lucky Tom moved more waddlingly, but his featherless head stayed a healthy bright blue and pink, with fleshy caruncles and a bright red snood hanging down over his beak.

No one knows for sure what the snood and caruncles are for, but it is widely assumed they are attributes to attract mates. Lucky Tom never got *that* lucky, but over the years, the beard of long hair-like feathers in the middle of his chest grew longer and longer, and he seemed prouder and prouder of it as it swayed from side to side. Wherever Dad would go, even outside the pasture, there was Lucky Tom. It was an interspecies kind of love, perhaps one of those that still dares not speak its name, but one that warms the cockles of the caruncles and the snood.

WEEK 3. Icy Harvest Arrives

WE RISE IN DARKNESS AND DON THE VESTMENTS OF THE season: long underwear, undershirts, T-shirts, flannel shirts, sweatshirts, hooded sweatshirts, sweaters, sweaters, sweaters, coats, rain gear, hats, and scarves. If ever there were a week of "so much to do and so little time," this would be it—the week of the last CSA delivery and the last farmers' market.

There are stages and phases to the end of the season. And as with nearly all endings, there are varying degrees of reprieve, although we know the ultimate conclusion: this world of verdant life will end not in fire, but in ice. Due to the bitter cold forecast for the end of the week, this will be our last chance to harvest vegetables to sell at the last market, provide to our CSA members, and keep the extended family well fed all winter long. And so we begin the seven-day marathon that will end only when we pack the last empty crates back into the truck after the last market in Evanston on the Saturday before Thanksgiving.

Shakespeare wasn't talking about this epic week, or even about farming, when he wrote about that "tide in the affairs of men, which taken at the flood leads on to fortune," but he could have been. Most people know that farmers have to make hay while the sun shines (or the rain will ruin your hay and you won't have anything to feed your livestock over the winter), but fewer know you have to harvest everything out of the ground before the last great freeze.

Gardeners who plant only heat-loving summer crops, such as basil and tomatoes, and wake to find them blackened and limp after the first night in the mid-thirties often assume that frost equals death. But although that first September frost lays the basil low by causing the water within the cells to freeze and burst the cell walls, other greens shake it off and begin employing a number of biochemical strategies to stay alive.

The hardiness of most vegetables gradually increases in the fall and early winter in response to the shorter days and/or the low temperatures. No plant can survive the formation of ice within its cells, but cold-tolerant plants devise ways to ensure that the only water that freezes is outside the cell walls. In this process, water inside the cell migrates outside the cell wall, where it can freeze without injuring the plant. As water moves out of the cell, sugars and protein molecules become more concentrated within the cell, forming a natural antifreeze. Pure water freezes at 32 degrees, but a strong sugar–water solution may not freeze until the temperature reaches the teens. We have already had countless nights below freezing through October and November, and several nights down in the low twenties, yet the lettuces and chois are still doing fine. But we know the plants' natural antifreeze can only preserve life so long. Once the nighttime temperature falls into the mid-teens, which the weatherman said will happen this Thursday night, even the most hardy crops will succumb.

So we are taking Shakespeare's advice to heart this week, "taking the current when it serves," and harvesting out as much as we possibly can. Although we will dig, pull, pluck, cut, wash, bunch, wet down, and pack from before sunup until after sundown each day, the week will not be a haphazard flurry of activity. Henry orchestrates our harvest activities as carefully as a top cyclist and his team plan out their strategy for each stage of the Tour de France.

The plan for this week is finely tuned to match a cold front followed by a brief warming just before the coming of the season's first frigid Canadian air mass, which will lower the final curtain on our harvest. The work will begin on Sunday, with an early harvest of CSA greens plus the harvesting of freeze-sensitive root crops in order to get them in before Sunday night, when the temperature will reach the low thirties.

Monday, we will dig out all the remaining potatoes, wash them, and set them out to dry overnight; the low temperatures will be in the high thirties, so the drying potatoes will not freeze. Tuesday is set aside for digging all the carrots, parsnips, salsify, leeks, and scallions. On Wednesday night, temperatures are forecast to bottom out at 18 degrees, so Wednesday will be the day to harvest all the greens for market. Any greens left in the field at the end of the day will be toast, or rather, compost. Thursday is the day for pulling any remaining hardy roots, such as beets, rutabagas, fall turnips, and winter radishes, and for digging any carrots or potatoes missed on Tuesday.

It is supposed to get down to the low teens Thursday night and then only up to 32 on Friday, so the ground will freeze. Any roots left in the soil will freeze, too—except for those with high levels of natural antifreeze, such as parsnips, sunchokes, and burdock root. These can be left in the ground all winter and dug up in the spring in perfect condition. But any other root we leave in the frozen ground will rot when thawed out.

All week, our eyes will be on that final deadline of Thursday night, when the cold air mass coming our way will put an end to this season. From the perspective of Sunday morning, that finish line seems impossibly far away. Except in extraordinary circumstances, Sundays are a day of, if not complete rest, then rest combined with housework and deskwork, and not field work. Henry and Hiroko earn extra money by translating Japanese news articles into English, mainly on Sundays and through the winter. So Sundays are usually the time to sleep in a bit, and then spend the day at the desk or kitchen table, translating, answering e-mails, paying bills, and reviewing the past week's field notes.

Not so on this Sunday before Thanksgiving. It truly is the time when, as Shakespeare wrote, "wasteful Time debateth with decay," or more simply, as our Grandma Henrietta would put it, "waste not, want not." She was usually talking about wasting food or money, not time, but if we were to waste a moment of this week, we would have less to sell this Saturday, and we would also most likely run out of storage vegetables over the winter and would want for them in the spring.

Of course, Grandma had a saying for every occasion. She just as well might be scolding us with, "What you gain on Sunday, you lose on Monday," as she was a staunch believer in the Day of Rest, but at this time of year, I think she would be lending her capable hands to our urgent work. She is about to turn 101 and is slowly fading away in the Lutheran nursing home in Danforth, but her spirit seems close by as all the family members and apprentices get up hours before dawn to converge at the barn.

The CSA delivery is always on Tuesday evening, and all season long, the CSA shares are harvested on Tuesday morning. At this time of year, however, we cannot take even a single day for granted, and besides, we can easily keep everything crisp and fresh until the Tuesday delivery. The CSA this year has 186 full shares, which serve about 230 local families. That means we need to harvest 186 quarts of Japanese turnips, 186 quarts of potatoes, 186 bunches of arugula, 558 heads of lettuce (each share gets 3 lettuces this week), 372 bunches of choi (each share gets 2 chois), and some 500 pounds of roots so each family can choose from Chioggia beets, daikon, burdock, sunchokes, and radishes.

When we reach the bottomland, Henry sends us off in pairs to harvest the cold-sensitive roots, which are those with exposed shoulders—the Japanese turnips, daikon and other winter radishes, celery root, leeks, and scallions. Like lovely ladies in strapless evening gowns, these roots are the most susceptible to the cold. The soil is warmer than the air now, so the underground portion of the roots are fine. But when the nights get down into the twenties, the shoulders sticking up above ground begin to freeze. They thaw during the day, and the plant keeps growing, but once they're frozen like that, the root won't store nearly as long, and the frozen part loses some flavor and texture.

As I pull the turnips, their cold white shoulders seem to be affecting mine. I try to ignore the cold and work on finding the most efficient rhythm—pull, tear, and toss into the box; pull, tear, and toss; repeat. But the cold keeps seeping in until finally it lodges in, of all places, my collarbones. I think, "I've never felt cold there before," and a phrase comes floating through my frigid brain: *edad de las nuncas,* the "age of the nevers." I heard this from an author I worked with in New York who had lived in Mexico for many years. She was then about my age now, and she explained that you know you've arrived at the age of the nevers when you start to say things like "I never felt this pain in my knees before," or "Until now, I've never had to get up at night to go to the bathroom," or "I've never felt cold in my collarbones before."

Henry's counsel for just about any such complaint is to work faster. The quicker you move, the warmer you'll feel—and, of course, the more food you'll harvest.

When the turnips are done, we start in on the winter radishes—black, rose-heart, German beer, and Japanese daikon. We break off their tops as we go and put the loose roots in boxes. We do the same for the Chioggia beets the CSA members will choose from. Root crops store best with their tops removed. If the leaves are left on, they pull water and nutrients out of the roots in order to keep growing, making the root begin to shrivel and turn mushy. So we quickly tear off the tops and leave them in the field for the fungi and bacteria to work on.

All morning long we fill box after box. Sometimes the boxes are so heavy it takes two of us to haul them to the end of the row. The exertion and the rising sun cause us to gradually slough off our outer layers of clothing. Every hour or two, Matt drives the pickup around the field to collect the crates of roots. He stacks them two or three layers high in the bed of the truck, lashes them down with rubber bungees, and drives back across the creek and up the hill to the barn. He unloads the crates and stacks them near the wash area, where Henry will do all the washing after dark, and immediately returns to the field.

Around 11 a.m., Henry sees that the white frost has melted off the leaves and stems. He pinches a few stems of turnip greens and chois and determines it's safe to move from harvesting roots to greens. Leaves that are just frosty on the surface will go all limp and mushy if harvested while still frosty, but they'll be fine if left to thaw first—perhaps because water that migrated out of the cells has then had a chance to migrate back. Leaves and stems that have frozen solid, on the other hand, will remain soft and spongy to the touch and are not suitable for bringing to market. I have never seen the mechanism of limited resurrection elucidated anywhere, but my theory is that had we tried to harvest the greens just a few hours earlier, we would have mashed ice crystals into the plant cells, rupturing them and causing the greens to turn mushy, with no hope of ever returning to their crisp former selves. But having waited patiently for the extracellular ice to melt, the plants can now be harvested without damage.

Most of the late-autumn greens—the different chois, kales, turnip greens, mustard greens, rapini, and lettuces—are very cold-tolerant. They may look fragile and delicate, but they will not be fatally harmed until the temperature falls into the teens. Fatal damage is hard to detect in these greens, because they don't turn black like the frost-sensitive basil or tomatoes. As a matter of fact, from a distance, they look just fine, but when you go to pick them the leaves are limp and the stems are spongy. At a certain temperature, despite the antifreeze, the water in their cells finally turns to ice and bursts the cell walls.

Lettuce, which the uninitiated generally assume is a tender green, is actually one of the most cold hardy. Long after the chard and turnip greens have been damaged by frost, lettuce is looking good and tasting even better. One year, an apprentice asked Henry which was better, the spring lettuce or the fall lettuce. Henry immediately said the fall lettuce, because it is thicker, crunchier, sweeter, and has a more developed character. When a plant is forced to overcome hardship, whether due to insects or weather, it develops amazing flavor and more nutrients. For vegetables, this is the result of perseverance through adversity—a sign of true character.

We, too, persevere, and perhaps better develop our own characters as we harvest the turnip greens, mustard greens, rapini, chard, and lettuces. As dusk falls, we begin to don the multiple layers of clothing we'd shed earlier. As the evening chill settles in, our fingers and toes turn numb. The bitter irony of this week is that, although it is the coldest harvest week of the year, we can't wear mittens or gloves. We need all our manual dexterity, compromised as it is by the cold, to dig, pull, cut, wash, bunch, and box.

As darkness descends, we head home to food and warmth, and we leave Henry alone at the wash area, dunking the greens and spraying the roots to wash the mud off. Two or three hours later, everything has been washed, and Henry loads the full crates on the truck. He leaves the truck door open a little on this first night to let the cold air in and bring everything down to as close to 32 degrees as possible.

"The great thing about this time of year," says Henry, "is that the whole world is a refrigerator." At 32 degrees, plant metabolism is extremely slow, and the vegetables keep all their nutrients and crispness for days. But if the temperature falls below 32, everything in the truck will freeze.

"The bad thing about this time of year," says Henry, "is that at night, the whole world is a freezer." Frozen produce in the field is one thing, but once picked and then frozen, resurrection is impossible.

On Monday morning, Henry gets up around 5 a.m. and immediately goes outside to shut the truck door. This will hold the cold in as the day warms to the forecast high of 55. The thermometer outside my kitchen window says it's 32 degrees, exactly what the weatherman predicted for our low.

It's still pitch dark outside, but with so much to do and so little daylight to do it in, Henry uses the predawn hours for barn chores such as shelling popcorn and cleaning garlic, the daylight hours for field work, and the post-sunset hours for washing vegetables. Our day's work begins under the cold fluorescent barn lights, with Henry as the master garlic braider and the apprentices and family serving as his prep team. We sit on hay bales with piles of the last hard-neck and soft-neck garlic all around us. The rafters are bereft, but we're happy that most of the seed garlic is nestled in the ground, and the remaining garlic for sale and for our winter use is piled at our feet. Some of us are cleaning the hard-neck bulbs for bulk sale at the market, while others are preparing the long-stemmed soft-neck garlic for braiding. I grab a dried soft-neck garlic plant and pinch it lightly, near where the stem joins the bulb. Then I pull upward along the entire length of the stem to remove one layer of dry stem, leaving plenty of supple stem for braiding. I use my

thumbnail to scrape away a layer of dirty skin around the bulb. Once the outer layer is gone, the perfect white paper below glows like old parchment, sometimes with accents of red or purple.

The cleaned garlic goes into a bushel basket, which, as fast as we fill it up, Henry empties out on the hayrack. He works the garlic into short braids of 12 heads and long braids of 18 heads. He also makes decorated braids in which he weaves in colorful straw flowers, globe amaranth, or statice. This year, he is making some holiday garlic braids with evergreen sprigs and red cayenne peppers woven in. And for the first time, he is making a few super-long braids with 40 heads each, stretching four feet in length, hoping to sell them to true garlic lovers.

One of these true garlic lovers is John Swenson, a Renaissance man who is a historian, singer, and point man for alliums and hot peppers at Seed Savers Exchange. John has been shopping at the Evanston Farmers Market for years, and he often brings Henry unusual varieties of alliums to try out. Because of John, we are perhaps the only farm in North America producing rare alliums such as rakkyo and Mongolian chives. We also grow John's Speckled Roman tomato, a variety he developed by crossing Antique Roman and Banana Legs. Those tomatoes, and all the rest of the summer crops, are long gone, but many are in suspended animation in our freezers—a little bit of the summer waiting to be revived on a cold winter's night. We need our chest freezers and Henry's storage pit to get us through the winter without committing what Henry calls "a sacrilege"—buying produce from the store.

An hour or so after daybreak, we brush the garlic skin from our clothes, stamp our feet to get the blood moving, and go down to the field to dig the last of the potatoes. Potatoes are the priority today, because, unlike the other roots, they will rot if put away wet. So after spending most of the day digging up over a dozen different varieties and washing them, we lay them out in trays to air-dry before boxing them up.

The warm front has brought in cloud cover. The late afternoon light grows yellow, then gray; soon, only the outlines of barren trees are visible. We pack up and go home to warm showers and hot food, while Henry is again stationed at the wash area until long after dark. Returning home, he glances up and is reassured to see the cloud cover is still unbroken. We'll have another mild night, with a low in the high thirties.

The air is still warm Tuesday morning, but we feel a change coming. It is cloudy, rainy, and blustery. Henry says that today we must dig the rest of the roots. This will clear the decks for the Great Greens Harvest on Wednesday, which must be done before the killing cold comes on Wednesday night. The day before any really cold weather hits is typically cold and blustery, like today, because the cold front is pushing out the warm front. Once the cold front arrives, the weather will turn clear and dry, and that's when the temperature drops drastically at night.

Just after sunrise, after we've worked on the garlic for only an hour, Henry says it's time to go down to the field. The temperature is in the low fifties, but in addition to the clouds and gusty winds, we now have on-again, off-again light showers that quickly leach away our body heat. Luckily, digging carrots, parsnips, salsify, and sunchokes is good aerobic work that keeps us warm, even in the rain. Except for our hands, that is.

I work with Matt on the carrots. He loosens the roots by stomping the digging fork as deep as possible next to the carrots and then prying back until the carrots heave an inch or two out of the soil. I follow behind, pulling the roots from the ground by their tops and breaking off those tops with one hand, while in the same movement throwing the tops onto the field and the roots into a crate. This is normally one of the few jobs that can be done while wearing gloves, but the rain has turned the dirt to mud, which sticks to gloves and makes them unusable within minutes. We rotate jobs so I get a chance to warm up a little from the digging before going back to fighting with the cold mud. We usually try to schedule jobs like this for dry days, but we no longer have such luxury.

Storage carrots grow slowly over a long season. By fall, most are two inches in diameter at the top and more than a foot long. They are sweet and crunchy and will easily last until spring in a refrigerator or the coolest part of your house—basement, garage, or back porch—as long as the space doesn't fall below freezing. Henry stores all of our winter roots in a deep pit out in the field that he constructs after the season is over. When one of our Evanston Farmers' Market customers asked for the best way to store roots, Henry mentioned the perfect temperature and humidity of his storage pit and inspired the person to dig a hole in her suburban lawn. As I pull the carrots and toss them into the box, I imagine root cellars making a comeback as a fossil-fuel–free way to keep vegetables for months.

We continue digging and filling crate after crate, tossing in mud-heavy roots with our cold-numbed hands. Matt then brings pickup load after pickup load back up the hill to the wash area for Henry to work on after dark.

We wake on Wednesday to 35 degrees and a light coating of frost on everything in the lower field. The day will be calm and sunny, and we expect a high of 45 degrees. After that, the mercury will fall precipitously to a fatal low of 18 degrees overnight. All the greens need to be harvested, washed, and put into the back of the truck by this evening, but we cannot start the harvest until the sun has had time to heat the air and melt the frost on the greens, allowing them to be harvested safely. We work longer in the barn this morning, cleaning garlic and preparing popcorn. By the time we leave for the fields, the air is much colder than it's been the past two blustery days, but it's calm and sunny and dry, and we feel relatively warm.

Henry deploys the troops with understated urgency, telling each person where to go and what to do. We work as fast as our cold hands will allow, starting with the chard, arugula, mizuna, cilantro, and dill, then moving on to the dandelion greens, lettuces, mustard and turnip greens, and finally, the most cold-tolerant greens—the chois, napa cabbage, rapini, kales, and collards. This way, if we don't finish before sundown, at least all that will be left will be the most hardy greens.

All year long, and even on the previous Sunday when we harvested for the CSA, we bunched the greens as we harvested them. Now there is no time to waste wrapping a twist-tie around each bunch. More importantly, if we harvest without bunching, everything keeps better as it waits out the days before market. Because the greens will sit in boxes for a few days, we put them in upright. If we were to lay them flat, as we would on a summer harvest day, they would soon bend upward.

In the plant world, as in the human world, there are various kinds of "tropisms," or yearnings. I have yearned for a quiet life of meaning, but so far, the quiet part has mostly eluded me. Things are simpler in the plant world. Heliotropism, or phototropism, is what causes plants like sunflowers (most obviously) to turn toward the sun. You've probably noticed this even among houseplants that turn toward your windows.

Another tropism, this one first described by Darwin, is geotropism. Darwin noted that plants detect the earth's gravitational pull; their roots respond with positive geotropism, while their leaves and stems respond with negative geotropism, moving against gravity. This means that if greens are laid horizontally in a crate, they will seem to levitate, moving against gravity and curving upward in the box. In order to not have the greens bent at a right angle when they arrive at market, we put them in the crates with their cut stems down and their leaves up—their gravitational orientation exactly as it had been in the field. This vertical position is even more important for the cilantro, dill, turnip greens, and mustard greens, which are pulled up by the roots to keep them fresh as long as possible. As long as they are kept moist and cool, they will hardly notice they are no longer in the earth.

We harvest the chois and kales late in the day and continue until we are doing it more by touch than by sight. On these short days, we seem to go directly from the slowly rising to the slowly setting sun. At some point, you notice things are less distinct and you glance up, surprised to see it's nearly dark.

In early fall, Henry washes the just-harvested burdock (left) and black radishes (right), and prepares to load them into the truck for the weekly CSA delivery to more than 200 families. In the background, winter squashes cure on a hayrack in the bright autumn sun.

Henry starts washing at around 5:30 and finishes up around 8:30. But as he is putting the last crates of clean vegetables onto the truck, he notices ice forming close to the truck door, which means the temperature inside the truck is very close to 32 degrees already. That's fine during the day, but it signals danger at night. With stiff hands and aching shoulders, Henry pulls all the crates from the previous three days of harvesting out of the truck, dunks each one in the water tank to warm it, and restacks them back in the truck. Our well water comes from hundreds of feet underground, and it's always 50 degrees. Back in the 100-degree days of summer, this water felt ice-cold, and we used it to wash and quick-chill the summer produce and to revive ourselves. The same well water now feels positively warm, being some 30 degrees warmer than the air. Now we are using the well water not to take the field heat out of the greens, but to put some of the warmth of the earth's core back into them. Vegetables hold on to a lot of water, and it takes a long time to cool that water down—even when it's 20 degrees outside. Feeling better about his vegetables' ability to survive the night, Henry puts a thermometer inside the truck and closes it up.

At 10 p.m., home at last, Henry has a quick meal and checks the weather radio. A low in the high teens is predicted, so Henry sets his mental alarm clock to wake up around 1 a.m. to check the temperature in the truck. It is a good thing he does, because—as he tells us the next morning—the thermometer read exactly 32 degrees. He plugged in the electric space heater and ran it at the lowest setting. When he checked again at 4 a.m., the temperature was up to 38, so he turned the heater off and went to the barn to get an extra-early start on the garlic.

He's been working for hours when I awake. Before I even get out of bed, my nose—the only part of my body outside the blankets— knows that overnight the clouds were pushed along by the cold front, which is here at last. I get to the barn by 7 a.m. and Dad is there, although he should be at home looking after himself. He reports that the overnight low slipped down to 18, and that tonight will be even colder. The high, he says, may get to 40 today, but only 32 tomorrow. That means *everything* else in the field must be harvested out *today* and put into the market truck, where it'll be safe from freezing until it reaches the market.

We put on all our extra layers of clothing today, but we still feel the chill and pull our hats lower over our foreheads and wrap scarves around our necks as we head down to the fields. The apprentices begin digging sunchokes while Matt pulls rutabagas, Henry pulls radishes, and family members work on the beets and turnips. Hour by hour, row by row, and bed by bed, we work our way through the root vegetables—an exercise in mind over matter as our extremities go numb.

Finally, the setting sun brings an end to our last harvest day, and we drag our nearly frozen bodies inside to warm up over hot soup in front of the fire. Once again, each apprentice, family member, farmhand, and friend moves into his or her own island of warmth and light while Henry stands alone in front of the wash tank. Everything takes longer to wash when it's very cold, because the frozen mud sticks tight. Over and over, Henry lifts four crates full of muddy roots into the washing tank and stacks them two on two. He lets them soak to loosen the frozen mud as he turns to the crates he's just lifted out. He sprays the vegetables as he slowly tumbles them from the dirty crate into a clean one, and then hefts the clean box of roots onto the truck. When he is finally done with the last box, he sprays water over the entire truckload of veggies, tucks them in with tarps, turns on the space heater, shuts the truck doors, and hobbles home.

Once in the warm house, his hands are so stiff with cold that he can't unbutton his rain coat or unlatch the suspenders on his rain pants. He calls to Hiroko for help, and she scolds him gently for letting himself get so cold.

"You're not a young man any more," she says.

Tomorrow comes too soon. Judging by the thickness of the ice on the water buckets, Dad says, it had to be close to 15. Today's high is only to be 32. It is too cold even to work on garlic in the barn, so we move into the basement instead, where we bag popcorn and finish up the last of the garlic. When the temperatures outside are getting up close to 32, we move out to the garage. This is where we will bunch all the greens we picked loose in the field. We begin by unloading all the boxes from the truck into the garage, then we get some twist-ties and start in on a stack—grabbing a handful of greens, pulling off any bad leaves, and making bunches of the right size.

It's impossible to bunch and twist the twist-ties with gloves on, so our fingers quickly turn red, then swollen, then numb working with the icy wet greens. Although the garage is about 50 degrees, the vegetables come off the truck at around 32, so it's almost like handling ice. When our fingers refuse to function, we run our hands under warm water or rub them together over the space heater. When your hands are this numb, you don't feel warmth but rather pain as your tissues slowly come back to life. We bunch all day long and into the night until we are done.

The evening before leaving for the last market, Henry sits over dinner, eyelids drooping, feeling the weight of the whole week of pushing to get one more bunch of greens, one more box of roots—feeling the air cool as the sun drops, knowing there is more to be done. The saving grace is that the last Evanston Farmers' Market starts at 8 a.m. rather than 6 a.m., which means we can arrive at 6 a.m. rather than 4 a.m., so we can wake at 3 a.m. rather than 1 a.m.

I always sleep fitfully before market—not trusting the alarm clock, and waking every hour or so thinking 1 a.m. has arrived. Henry used to have this problem, too, until he hit upon his sleep mantra. Hiroko wakes before he does to fix his once-a-week cup of coffee, so before falling asleep, he intones, "If I don't wake up, Hiroko will wake up." Then if, say, Matt and I are going to market that week, he continues. "If Hiroko doesn't wake up, Terra will wake up. If Terra doesn't wake up, Matt will wake up. If Matt doesn't wake up, I'll wake up. If I don't wake up, Hiroko will wake up ..." and round and round he goes until he falls asleep.

Soon, 3 a.m. is here, and we get up in darkness one last time and climb into the cab of the big box truck. I always bring a pillow and sleep at least an hour or two en route. Henry drives and thinks and plans. He tells me that no matter how tired he is after the harvest day, he is never tired while driving to market. He's mentally juggling the more than 100 different vegetables he has in the back of the truck, and thinking about how to display each to its best advantage.

Energy builds as we drive through the city to the market site. As we tumble out of the truck, the energy goes up another notch as, for the last time this season, we unlatch the back of the truck, push up the big door, and hop up to begin unloading.

First the six 10- by 10-foot tents come off and get set up, and then the homemade plywood tables with their folding steel legs. Next come the crates of produce, each going from the truck to the section of the stand where Henry has determined that item will be displayed—roots on one side, lettuces and salad greens toward the back, Asian greens along the other side, and in the center, bushel baskets overflowing with all the different potatoes, turnips, beets, celery root, and more. One last time, our fingers freeze as we unpack the bunched greens and display them, at Henry's direction, in the upturned crates—chard with brightly colored stems out, curly green kale with leaves out, bunched choi with fleshy butt ends out, and big white daikon radishes in one crate, rough-looking roots of burdock in another.

As we are setting up, before we've even had time to get out the clothespins we use to attach the laminated labels to each crate and basket, the first customers come and greet us. "Hey, Henry! Howya doing?" and "Where did you get all those greens?!" and "Here, we brought you some coffee and chocolate cookies."

Almost always, our first customer is slender, kindly Bud. He materializes quietly. We turn around, and there he is, making his careful selections. Van, who either rides his bicycle or takes the train up from the city, comes around the same time. Then, soon after, Joe and Paul are there with their spaniel, Lancelot. There are hugs and oohs and aahs at the sight of the late-season abundance.

Henry says, "I know we have done as good a job as we could to save as much as possible. We could have gotten more greens if we had had more hands or more hours in the day. But I'm satisfied."

The customers are more than satisfied. Words of thanks wing back and forth over the potatoes, the lettuce, and the rutabagas. They thank us for a season of good food, and we thank them for making it possible for us to keep growing this kind of food. The sense of completion and satisfaction we feel at this time of year stems in large part from the

Gailan **Miracle**
(Basic Stir-Fry with Peanut Oil and Garlic)

On one of our marathon harvest days, the sun set before Henry could pick the gailan *(Chinese broccoli). The next morning, he was disappointed to see that it seemed too damaged to harvest. But lo and behold, by afternoon it had recovered. Somehow, it had repaired the damage to its frozen tissues, and so all of it made it to the last market and on to dinner plates throughout the city as the* Gailan Miracle.

> **1 pound** *gailan* **(Chinese broccoli), or a mixture of different choys**
>
> **2 tablespoons peanut oil**
>
> **1 teaspoon sugar**
>
> **1 teaspoon minced garlic**
>
> **Salt, or soy sauce, to taste**

Cut the *gailan* stems into 1-inch pieces and coarsely slice the leaves.

Heat a wok or heavy frying pan. Pour in the oil. Add the stems and toss over moderately high heat until somewhat softened, about 2 minutes. Reserve the leaves.

Add the sugar, garlic, salt, and soy sauce. Add the reserved leaves. Toss for another 2 minutes and remove from heat. Serve.

symbiotic relationship between us and our customers, who are much more than customers. They are what Carlo Petrini, the founder of the Slow Food movement, calls "coproducers." It's true that their hands do not work the soil, plant the seeds, hoe the long rows, mulch the potatoes, stake the tomatoes, and harvest, harvest, harvest—but those of us whose hands do the work could not produce this food without their financial and moral support.

Those hands belong to Henry and Hiroko; their children, Asa, Zoe, and Kazami; our parents, Herman and Marlene; farmhand extraordinaire Matt Ericson; the farm's apprentices (different folks each year); assorted drop-in friends and neighbors; and all the people who help us set up and tear down the stand and sell the vegetables each Saturday. All these hands combine with all our coproducers' hands to create a beautifully simple and perfectly transparent food chain that links us to each other and to the earth. They also create a mid-November farm stand that is overflowing with lettuces, collards, napa, kohlrabi, chois, kales, mustards and mizuna, cilantro, dill, brussels sprouts, rutabagas, turnips, carrots, radishes, beets, celery root, potatoes, sweet potatoes, parsnips, salsify, winter squashes, popcorn, garlic, onions, leeks, scallions, sunchokes, burdock root, and the last of the pears—all on a frosty, wintry morning. The trickle of customers suddenly becomes a flood, and there are only a few seconds to talk with each person as we weigh, add, bag, and wish each other happy holidays and a good winter. Our last words are always, "See you in the spring."

WEEK 4. **Wabi-Sabi Prevails**

THE LAST MARKET AND LAST CSA DELIVERY ARE DONE. THE hoophouses are vacant. The truck is full of empty crates. Braids of dry onions and garlic hang from Henry's basement ceiling over boxes of cured sweet potatoes. Stacks of crates filled with potatoes, carrots, parsnips, celery root, sunchokes, beets, turnips, rutabagas, daikon, and burdock sit in the garage, waiting to be transferred to the storage pit within the next month to feed us through the winter.

As if waking from a dream, we look up from this patch of earth and take in the larger world around us. On the one hand, things fall apart, as evidenced by the decaying remnants of vegetable life in the fields and the stacks of broken boxes outside the barn waiting to be fixed or broken down further for firewood. On the other hand, there is beauty—in the stark architecture of the trees and in the gentle gray dawns.

Those two hands are part and parcel of wabi-sabi, a Japanese concept that is hard to translate but is illustrated in the brief life of a cherry blossom, the earthy aroma of autumn leaves beginning to decay, or the emptiness of a field waiting for winter. It is hard to define wabi-sabi in English. In fact, from all I've read and heard, it's not easy in Japanese either. The concept correlates with the core concepts of Buddhism: all things are impermanent; all things are imperfect.

We are certainly imperfect. There are things we didn't get done last week. We left some kale in the field, some turnip greens, several full rows of chois and lettuce, but like good Buddhists, or good farmers, we accept that nothing is perfect, nothing lasts, and nothing is ever finished. And we embrace wholeheartedly the wabi-sabiness of the season, which Henry defines simply as "the beauty of sadness; the sadness of beauty."

This is perhaps why I have always loved eventide and wintertime—the wabi-sabiest times of the day and of the year—and the serene melancholy they bring. It's more complicated than the simple opposition of green life (good) versus black death (evil). It's been a good season, but a long one, and we're tired. As our bodies get older, they become more permeable to cold and damp and all the ills that flesh is heir to. Last week, I sliced my finger while cutting the turnip greens during the harvesting marathon, but I didn't realize it until I returned home hours later, because my fingers had been numb and almost bloodless. If you put yourself into the muddy boots and frozen feet of a person who has been doing hard manual labor out in the fields every minute of daylight for the past eight months—through the brutal heat of summer, through downpours, through freezing rain and wind, hour after hour, day after day, month after month—then you can imagine how pleasant winter begins to look.

The "wa" in wabi-sabi means subdued refinement or solemnity. In Japanese poetry and in the tea ceremony, it came to mean plain, simple, sedate. The best farmers I know are wabi people—quietly comprehending the wisdom of rocks and trees, earthworms and grasshoppers. "Sabi" comes from the character meaning lonely or sad, but when used in wabi-sabi it means the kind of beauty that flows from inside an old object, like the green patina on old copper, or lichens that transform an old rock into a beautiful swirl of patterns and colors.

The rural Midwest is full of wabi-sabi, the result of a half-century of farm policy that has unintentionally decimated farming communities. A drive through the countryside reveals wooden barns and corn cribs slowly collapsing in on themselves, old trucks left to rust behind a shed or in the woods, and here and there in the endless miles of corn and soybeans, a few old trees along the road, erect as tombstones, announcing where a farmstead once stood. The only thing proliferating in these rural communities, it seems, are the graveyards, slowly biting off more of the surrounding fields year by year. This is a thought more bitter than the bittersweet of wabi-sabi.

Wabi-sabi is a fact of nature—apple blossoms break apart petal by petal and swiftly blow away, corn cribs list like drunken sailors and then collapse in a heap, smiles crease ever-more wrinkled skin. These inevitable consequences of time are sad, but also beautiful, as John Donne understood when he wrote, "No spring, nor summer beauty hath such grace /As I have seen in one Autumnal face." Now, in late November, the world shows its autumnal face, and because we know its wintry face is coming, we appreciate it all the more, knowing, as Shakespeare did, that "all that lives must die, passing through nature to eternity."

As I rise each morning and go to open up the coop to feed and water my chickens and ducks, Grandma Henrietta's face floats in front of me. I remember how she always made sure we children thanked the hens when we gathered their eggs. Grandma just turned 101, and she too is impermanent and imperfect, her skin like gauze, hair fine as imagination, bones as beautiful as architecture. Her world has contracted to the size of a room at Prairieview Lutheran Home, which does not have a view of the prairie but of what the prairie has become over her lifetime—corn and soybeans, interrupted only by the interstate. Grandma was named after her father Henry, so my brother Henry is named after both his grandmother and great-grandfather. From a distance, generations are seasons too, cycling in and out.

Grandma cycled in on November 26, 1906, and the seasons of her life were eventful, from horsepower to gasoline engines, from the First World War to all the wars that followed, and from silent movies to the internet. Although Henrietta always claimed that she was "the runt of the litter," she was strong in body and spirit, and has survived all of her 10 brothers and sisters.

In 1927, she married my grandfather, Fred, and they settled in the small town of Ashkum, where they attended the Lutheran church. At that time, the men sat on one side of the church and the women on the other, but Henrietta insisted on sitting in the men's section next to her husband. When the pastor suggested she sit with the women, Henrietta declared, "If I can sleep with him on Saturday night, I can sit with him on Sunday morning!"

Fred and Henrietta moved to Fred's parents' farm northwest of Danforth in 1930 and began farming their 160 acres with mules and horses. They grew corn, wheat, oats, and hay and raised fruits, vegetables, cattle, hogs, sheep, chickens, geese, and ducks. In other words, they had a diverse and organic farm operation, as did all farmers at that time. At the holiday meals she hosted year after year, she rarely sat down until the meal was over. Then we would hear stories—of the past weeks and of many years ago.

Grandma had a taste for the macabre. Or perhaps those are the stories I remember most vividly. There was the one about the little girl who died during the spring thaw, whose grave filled with water so the casket kept floating up to the surface, despite everyone's best efforts to keep it covered with earth. There was the whole family that died in agony after the wife accidentally—Grandma always said *accidentally*, but there was a subtext that carried the opposite interpretation—put strychnine in their breakfast pancakes. There was the hired man who fell from the top of the big hip-roofed barn that Grandpa's father built in 1912. They revived him by dunking him in the horse tank, and then brought him to the upstairs bedroom, where he lingered in and out of consciousness for weeks. Then one day, without warning, he came downstairs for breakfast—a little shaky, but dressed and ready for work.

And then there was the story that always affected me the most (though my siblings say they don't remember ever hearing it)—the tale of the family on its way home from church in their horse-drawn sleigh that encountered a pack of wolves. The wolves leapt up to slash the horses' throats, and the family knew that once the horses were down, the wolves would surely and swiftly kill them all. Terrified, they decided they had no choice but to sacrifice someone, so the mother threw the bundled-up baby out into the snow. Satisfied with this sacrificial offering, the wolves were distracted, and the rest of the family returned home safely. Henry says it's just an old Russian folktale. Maybe he's right, but if it is, it's one I remember hearing Grandma tell, and it still makes my blood run cold.

We are all back safe in our homes now. But although the great vegetable harvest is done, the farm work is not. This morning, our first task is a wabi-sabi one: separating the bull from the rest of the herd, since he too will soon be harvested. Autumn is not only a time to reap plant life but a time to sacrifice animal life as well. Many of our neighbors harvest their winter meat by going deer hunting. We simply separate out one or two animals from my father's herd of cattle in order to feed our families.

Separating one herd animal from the others is not easy, and Henry and Dad have called on all the apprentices, farmhands, and family members to join in the task. I am the first to get to the upper pasture, so I park the truck across the gravel lane to prevent the cattle from trotting down to another of their many pastures when we move them. Our father has created a byzantine system of electric fences over this part of the upper pasture area. If you connect one gate in a certain way, the electricity will run to one pasture, and if you connect it a different way, it will run to another. In this way, the cattle can be easily moved to fresh pasture as often as needed, and they grow hefty and sleek with no grain at all.

After I park the truck, I grab one of the better-looking apples out of the basket of fallen ones I have brought to feed the cattle. It's so cold it makes my teeth hurt, but the sugars have concentrated in its cells—not only preventing it from freezing in the same way that our hardy greens protected themselves but also making it explosively crisp and exquisitely flavorful. I munch the apple as I walk down the lane to the cattle and observe them as seriously as they observe me in the watery dawn.

After my father, I may be the member of the family who loves cows the most. I was 12 when I got my first heifer, Frosty, a Charolais cross. She was stubborn and willful on a scale that has become legendary. I worked with her each day as I did my morning and evening chores, putting the halter on her, brushing her, and resting against her side and listening to the music of her quartet of stomachs. Cattle really do believe the grass is greener on the other side of the fence, and in the spring and summer she stood near the gate, waiting for me to get the halter and put it on her so we could walk together along the roadside.

Frosty turned out to be a good mother, fiercely protective of the fine calves she bore spring after spring. I looked after her through my high school years, but then she became one of my father's additional chores when I went away to college, and then graduate school, and then five years in Japan and eight years in New York. A dozen or so years after I had left home, she had twins two years in a row. Then she stopped, entering a rare phase of life for a cow—menopause. Most farmers bring their cows to the butcher when they are three-quarters or so through their reproductive life, before the likelihood of complications increases. But Dad kept Frosty all the way through her fertile years and beyond, a very un-farmerlike thing to do. Her feet were bad and her teeth were worse—so ground down by decades of chewing grass and hay that Dad began feeding her grain, food she could lick up and swallow without chewing. Although Dad treated her with loving kindness, Frosty was not a pet. But the fellow-feeling that farmers have for the creatures under their care cannot be underestimated. We take good care of them because they take care of us. No, Frosty was

never a pet, but she was the matriarch of our herd, and for that, she got special treatment until her dying day.

I don't remember exactly when Frosty died. I was living in New York when Dad had our neighbor come over with the front loader and bury her. But Frosty's face and frame and temperament are still easy to discern in our father's herd. He has selected cows that calve easily and whose calves put on weight quickly with their mother's milk, lush pasture, and no grain. There is only one reason for this herd, and for domesticated animals in general, to exist—and that is to feed us humans. It is sometimes difficult to convey this to people who seem to have but two file folders under "animals": pets and wildlife. When most folks observe a domesticated animal, such as a cow or pig, they generally file that animal under "pet." While we do care for these animals as if they were kings and queens, they are never pets. They are, ultimately, dinner—often the meat course for our winter dinners.

My reverie is interrupted by the arrival of Matt, the apprentices, Henry, Hiroko, Asa, Zoe, and Kazami. Henry grabs an armload of long sticks from the bed of his truck and hands one to each of us.

Dad gets water for the yearling bulls, who have been separated from the pregnant cows. Each year a few of the grass-fed cattle are slaughtered in December to provide family and friends with meat for the coming year.

Frost-Sweetened Kale with Garlic

Kale and brussels sprouts are the hardiest greens, able to survive until the end of November. Enjoying these last greens is a gustatory example of wabi-sabi, an embrace of the moment itself, impermanent and imperfect though it is, just before the frost that has sweetened the greens kills them. Knowing these are the last fresh greens until the first wild ramps and nettles appear in March and April makes us savor them all the more. This recipe is equally good with turnip greens, mustard greens, rapini, collards, or any of the chois.

> **2 bunches kale (any variety), stems trimmed and coarsely chopped**
> **¼ cup olive oil**
> **3 cloves garlic, chopped**
> **½ teaspoon dried crushed red pepper flakes**
> **Salt, to taste**

Bring a 4-quart pot of salted water to a boil. Boil the kale until crisp-tender, about 10 minutes, and then drain.

Heat the olive oil in a sauté pan. Add the garlic and pepper. Cook over a low flame until the garlic is just barely golden, about a minute.

Add the chopped kale and sauté for 5 to 6 more minutes, or longer, if you like. Add the salt, to taste. Serve as a side dish, or make a meal of it by placing it on toasted Italian bread rubbed with garlic and drizzled with olive oil.

They will help extend our arms' length and our effectiveness in separating out the bull who will become freezer beef—a quarter for Henry and his family, a quarter for Jill and her family, a quarter for Teresa and her family, and a quarter for me and my boyfriend, Joel. The first step toward that end is to move the calves and cows into another pasture, while keeping the bull back in this one. He is nearly two years old and has led a short but peaceful and full life—born and raised right here in these lush pastures, with trees to shade him in the summer and valleys to shelter him in the winter, and half a dozen cows to service.

Out west, cowboys separate cattle quickly and easily with their cutting horses. But we aren't cowboys and don't own a horse of any kind, so we need as many people as possible to form a human fence between the bull and the other cattle. Henry positions us midway between the north end of the field, where the cattle are grazing, and the southeast corner, where the gate is. Then he gets behind the animals and slowly drives them toward us, keeping the bull toward the back as the herd follows their trail up the hill to the corner.

As they reach us, he shouts for us to quickly move in and get between the main herd and the bull. We hold our arms out parallel to the ground, with the sticks increasing our reach, to create the illusion of a fence. For a brief moment, the bull is separated, but then a bull calf breaks through our porous human line. Henry says not to worry, but that we must make sure the bull and bull calf stay behind with us in the pasture as he opens the gate for the cows and other calves. They know this routine, and they trot across the lane over to their new pasture near the aronia bushes. The bull and bull calf stay back, behind our line.

I dump my half-bushel of apples on the ground to keep our captives occupied until the others are out of sight. Over the coming weeks, we'll give the bull treats—more windfall apples, some rotten pumpkins and squash—to train him to come into the small pen just outside the pasture. This is where our neighbor will eventually load him into a cattle trailer and drive the five miles to the Eureka Meat Locker, Illinois's only certified organic processing plant, to be butchered. We wait a few minutes to make sure all the cattle are settled in their separate pastures, and then we turn back to our separate vehicles and to the rest of the day's tasks.

Henry stays behind to walk the electric fence surrounding the pastures. He checks the current by angling a plastic-handled screwdriver against the wire and almost touching the metal pole with it. If the fence is intact and hot, a spark jumps to the pole. If it doesn't, he must find where the fence is broken and repair it. Henry sees no spark, which is not surprising this time of year. It's hunting season, and also the time when the white-tailed deer are mating. For both of these reasons, the deer are on the run, and they often break through the electric wire—sometimes several times a day.

But all of this—the broken fence, the fallen apples, the separated bull—is part and parcel of this wabi-sabi season.

Sugar Maple in Winter

II. LONG NIGHT MOON

WEEK 5. **Garlic Sleeps**

WITH THE GARLIC IN THE GROUND, AND THE OTHER VEG-
etables safely out of it, there's time to breathe. But we are not
quite out of the fields yet. Mulching garlic is the last major outdoor job
of the season. Or it's the first job of the next season.

Last month, after we plunged the garlic cloves into the moist soil,
the earth performed its magic spell, breaking the cloves' dormancy and
causing them to send down bone-white roots. These roots immediately
established each clove's purchase on a portion of soil from which it began pulling in water and nutrients on its way to new life. But now, it's
time to send the garlic back into dormancy by tucking it safely under a
thick blanket of straw mulch for the winter.

Mulch is simply a layer of insulation. If you put it on while the ground is still warm, it will hold the warmth of the earth and keep the ground from freezing. Sometimes we cover root crops with a thick layer of mulch before the ground freezes so we can pull the mulch off a section at a time and dig fresh roots from the ground all winter long. The principle behind mulching garlic in December, however, is to keep the ground cold, not warm.

So Henry waits for a series of clear nights cold enough to cause an icy crust to form in the top inch of soil. That icy crust plays a number of important roles. Physically, it forms a hard surface that will support Henry and Matt as they mulch the field, and they won't have to worry about where they are stepping. Functionally, the ice forms another layer of insulation that will help keep the garlic cool.

Together, the icy layer and the mulch will mitigate the up-and-down bounces in temperatures that characterize a central Illinois winter, where a week of below-zero weather can be followed by a week in the fifties—no matter if it is December, January, or February. Without the mulch, the garlic would also experience that fluctuation of temperatures, and during every warm spell, it would think, "Spring!" and shoot up its green stalk. In the following cold snap, that green shoot would freeze and die back. If the cycle is repeated too many times, the garlic clove will run out of food to fuel new growth, and it will die. Thus, a good mulch improves winter survival. If we mulch at the right time, and do it well, we should see every single clove planted in November send up a strong green shoot come March.

Matt has already moved to his winter quarters in town, but he knows there is one last farm task to be done before he can turn himself over to art for the winter. "Can you be out here at daybreak tomorrow?" Henry asks.

Garlic-mulching day begins with Henry getting up well before the sun. Time is of the essence, because very cold nights are generally followed by clear, sunny days. That sun warms our black soil quickly, thawing the icy layer on top; once that layer thaws, work has to stop. Henry bundles up in many layers because, as he likes to say, "The cold-

est place on the farm is the seat of the tractor." (And in the summer, "The hottest place on the farm is the seat of the tractor.")

Before the sun begins to gently illuminate the eastern sky, he drives the tractor over to the long row of big, round hay bales made from cutting the clover and alfalfa in the fallow field during the summer. He lifts the bales—six feet long, five feet wide, and five feet tall—with the bale fork attached to the rear of the tractor and carries them over to the garlic patch, dropping them at the ends of the rows. All the apprentices have gone their separate ways, and the kids are in school, so as soon as Matt arrives, it's just the two of them in the cold, quiet dawn.

Round bales are made by a baler that rolls up the swaths of mown, dried hay. Now Henry and Matt simply reverse the process. They cut the strings and push and pull on the hay bale, getting it rocking back and forth until, with a final heave, they get it rolling. Once the bale is rolling, they guide it down the rows, right over the top of the garlic protected under the frozen crust. As the bale rolls, the hay sloughs off in a thick layer down the length of the bed. Pushing the heavy bales soon warms their muscles, so the men begin loosening their clothes

Some of the hay cut from the fallow field each summer is used for feeding cattle and goats over the winter, and the rest is used for mulching garlic.

and taking off scarves and jackets. Their gloves stay on, however, since the hay is the same 12 degrees as the air.

Once the hay is rolled out, they grab their pitchforks and go back over it, pulling and forking the thick layer apart to spread it evenly over three beds at a time. They breathe in the scent of summer trapped in the dried hay. Each bale smells different. Ones with lots of oat straw have a hint of molasses from fermentation; those with lots of oat or wheat grains smell slightly of beer; and some others smell like finely aged cigars. As soon as one bale is spread out, Henry jumps on the tractor to retrieve and position the next one for rolling out. Gradually, an even blanket begins to cover the icy ground where the 20,000 garlic bulbs rest in dormancy.

By 11 a.m., even though the air temperature is still below freezing, the ground is getting slippery on the surface where the bright sunshine has melted the ice. As soon as Henry feels his boots break through the icy crust mulching stops for the day so as not to damage the garlic or the soil. They'll finish up tomorrow if another cold night is in the forecast.

As Henry and Matt drive back up the hill, the patch of black earth is now covered with a golden blanket that glistens in the sun. Mulch is a beautiful thing. It suppresses weeds and prevents soil erosion. When the spring rains come, they will leach nutrients from the mulch into the soil, fertilizing the plants. The mulch can also increase the size and overall yield of our garlic bulbs by keeping the soil moist when the hot summer months come. Garlic pulls up huge amounts of water during its growing period, and since Henry doesn't irrigate (except as needed to ensure germination of fall crops in the hottest part of the summer), he needs to keep water evaporation at a minimum. Furthermore, garlic quits growing when the soil temperature reaches 90 degrees, so this mulch is protection not only in winter but in summer as well.

When the soil begins to warm in earnest in March, all of the energy slowly gathered and stored by the roots and cloves all winter long will pour into their green shoots and thrust them up like a rocket, through the mulch and into the sunlight. Each day, the garlic will grow with time-lapse rapidity; by mid-May, the stalks will be two feet tall, and we will be enjoying the first fresh green garlic of the season. But for now, as noon rolls around and we've tucked more than half of the garlic cloves under their straw blanket, we say goodnight, and return to our winter tasks.

WEEK 6. **Seed Catalogs Bloom**

"Mommy, where do tomatoes come from?"

"Well, honey, it all starts in December, when Mommy and Daddy sit very close to each other, reading the seed catalog."

THIS IS HOW A MARKET CUSTOMER CHARACTERIZES THE IM-maculate conception of Henry's tomatoes. It is not far from the truth. After garlic mulching, the final major outdoor job of the season, Henry immediately begins his first desk job: evaluating the season that just ended and preparing for the season that has just begun. He needs to do this quickly so he can be one of the first farmers to get his seed order in, thus ensuring he will get nearly all of the 650 varieties he will be ordering.

We've all heard of glossy "food porn," but seed catalogs are just as seductive, beckoning with bright pictures of fetching red ruffled lettuces and juicy melons of every description. Katharine White, another seed-catalog addict, wrote in her book *Onward and Upward in the Garden* that "snow is falling, but indoors half a hundred catalogs are in bloom."

Before Henry can turn his attention to the stack of 30-some seed catalogs on his desk, he gets out his field notebooks and market notebooks to review the year. These notebooks refresh his memory about everything he grew. He is particularly interested in the varieties he tried for the first time and will decide this year whether to keep them at the same level, increase or decrease their amounts, or eliminate the varieties altogether.

Henry has three field notebooks for the bottom field—one each for the east, middle, and west sections—and one for the upper field.

Each page is numbered and refers to a specific bed within that portion of the field. Thirty-six beds make up an acre, so Henry has some 360 separate pages to keep track of in his four field notebooks. Over 60 percent of his beds are double-cropped, adding to the complexity of the ecosystem of his fields—and to the complexity of the bookkeeping. On each bed's page, he records what was planted there, and when. Throughout the season, he jots down notes: how different varieties germinated and grew, what their productivity and taste quality were, any insect or disease problems that occurred, when the harvest started and ended, and any other data and observations.

After reviewing the field notes, Henry gets out what Matt calls "the Holy Grail," the market notebooks. These would look at home in a library of rare manuscripts. Long ago, the pages relinquished their cutting edges. Today, they are frayed and fuzzed by the many thumbs that have turned them. The three- by-five-inch looseleaf notebooks have six small rings inside to hold the custom pages Henry makes each year. These pages have a line for the date at the top, and then five small columns—for the crop name, amount picked, amount left (written in Japanese—*no-ko-ri*), and then a space for noting which bed they were picked from and their quality.

The main market notebook is quite sturdy as notebooks go—brown vinyl with metal corners—but the folding joint where it opens and closes gave way long ago. The vertical binding has been taped over with green duct tape, and then again at the top and bottom edges with blue duct tape. The colored tapes were then covered at some later date with a three-inch wide strip of heavy, clear packaging tape running vertically over the outside cover and then the inside cover. This tape is covered in earth and specks of plant matter. It's not pretty, but like everything and everyone else on Henry's Farm, it works.

Henry also has his "decade diary" at hand. This is a bound volume with each month and day indicated in the top corner of a full page, and the length of the page divided into 10 strips, each strip with four lines for the year's notes for that day. It is a brilliantly designed farmer's diary, although it was made in Japan for Japanese businesspeople and a wholly different sort of accounting. Each day, Henry records the

weather and what tasks he did, plus any special observations, using his own peculiar abbreviations: "tm" = too much (i.e., he grew more than he needed), "py" = poor yield, "nh" = no harvest, "fb" = flea beetle damage, "dr" = drought damage, "fr" = frost damage, "td" = too dry, and "tw" = too weedy.

With this wealth of encoded data about the past season in front of him, Henry begins to determine how much he grew of all the different vegetables, how much he brought to market, how much supplied the CSA, how much was sold and at what price, and how much was picked but went unsold. For example, one week last year, we picked and packed 500 heads of lettuce, and as they went onto the truck Henry noted "500" in the "picked" column. When he rumbled back down the gravel lane after the Evanston Market, he had but one lonely raggedy lettuce, which he threw into the chickens' box, and then entered "1" in the *no-ko-ri* column.

The chickens only get the leftover vegetables that are too tattered for the family. Most of the *no-ko-ri* that comes back from the market is divided among the family and apprentices. The whole routine of Henry's return from the Saturday market has turned into something of a weekly pageant, and begins with our mother (who must have had a Roman town crier in her family tree) declaring, "Hail, the conquering heroes!" as the market truck pulls to a stop behind the barn and Henry and his market helpers emerge, slightly battleworn.

On a hot summer harvest day, Henry notes the amounts of different types of hot and sweet peppers he's harvesting. In December, he'll use the numbers to decide how much of which varieties to order for the next season.

Our dad then backs his pickup up against the back of the big truck, and we line the bed of the pickup with empty crates. We order the crates left to right and front to back in alphabetical order—Henry and Hiroko, Jill, Matt, Mom and Dad, Teresa, Terra, and Trailer (the apprentices). If other helpers or friends are around, they get a crate too, whether they need one or not. Then Henry begins to unload the truck, counting how many of each vegetable went unsold and entering that number in the *no-ko-ri* column.

At his desk in December, Henry can calculate how much of each crop he sold by subtracting the number returned from the number picked, and he uses these data to calculate how much money he made from lettuce, and every other crop, that week. He then adds the weekly numbers and determines how much each vegetable brought in over the 26 weeks of the season. By the end of the exercise, he'll know the gross amount that each different vegetable brought in over the whole year.

You may think that Henry would use this information to drop the low-gross-revenue crops or varieties—but you would be wrong. Henry's goal is always diversity—the kind of diversity that mimics nature and keeps pests guessing; the kind of diversity in which one crop removes nutrients from the soil, and another puts them back; the kind of diversity that yields not only a healthy farm but also a healthy bank account. Joel, who identifies himself as a "quant" (a guy good with numbers), articulates what Henry intuits on that last point: "to examine each crop's dollar yield in isolation would be a flawed analysis, since the value of a low-yield crop plays itself out across the entire field and contributes to the higher economic fortunes of those with which it lives in balance."

The numbers help Henry discern how much he's producing and how much people are buying, which helps him determine what he might want to plant more or less of next year. He would never stop growing a vegetable just because it didn't make the top 10, or even the top 100. He only eliminates things that don't grow well or taste good. If something does grow well and taste good, but doesn't sell well, Henry may put it on the bench for a few years. But out of sheer perseverance and the conviction that there's an audience out there for any good vegetable, no matter how unfamiliar, Henry generally succeeds in reinstating it. New Zealand spinach, Malabar spinach, and bitter melon are examples of vegetables he dropped for a few seasons, only to restore and have them work out later.

Once he has his data, both quantitative from the market notebook and qualitative from the field notebooks, he reviews the seed order he placed for the year just past. That previous order is the basis for the next seed order, with slight modifications—some drops, some adds, some increases in amount ordered, and some decreases.

Now it's finally time to turn to the seed catalogs, which are beautiful things, and dangerous, too. There are so many luscious and compelling vegetables but so little time and space. How can one possibly choose between the Genovese basil, the Napoletano, the Italian Large-Leaf ("a sweeter pesto type with high yields"), or the SuperBo ("NEW! Ideal example of classic Italian basil."). And that's not even looking at all the Lemon Basils, Thai Basils, Purple Basils (Amethyst Improved, Ararat, Dark Opal, Osmin Purple, Red Rubin, Purple Ruffles ...) and more. Who can possibly resist a purple-podded shelling pea, Egyptian walking onions, or a tomato known as the "Mortgage Lifter"?

To prevent himself from ordering every single seed from every single catalog, Henry imposes rules. "I'm not going to increase the total at all," he says. " No more than 50 varieties of lettuce this year," he declares. "If I add a new one in, I have to drop an old one out," he sternly intones. Oddly enough, however, the total number of varieties grown on Henry's Farm continues to creep up, year after year.

WEEK 7. **WINTER SOLSTICE:**
Time Stretches

THE LONG NIGHTS THAT COME AT THE WINTER SOLSTICE ARE perfectly suited to reverie, and the bottom field is the perfect place to rest and daydream now that it, too, is resting and regenerating. I visit my dad, who is scheduled to have gallbladder

surgery soon, and then walk down the hill that bottoms out near the rhubarb patch. Kinder Creek gurgles by softly under a thin layer of ice. I cross the lane and move into the main field, where a few scare-crow stalks of okra punctuate the otherwise smooth sweep of new snow. The center of the field calls to me, and I lay down in the sweet, soft silence to watch the stars swirl in the heavens and to commune with the past and present spirits of this place.

Just six months ago, as I bent to plant the okra seeds whose spent stalks now poke through the snow, I felt at my side my bespectacled 13-year-old self, serious and awkward, helping Dad plant peas de-cades earlier. Later, I walked beside my 17-year-old self, strong and lithe, hauling a bushel of freshly picked peas up the hill to be shelled around the kitchen table and frozen for winter.

It's not just my ghosts that inhabit these fields. One day early in Henry's farming career, as he was hoeing in the field alone, a man dressed all in brown appeared next to him. Head lowered to his work, Henry suddenly became aware of the man. He stopped short, looked up, and said "*Bikkurishita!*" (Which means, in Japanese, "You

surprised me!" or more colloquially, "I didn't know you were there!")
As soon as Henry became fully aware of the brown man, he faded
away, but his quiet presence still dwells in the sheltering bowl of this
small Eden cupped in the hands of God. I hope that future generations
will meet these ghosts, and others too, and that this place, this patch of
earth beneath me, will be the polestar for others that it has been for me.

Lying back in six inches of new snow, I remember how the circle
that centers me on this piece of earth began to be drawn in the late
1960s, when my parents bought what we simply referred to as "The
Land." For years before the house was built, we continued to live in
town, but on weekends and in the summer, we'd pile into our big white
Chevy van to go out to the 50 acres of The Land. Once we were settled
in, with seat belts fastened, Dad would turn around and count all of
us kids, "one, two, three, four, five," and, triumphantly, "six." Then he'd
turn the key in the ignition.

Twenty-five minutes later, after crossing the Mackinaw River and
winding our way up into its bluffs, we'd turn a corner and go down
what seemed to us flatlanders like an impossibly steep hill and up the
mountainous other side. At the crest of the hill, we turned into the
beginnings of a gravel lane, parked, and escaped—from the confines
of the car, and from our parents, who set about determining where
the house would be built and the well drilled, and all the other adult
things they worried about.

For us kids, The Land was a worry-free zone of infinite variety
and possibility. Hidden beyond the rolling hills was flat bottomland,
the fertile fields of what is now Henry's Farm. Back then it was over-
grown with multiflora rose bushes and underbrush, which we pushed
through to wade in the small creek. We followed it downstream, eyes
searching for minnows or turtles, to where it flowed into what we took
to be a big river, but was really only the midsized Walnut Creek. There
we examined the geologic strata in the cutaway banks and sniffed the
sharp root-beer smell of the sassafras tree roots washed clear of the
soil that had once anchored them.

Oblivious to the eventual fate of these trees, which would soon
be uprooted and washed downstream, we hiked back up out of the

bottomland and into the steep, forested ravines with tiny streams trickling through their deep Vs. Along the trickling water, we saw tracks in the black mud—evidence of the deer, raccoons, possums, weasels, and field mice that had come to drink. My brothers and sisters and I would follow the tracks until they petered out, and then explore further.

We finally moved out to The Land in the early 1970s, and ended up living in the basement of the partially finished house for the next decade. But even before that, one of our first human imprints on The Land was to plant our large family garden in a patch of bottomland far west of the house, south of where Henry's Farm now flourishes. To get down and back from the garden, we would walk the twisting deer path, dodging the hawthorns, delicately pinching the canes of multiflora rose and wild black raspberry that crossed the path, pulling them aside to let us pass, and sometimes letting them snap back to catch the next sibling coming down. We emerged from the woods at the lip of a cutaway hillside our little Kinder Creek had gouged out thousands of years earlier when, in its former life, it was a major waterway. Where the hill ended, we'd make a right-angle turn, scamper down, jump the stream at the bottom of the hill, turn left at the weeping willow ... and there we were.

The garden seemed enormous then, although it was a mere fraction of what Henry's Farm is today. But it was big enough to provide year-round vegetables for our family of eight. The garden plot extended from the base of the cutaway hillside south to the two giant cottonwood trees that stood sentry at the next bend in the stream. Beautiful as it was at ground level, it was even lovelier from above, and never more than when I visited it alone.

I would come here at random times, often before or after feeding and watering my cow, Frosty, and her offspring. I would leave behind the shade of the shagbark hickory, sugar maple, oak, and locust trees and emerge from the fabric-tearing, skin-pricking undergrowth. Then, suddenly, the world spread out in front of me, legible at last. Sometimes I would stand and muse. Other times I would sit and dangle my feet over the brown clay cliff, watching the stream flow below and the birds fly above. Other times I would lie in the grass and feel myself sink into the earth, becoming part of the buzzing flies, crawling ants, tickling grass, and great sky.

Before I had ever heard of Virginia Woolf, I knew this was my "room of one's own"—a private space with a bird's eye view of a calm world without self-consciousness. This is where I escaped from the stresses of life in a large family, the frustrations of a shy childhood, and the indignities of puberty. This is where I came in the summer to feel the cool breeze blowing up from the stream. This was my favorite spot in the winter, where I would escape the bitter winds by lying down in the snow, feeling kinship with Jack London and his ill-fated protagonist in "To Build a Fire," who finally gave up his struggle with the cold and calmly released himself back into the elements. And this is where I planted, year after year, those bare-root seedling trees they gave us at school each Arbor Day, a child's naive attempt to keep the stream from eroding the hillside even further. One of them—a single white pine—stands there today, 50 feet tall. I did not know it then—I am not sure of it now, even though my 50 years echo its 50 feet—but perhaps one tree planted in blind faith *can* hold up a hillside.

WEEK 8. Goose Music Continues

A FEW LACKADAISICAL CANADA GEESE FLY OVERHEAD LATE one evening. Their calls echo out above the soft crackle of the fire as Henry, Hiroko, and their children, Asa, Zoe, and Kazami, sit around the woodstove reading.

In mid to late December, after the seed orders have all been sent off, Henry asks me for books. I look over my shelves, through classic literature, modern poetry, and recent nonfiction, and pack up an armload of possibilities for him. One winter, he devoured all my Virginia Woolf, and later Septimus Smith from *Mrs. Dalloway* crept into his writings about taste and nutrition. Another year, he read every recent book on genetically modified organisms (GMOs), including Vandana Shiva's firsthand knowledge of their impact on poor farmers in India in *Bio-Piracy,* scientific explanations of how GMOs are created and their potential risks and benefits in *Against the Grain* by Marc Lappe and Britt Bailey, and *Pandora's Picnic Basket* by Alan McHughen. He spent part of one winter on multiple biographies of totalitarian leaders—Mao, Stalin, Lenin, and Hitler. Last year, Henry read the Bible, top to bottom. This year, he is revisiting Dostoevsky and rereading Aldo Leopold's work, heartened by his strong, clear writing, and disheartened that we have progressed so little that his writings are still relevant.

The geese break through our reading, reminding us of the year a sociable Canada goose landed in Henry's field and kept us company for a few weeks during the summer. Like a dog, but more waddlingly, he would trail us as we weeded the carrots or dug the potatoes. Then, as mysteriously as he had appeared, he was gone, leaving only echoes of his honking.

Aldo Leopold wrote, "And when the dawn-wind stirs through the ancient cottonwoods, and the gray light steals down from the hills over the old river sliding softly past its wide brown sandbars—what if there be no more goose music?" I imagine Leopold would be heartened with all the goose music we hear now, half a century after his death.

Early in the autumn, it comes haltingly from the half-hearted practice Vs that are more like a first-grader's wavering Ws. By mid-November, it comes full-throated, from the serious Royal Air Force formations. By this time, after the winter solstice, the geese are usually in their winter grounds further south.

A fellow midwesterner, born in Iowa and living the latter half of his life in Wisconsin, Leopold was the father of wildlife ecology. In his book *A Sand County Almanac,* Leopold defines his "land ethic" as an extended and cooperative kinship that "simply enlarges the boundaries of the community to include soils, waters, plants, and animals, or collectively: the land." This is the philosophy that has guided the five generations of our Illinois farm family, from our great-grandparents through Henry's children and our nieces and nephews.

Leopold is one of our father's heroes. When our father retired from the Department of Biological Sciences at Illinois State University in 1998, after 35 years of teaching and research, our father wrote in his farewell address:

I have had many strong environmental influences, but all of my genome came, of course, from my father and mother, German and Dutch gene pools, respectively. And, of course, the environmental influences were great. First, from them I received my great love of nature, especially of the farm—of the soil and all that it nurtures. They seemed to have known instinctively that which I later learned from Aldo Leopold in his *A Sand County Almanac*, which is his famous "land ethic."

This Canada goose followed us around for a week—happy, it seemed, to be in an ecological farm that welcomes wildlife, pollinators, and biodiversity.

Dad's appreciation of the land ethic began on his family's 160-acre farm built on the drained wetlands of Iroquois County in the 1880s. He was born in the old white farmhouse, in the same room where his father had been born. Today, my little sister Jill lives there with her husband and their four girls, who will be the fifth generation to steward this particular patch of land now known as the Brockman Centennial Farm.

In July 2008, the Land Connection, the nonprofit I founded in 2001, sponsored an organic field day that featured a tour of the family farm. Rain clouds blew in just as the talks were about to begin, so we all moved up into the hay loft of the old barn, which was built by my great-grandfather in 1912. There Dad gave a brief address that told the history of the Brockman Centennial Farm, including its trajectory from a diverse, sustainable farm that fed the family and community, to a chemical-based monocrop farm that fed the industrial food supply—and then back to true sustainability:

My grandparents, Herman Brockman and Maria Zachgo-Brockman, bought this farm (then 160 acres) and the house (only the small south section existed then) and farm buildings in 1898. My father, Fred Brockman, was born here in 1905. In 1912, Herman Brockman had the big red barn, with the then unheard-of concrete floor, built. From this and other evidence we have, I judge him to have been an industrious and progressive farmer. He died in 1917, when my father was only 12, suddenly and painfully, perhaps of a ruptured appendix. Dad's mother died five years later.

The farm was rented until Dad and Mother (Henrietta Zeedyk-Brockman), who were married in 1927, started farming in 1930—just in time for the real tough times of the Great Depression and the dust-bowl drought. Dad was a man of few words, but Mother told me how Dad worked to build up the soil fertility. He pitched manure into a hayrack (they couldn't afford to buy a manure spreader), and then pitched it off "at the back 40." He raised sweet clover and plowed it under to feed the soil. He grew timothy for the horses and red clover for the cows and sheep.

In retrospect, Dad, and his father before him, were organic farmers, as were all farmers at that time. Dad, and especially Mother, never embraced enthusiastically the new ways of farming that came to be after World War II. Mainly, they continued to rely on a crop rotation that included legumes for pasture and hay, and lots of manure from the horses (in the early years), cows, sheep, hogs, and chickens. They also applied limestone, rock phosphate, and potash as needed. It was highly diversified and sustainable farming, with cream and eggs sent to Chicago by train.

Unfortunately, Dad had to stop doing the fieldwork and having farm animals after he crushed his leg while harvesting corn in 1963. He was in the hospital for seven months, and didn't get rid of the bone infection for another three years after that. But Mother and Dad continued to live on the farm, to act as landlords, to have enough hens for their own eggs, and to grow their own vegetables and fruit for about another 30 years.

During those decades when Mother and Dad rented the farm, the tenants insisted on mainly a corn–soybean rotation and high inputs of commercial fertilizers and pesticides. The folks were never happy with that kind of farming. Mother often railed against "all of those darn chemicals."

It is easy to understand why the tenants, and nearly all farmers from the 1950s onward, used "those darn chemicals." The experts—from university professors to government agents to farm bureau officials to professional farm managers to the owners of local feed and seed stores—all said chemicals were needed to make the farm efficient, like a factory. So my grandparents' farm, like most others across the country in the 1950s and 1960s, became a chemically managed monocropped farm. The pear orchard was bulldozed, and little by little, the hayfields and pastures were plowed under for corn and soybeans.

The postwar years, around the time Leopold was writing about his land ethic, were precisely when the practices of midwestern farmers went out of alignment with their values. Farmers still professed their traditional values of land stewardship, independence, and self-sufficiency, but there was a breach between their values and their farming practices. Leopold's basic premise—"the individual is a member of a community of interdependent parts"—was ignored for the first time in the 10,000-year history of agriculture. Instead of a relationship among a community of interdependent parts, farming was recast as a struggle among warring factions; farmers were told they must use chemicals to wage war against offending pieces of the community—insects and weeds, in particular.

Leopold would be pained to see that today, more than 50 years after his death, the guiding philosophy of mainstream agriculture remains short-term economic gain at the expense of long-term sustainability. He would be outraged to see the layer of fine black soil that covers the drifts immediately after a snowfall or to hear the endless buzzing of planes as they dive-bomb fields with chemicals all summer long.

A system of agriculture that leaves the soil bare half the year, allowing it to be blown or washed away, is not sustainable. Neither is a chemical-based agriculture dependent on cheap, abundant fossil fuels to make its fertilizers and biocides, poisons innocuously known as "inputs." A system of agriculture that ignores the web of life—the interconnections between plants and animals, sun and water, bacteria and air, roots and fungi   is doomed.

When I attend agriculture meetings in Illinois, someone in the room usually goes to great pains to say *we are all in this together*—from large-scale monocropping agri-chemical farmers to small-scale, diverse, organic farms catering to local markets—and that we shouldn't argue about whose practices are better. I generally keep quiet, but I remember the questions the ancient Egyptians knew they would have to answer when they crossed over the River Styx from this life to the next: "Did you lie?" "Did you steal?" "Did you pollute the Nile?"

Chemical-based agriculture pollutes *our* Nile, the Mississippi. And it pollutes the groundwater your children and their children will have to drink. It may not be gracious to say so, but some farming practices *are* better than others, and the best ones adhere to Leopold's land ethic.

At the same time mainstream chemical agriculture has moved further and further from Leopold's land ethic, however, that ethic has taken root among a growing number of farmers using sustainable or organic practices. I am sure that tasting locally produced vegetables, fruits, herbs, meats, eggs, and other bounties from the well-stewarded farms of central Illinois would cheer Leopold as much as hearing his beloved goose music, knowing that both spring from the very same "community of interdependent parts."

WEEK 9. **Christmas Guesses**

As December draws to a close, there is plenty of time to indulge in reading and eating. On Christmas Eve, ten children—Henry's three, Teresa's three, and Jill's four—are sitting around a long row of card tables perpendicular to the adult table. It is odd, perhaps, that of the six children my parents had, the first three did not have their own children, but the last three did. If our mom and dad had stopped with two or even three children, they would have had no grandchildren. As it happened, they had six children ("and not one of them a dud," as my mother is fond of saying), and they now have ten grandchildren.

The children are digging into the traditional Christmas Eve meal at the "kids' table," as the rest of us pile food onto our plates and sit down at our table. Dad, thin and walking gingerly these days, sits at its head. The doctors removed his gallbladder a few weeks ago, but the surgery has only slightly alleviated his symptoms. There is a chair for Mom next to him, but she is shuttling back and forth across the room, a five-foot bundle of electric energy. Her dark brown eyes are bright as ever, but her dark curly hair has turned mostly gray. That hair has always been unruly, but it suits her, a visual representation of the thoughts, ideas, and words that constantly bubble and burst forth unedited.

All these years Henry has been farming, it has been our mother whose energy put us all (other than Henry) to shame. Although she's not an early riser, and although she is in her 73rd year, she is impossible to stop once she gets started. No matter if we're transplanting in spring or harvesting on a long, hot summer day, it is always Mom who refuses to take a break, saying, "Oh, we can do one more row."

Mom's driving has also become legendary, expressing the same level of energy as her hair. Whenever the grandkids see a cloud of dust coming down the lane, they know Grandma is behind the wheel. For their 50th wedding anniversary, Zoe captured her paternal grandparents in two stanzas:

I have a grandma
That drives real fast
I have a grandpa
That lectures me on chloroplasts

Though normal people have grandparents
All perfect and loving
I'm glad I have grandparents
That care about something

Perhaps it is my mother's Italian heritage that has given her a highly refined ability to judge the quality of vegetables, particularly tomatoes and eggplants, and to ensure that each bag of mesclun salad mix is perfect.

Slowly, the table fills up. Our older brother, Fred, is in Washington, where he works as a research microbiologist, and our middle sister, Beth, is in Baja, where she rescues animals and mostly relaxes after her years as an emergency veterinarian in Santa Monica, but there are still eight of us: me, Teresa, Henry, and Jill, plus our significant others. We keep calling our mother back to the table to make 10, but she keeps flitting about. Our Christmas Eve dinner is in the tradition of my maternal grandparents, landless peasants from Calabria. It is spartan: spaghetti baccalà and a vegetable side dish or two. Although there is not much to tend to, it's nearly impossible to get Marlene to sit down. Finally, she does, and we raise our glasses in a toast to the parents and grandparents and all who helped bring this food to our table.

Halfway through the meal, someone asks Henry how the year went. This is his cue. Christmas Eve has come, and with it, our now-traditional Christmas Eve guessing game. Henry unfolds his large, handwritten spreadsheet consisting of eight pieces of paper taped together to form one large square. It contains the results of the past few years' end-of-year totals and the results of the past few weeks' calculations of this year's results.

"Okay. What was number one?" he asks.

"Tomatoes," our mother volunteers.

Henry shakes his head no.

"Lettuce," Teresa says.

Henry nods. It's an easy win. Number one has been either tomatoes or lettuce ever since Henry started farming, so it is no surprise when Henry announces that lettuce was the top moneymaker due to the cool, wet year.

Number two is a foregone conclusion, but Henry asks anyway, and Mom repeats, "Tomatoes!"

It is amazing that even in this wet year, tomatoes came in second, despite the fungal infections and early dieback caused by the damp. On top of that, their season was abruptly ended a month prematurely when the tomato patch flooded in an early September nine-inch rainstorm. Still, we have bags and bags of frozen tomatoes in all of our freezers, and those are just the ones that weren't good enough to take to market. That we have plenty of tomatoes for winter soups, and that they held on to second place in the Top 10, is a testament to the benefits of biodiversity—among the 77 varieties Henry plants, there are always some that do well in less-than-ideal conditions.

"Number three?" Henry asks.

"Carrots."

"Basil."

"Potatoes."

The answers ring out, and to each Henry gives a little shake of his head. You'd think we would remember more from year to year.

Finally, our mother says, "Beans!" and Henry nods in confirmation.

In his calculations, Henry groups all the beans together—green, purple, yellow, French, Italian, and the Dutch heirloom Dragon Tongue. Only the Japanese soybeans, *edamame*, are a separate line in his accounting. Even though beans are my least favorite crop to pick, and I am always lobbying for Henry to plant less of them, he has no plans to change. He doesn't sell that many beans volume-wise, but since handpicking is so labor-intensive, he charges a lot for them— three or more times as much as the farmers who pick them with machines. But the varieties that are bred to mature all at once and be tough enough to withstand machine-harvesting are not as delicious and tender as the varieties Henry plants. So as the quality of main-stream produce declines year by year, our customer base increases and our beans leap off the stand.

"Number four?" he asks. A chorus of guesses ensue. "Beets?" No. "Carrots?" No. "Potatoes?" No.

We are not doing well. I think back to the things we sell all year long, and it hits me ... "Garlic!"

Yes, Henry says, garlic was number four. This includes the green garlic we sell from mid-May to mid-June, as well as the dry garlic we sell from early July clear through Thanksgiving. Garlic is the only crop we can bring to the market in one form or another every single week of the season—as long as we don't run out at the end of the year.

"Number five," Henry continues. The same vegetables come up again, in a slightly different order, but eventually my father answers correctly.

"Potatoes."

When Henry first started his vegetable operation, potatoes were a crop he thought he would plant only for the family. He assumed that when people could buy a 10-pound bag for a couple of dollars at the store, they'd have no interest in paying a couple of dollars a pound at his stand. But, as with the beans, Henry found that once people tasted the amazing flavors and textures of high-quality potatoes, they wanted more, and year after year, potatoes have been in our Top 10 best sellers.

"Number six," Henry says, looking over his chart.

"Peppers," Teresa guesses.

"Basil," says Joel.

"Carrots," says Dad.

But Mom nails it with, "Beets!"

Dad gets number seven: "Carrots."

Both beets and carrots are crops that Henry sells at almost every market of the year, especially now that he sneaks an early crop out of the hoophouse.

"Number eight?"

"Basil?"

"Peppers?"

"Parsley?"

"Chard?"

"Kale?"

We're flailing, so Henry finally gives us a hint. "It used to be higher up in the ranking."

Hmmmm, I think. Lettuce and tomatoes are always number one and two because they're things everyone likes. Even people who "don't like vegetables" buy lettuce and tomatoes for salads and sandwiches. Suddenly, it hits me. "Mesclun!"

"Yes," Henry nods.

Henry's ever-changing mix of mesclun salad greens was one of our top three items throughout the early years of the farm, but it's been slipping down the ranking.

"Number nine?"

I guess basil, which I've been guessing at every turn because we pick 200-plus bunches of it every week through most of the summer. But I forgot how cool and wet it had been, and how basil plants, like tomatoes, dislike cool, wet weather.

Jill gets it right: "Peppers." This includes all the hoophouse colored peppers, the field green and yellow Hungarian Horvath peppers, and all the hot peppers.

And, finally, just squeaking in at number 10—basil.

As we finish up the Top 10, we finish up our meal. Except for the spaghetti baccalà, we grew everything we are eating. A lot of talk and column inches have been devoted to local foods in recent years, but too often it's covered as a curiosity or a trend, and not as a matter of national security and public health. The prevailing system of commodity agriculture encouraged by national policy, itself the result of influence by agribusiness and processed food concerns, holds us hostage to the fossil fuels this system depends upon. At the same time, our agricultural policies have turned the U.S. into a net food importer, meaning we are becoming dependent on other countries for our food. We all know where the dependence on foreign oil has gotten us. The fact is that we can live without oil. We cannot live without food.

This immature Jonafree apple was bred to be resistant to scab, fireblight, and mildew. The white dots on it are remnants of the kaolin clay slurry that Teresa sprays on as a physical barrier to insects.

What, then, is the value of local food? Leopold explored how we value things in his essay "Goose Music":

> If wild birds and animals are a social asset, how much of an asset are they? ... In short, what is a wild goose worth? ... Worth in dollars is only an exchange value, like the sale value of a painting or the copyright of a poem. What about the replacement value? Supposing there were no longer any painting, or poetry, or goose music? It is a black thought to dwell upon, but it must be answered. In dire necessity somebody might write another *Iliad*, or paint an "Angelus," but fashion a goose?

Leopold's question, "What if there be no more goose music?" is no longer nearly as urgent as when he wrote it a half century ago. We hear the goose music in louder strains each fall. The real question now is, "What if there be no local farmers growing food? What if there be no more fungicide-free strawberries? What if there be no more apples grown in the U.S.?" The way things are trending, a future without farms stewarding the land and growing healthy foods is possible, and it is indeed a "black thought to dwell upon."

But there is hope. Back at the organic field day on the Brockman Centennial Farm, my father ended his talk with a few thoughts about the future of his house and farm.

> I hope that this house will be home or a treasured place to visit for many future generations of our family. I hope that this land will be farmed with the same respect and love that Dad and Mother gave it. I would like to see part of it restored to tall-grass prairie, as close as possible to the way it was when Native Americans were here. I would like to see this farm be a demonstration farm of the type that would educate others to the benefits of sustainable farming.

Teresa's Priceless Apple Crisp

(Makes one 9 × 13 pan)

For the Topping

- **3 cups old-fashioned oats**
- **⅓–½ cup brown sugar**
- **½ cup chopped pecans**
- **½ cup butter or margarine, melted**
- **½ teaspoon cinnamon**

Preheat the oven to 350°F.

In a medium mixing bowl, combine the oats, brown sugar, pecans, butter, and cinnamon; set aside.

For the Apples

- **¼ cup brown sugar**
- **¼ cup flour**
- **1 teaspoon cinnamon in ⅓ cup water**
- **8 cups sliced apples**

In a second large mixing bowl, combine the brown sugar, flour, cinnamon in water, and apples, tossing to coat. Spoon the brown sugar–apple mixture into a 9- x 13-inch baking pan. Add the topping.

Bake at 350°F for 40 to 45 minutes, or until the fruit is tender.

I know that Mother and Dad, and my grandparents, would be very happy to know that fourth and fifth generations now live in the farmhouse, that the barn and chicken shed are once again a home for farm animals, and that Harold and Ross Wilken are farming their beloved land organically—for the benefit of the environment, and for the future of all of us.

For dessert, two big pans of apple crisp from Teresa's late-season apples—the tart Freedom, sweet Red Delicious, and crisp Cox's Orange Pippin—come to the table, and I think about the social-asset value of an organic heirloom apple. How can we place a value on an explosion of flavor, in knowing where and how an apple was raised? In a world where most of our apples come from China, and how they were raised is hard to document, the question is not rhetorical.

Mom scoops apple crisp onto the dessert plates, and Dad adds a scoop of vanilla ice cream to each—the amounts exactly the same, he says, "within 5 percent human error"—before they get passed around the table. I am sure Aldo Leopold would have enjoyed having some, heartened that more and more people—farmers, landowners, and consumers—value the interdependent community of life that provides goose music, healthy farmland, and juice-oozing, poison-free apples.

Moon

III. OLD MOON

WEEK 10. **Plastic Lapses**

AFTER HENRY GETS THE ALL-IMPORTANT SEED ORDER OUT THE door in December, he begins to take stock of his quart and pint containers, harvest knives and sharpening stones, clippers, pruners, hoes, pitchforks, potato forks, twist-ties, small plastic bags for the mesclun salad mix, and larger plastic shopping bags for customers' purchases—all in preparation for his early January supply order for the coming year.

Those last two items, the only ones made out of plastic, have always been a thorn in our side. Back when Henry was just starting out and his produce filled only one 10- by 10-foot tent, we were able to reuse plastic bags from other stores. Then, as his production and customers increased, Henry started buying plastic to bag his customers' produce. Each year, the demand increased, until he was handing out more than 1,000

HENRY'S FARMSTAND IS NOW **BYOB!**

Bring Your Own BAG!

We don't have to tell you how much plastic bags harm the environment in their production and in their disposal.

And we know you have all sorts of paper, plastic, and canvas bags at home. Just stash some in your car and they'll be there when you need them.

If you show up at the market without a bag, don't worry, **we have Biodegradable Plastic Bags that we will sell you at our cost: 4 bags for 25¢.**

Help us be part of the solution → BYOB!

Encouraging customers to BYOB provided them with an opportunity to not pay for plastic bag costs embedded in produce prices. Henry's plastic bag policy quickly led to a 90 percent reduction in our plastic bag use.

plastic bags each Saturday. That added up to 30,000 plastic bags per season, meaning we were part of the huge problem of the 100 billion plastic bags Americans use each year, 97 percent of which are not recycled.

While most of the supplies are necessities, the plastic bags are finally becoming optional. This came about as a result of Henry's plastic-bag policy. I had always thought of policy as something abstract and wonkish, but at the Evanston Farmers' Market, I saw firsthand the impact a policy decision can have on peoples' daily lives, as well as on the community and the environment.

The new plastic-bag policy started quite innocently: a friend suggested we use biodegradable plastic bags. Even when we found out that the biodegradable bags were four times the price of regular bags, we still thought it was a good idea.

So on Henry's way back from the first market, he picked up a truckload of biodegradable bags. At first blush, it seemed a perfect solution. But the more we looked into it, the more this quick fix to our plastic problem began to breed its own host of problems. First, we learned there is considerable doubt that biodegradable bags really do degrade under the conditions they are supposed to—including water, sun, and underground (e.g., in a landfill). Second, the renewable resource used to make most biodegradable plastic bags is corn, the chemical-intensive production of which has its own set of negative environmental impacts. To add insult to injury, we learned that the corn used to make the bags we purchased was grown in China. Thus, our "green" bags were contributing to soil loss, polluted wells, damaged ecosystems, and food insecurity in China—not to mention all the fossil-fuel use and concomitant pollution that started in a field in China, continued at a bag factory there, and then went on with emissions from trucks, ships, planes, and trucks again to finally get into our hands.

Once in our customer's hands, the biodegradable shopping bags were even more problematic. If a person brought them along with other plastic bags to a recycling center, they would contaminate the recycling stream, rendering entire batches of recyclable plastic useless. They also promote littering, as people assume the bags break down quickly in the environment when in fact it takes most biodegradable products at least 18 months, and sometimes much longer, to break down. Until they do, they have the same potential to harm wildlife and create litter problems.

On top of all that, biodegradable bags rarely get the chance to biodegrade, since most consumer waste goes into a plastic garbage bag, inside a garbage can, into a dumpster, onto a garbage truck, and finally into a landfill. There it is effectively entombed and preserved for thousands of years. In the end, we realized that unless you have a composting center nearby, your biodegradable plastic bag is no better—and often worse—than a standard plastic bag.

"Get over it!" I imagine someone saying. "If you think there is some magical shopping bag out there that doesn't consume vast natural resources and contribute to pollution, and that disappears harmlessly when its useful life is over, you're dreaming!"

Well, after some 16 years of selling at the market, we knew we weren't dreaming, and that such a thing *does* exist, because we'd seen lots of customers using them every week—sturdy, stylish canvas bags that last far longer than most relationships. When they do wear out (after, say, 20 or 30 years), they biodegrade with no harmful side effects.

Noting that many of our market customers already brought their own canvas, paper, plastic, or string bags, Henry thought it would be unfair to make them pay more for plastic they never used. We also knew that, human nature being what it is, the stick (paying for a bag) could be a more effective tool than the carrot (refunding people a nickel when they bring their own bag). So rather than pass his higher bag cost on to all the customers through higher vegetable prices, he decided to pass on the cost only to those who needed a bag.

And so we announced our plastic-bag policy in the weekly *Food & Farm Notes*, explaining its origins and inviting our customers to join us in making real change every Saturday morning by making Henry's market stand BYOB—bring your own bag. We encouraged everyone to dig up their bags and throw them in their cars.

"But don't worry if you forget," we added, "because we still have those biodegradable plastic bags and will sell them to you at our cost: four bags for 25¢."

Well. You would have thought we had uttered heresy. Pay for a plastic bag? That seemed downright un-American to some folks. While most customers applauded our policy, I often felt wounded by those who took umbrage. But Henry found all the reactions absurdly and hugely hilarious. Within a week, we had moved from *The Graduate* and the all-important word "plastics" into Harold Pinter territory:

Scene 1
Henry: Do you need a bag?
Customer: Yes.
Henry: Okay. They're four for a quarter.
Customer: What?!

Henry: We're encouraging customers to bring their own bags, but if you don't have one, we'll sell you up to four for a quarter, which is slightly less than our cost.

Customer: Why should I pay for the bag?

Henry: Why should I pay for the bag?

Customer: Well, why should I pay for these carrots?

Henry: Because you want to eat them.

[Customer exits stand left, pondering this economic reality.]

Scene 2

Market salesperson: That's $26. Do you have a bag?

Customer: No.

Worker: Okay. Here you go. Your total is $26.25.

Customer: [look of annoyed disbelief] You're charging for the plastic bags?

Worker: Yes. We're passing on our cost and encouraging people to use other bags they already have.

Customer: I can't believe it!

[Customer exits stand right, muttering and fuming]

Scene 3

Worker: Bags are four for a quarter.

[Well-to-do middle-aged man storms over to Henry.]

Customer: Henry! I always bring my own bags but forgot to today and also didn't know I would be charged for bags. If I had known, I would have brought my own. You know I've been a loyal customer for ages, and I'm a great environmentalist. Can't you just this once give me a break? C'mon, give me a bag.

[Henry listens patiently.]

Henry: Come on, you can afford a quarter for a bag.

Customer: But it's the principle of the thing.

Henry: Precisely.

The plastic-bag story had legs, getting onto various blog sites, and eventually making its way onto the front page of the *Chicago Tribune*.

That article generated more heat than light, but by the end of the season, the plastic-bag policy was old news. We had lost some customers, to be sure, but we had fostered greater loyalty from many more.

By the end of the season, we seldom sold a biodegradable plastic bag, and Henry had decreased his plastic-bag usage by 90 percent. It occurred to me, as I watched customers pull bags out of their backpacks or purses and happily fill them with turnips, potatoes, parsnips, and more, that we have wall-to-wall corn and soybeans in Illinois as a result of certain policies, and that a change in those policies could mean more apples and carrots available to low-income families, or less chemical runoff into our rivers and streams, or more permanent pastureland to sequester carbon. Positive change from policy change, while sometimes painful, is possible, and what seemed heretical a few months before now seemed merely practical.

WEEK 11. **Winter Keepers**

THE FEELING OF SECURITY ENGENDERED BY FREEZERS FULL of summer's bounty is, for me, better than that of having money in the bank. Every time I look into our chest freezers—one full of a rainbow of quart bags of green peas, gallon bags of yellow corn, and two-gallon bags of red, yellow, green, and striped tomatoes, and the other one full of white-paper-wrapped packages of beef and pork, with a few chickens and goat bratwursts thrown in for good measure—I feel almost euphoric.

But of all the fruits of our labor, none shines brighter and holds more promise than those red and gold orbs in the bottom drawer of the refrigerator. The autumn sun still shines from the last apples we picked as fall was turning to winter—Teresa's Black Oxford and Henry's Gold Rush. These and many other varieties—Winter Banana, Stayman, Rome Beauty, Roxbury Russet, and Esopus Spitzenburg—slowly sweeten after they are plucked and keep well for months with no decline in texture or flavor, proving that it's not only fine wines (and some people) that improve with age.

These apples are also proof that there is no need to partake of the Faustian bargain by which, in exchange for having *all* fruits available *all* the time, we sold not our souls but our taste buds. Most of the fruit varieties available in stores are bred for color, size, shape, and transportability, not taste. Yes, we can have an apple (or a peach or a tomato) any day of the year, but chances are it will be mealy, insipid, and stale. Luckily, more and more people are taking matters into their own hands and resolving (this is, after all, the season of resolutions) to discover local producers and winter apples. Once you taste the rich, tangy, sweet and tart flavors of these winter keepers, you will understand why the apple was so tempting to Eve.

In addition to being the season of resolutions, this is the season of wassailing—the perfect time to make mulled cider. In Europe and early America, Twelfth Night, January 5, was the traditional night for wassailing, but the word and the tradition are much older.

Wassail is an ancient Saxon greeting, a contraction of *wæs hæil*, meaning "be healthy." The second word is the same as our currently underused English word "hale" as in "hale and hearty." By the twelfth century, *wassail* had morphed into the salutation you offer as a toast, to which the standard reply was *drinc hail*, "drink good health." It then came to refer to the alcoholic beverage itself.

Over time, a different sort of wassailing emerged—one deeply rooted in gratitude for the earth and its plants and animals. Farmers would go out on Twelfth Night to wassail their crops and animals and

Our youngest sister Jill and friends go out on a bitterly cold January night to give thanks to the apple trees by wassailing them with wassail-soaked bread and song. Our parents planted the Ozark Gold apple tree at our grandparents' farm in 1963. Forty-five years later it is still bearing golden fruit for Jill and her family.

drink to their health. In eighteenth-century Britain, the practice took place most often in orchards, where the townspeople gathered to toast the good health of the apple trees and promote an abundant crop the next year.

This is the tradition my sister Teresa revived for us a few years ago. We made a big pot of potent wassail, and at midnight on Twelfth

Traditional Winter Apple Wassail

10 small winter apples

10 teaspoons brown sugar

2 bottles dry sherry or dry Madeira

½ teaspoon grated nutmeg

1 teaspoon ground ginger

3 cloves

3 allspice berries

1 1-inch stick cinnamon

2 cups superfine sugar

½ cup water

6 eggs, separated

1 cup brandy

Preheat the oven to 350°F.

Core the apples and fill each with a teaspoon of brown sugar. Place the apples in a baking pan and cover the bottom with ⅛ inch of water. Bake at 350°F for 30 minutes, or until tender. Remove the apples from the oven and set aside.

Combine the sherry, nutmeg, ginger, cloves, allspice berries, cinnamon, sugar, and water in a large, heavy saucepan and heat without letting the mixture come to a boil. Leave on very low heat.

In a large mixing bowl, beat the egg yolks until light and lemon-colored. Beat the egg whites until they are stiff, and fold them into the yolks.

Strain the wine mixture and add it gradually to the eggs, stirring constantly. Add the brandy. Pour into a metal punch bowl, float the apples on top, and serve.

Night, a bitterly cold night of about 5 degrees with a biting wind, we bundled everyone up and gave the kids all manner of pots and pans and kitchen implements to bang them with. We traipsed out of the house, a ragtag parade, with the kids leading the way with their culinary noisemakers, banging loudly enough to wake the dead, and the adults bringing up the rear with the wassail bowl and toast. Out in the orchard, we impaled wassail-soaked pieces of bread on the bare branches to bring forth good spirits (birds). Then the kids banged the pots and pans to ward off evil spirits. We splashed the wassail at the base of each tree, formed a circle around it, and sang the old song:

> Let every man take off his hat
> And shout out to th'old apple tree:
> Old Apple tree, old apple tree;
> We've come to wassail thee,
> And hoping thou wilt bear
> Hats full, caps full, three bushel bags full;
> Barn floors full and a little heap under the stairs.

It seemed a fitting gesture of gratitude—returning some of nature's bounty to water the tree and feed the birds—a heartfelt thank you to the tree and the earth and all its creatures for sustaining us year after year.

WEEK 12. Digging Deep

WHILE THE BOTTOM DRAWERS OF THE REFRIGERATOR ARE perfect for keeping the winter keepers, more space—and different conditions—are needed for all the root vegetables we dug in mid-November. There was a time, not so very long ago, when everyone knew you could store vegetables for months without using any fossil fuels. Ask your grandmother. If she grew up in a temperate zone anywhere from Vermont to Poland to Japan, she probably had a root cellar and made good use of it during the winter months.

Apples keep best at 30 to 32 degrees, with high humidity and good air circulation. Winterkeeper varieties, such as Melrose, Fuji, and Mutsu, will keep well even under less-than-optimal conditions.

Neither my dad nor I remember the root cellar my great-grandparents had, but my grandmother says it was huge, with bins all along one side for potatoes and bins for apples lining the opposite wall. Between them were large crocks. In some of the crocks were carrots, buried in damp sand to keep them at the right temperature and humidity level. Most of the other crocks were filled with sauerkraut, each with a cover made of wood. The wood covers were made to fit exactly into each different crock, and they were weighted down with a brick that lowered as the sauerkraut was gradually eaten over the winter. By spring, the covers and their bricks would be resting on the bottom of the crocks.

My dad remembers his mother, my grandmother, saying it was her job to gather vegetables and apples from the cellar every few days during the winter when she was a child. Each time, her mother would remind her, "Now, don't eat any sauerkraut," and each time, my grandmother could not resist lifting a wooden lid and taking a little pinch of it.

Dad clearly remembers his own parents' root cellar. They used the deep, concrete-lined pit that housed their well pump. In this underground room, which was about 12 feet by 12 feet, Grandma and Grandpa kept apples, pears, and assorted vegetables all winter long. To get to the produce, you removed the aluminum cover of the well housing and climbed down a ladder. Below, you were in a small, concrete-lined area that had one bare lightbulb hanging from the ceiling. Dad told me the bulb was kept on during cold spells to provide a bit of heat and keep the produce from freezing.

Now that root cellars have gone the way of the dinosaur, the typewriter, and the card catalog, you may think there is no point in rooting around in the past. But in this mote of quiet time after six nights of snow in a row, the words of Henry James come floating through my mind: "To take what there is, and use it, without waiting forever in vain for the preconceived—to dig deep into the actual and get something out of *that*—this doubtless is the right way to live."

This is the season for digging deep—not only into your own thoughts but into the earth, or in my case, into the storage pit down in the bottomland. This is where we store all the roots that we dug from the earth before the hard freeze: turnips, parsnips, salsify, celery root, burdock, carrots, beets, potatoes, and winter radishes.

Henry's storage pit is more low-tech than our grandparents' and great-grandparents' root cellars, but just as effective. Its starting point is the burdock pit, the hole in the ground that was created as he harvested out the deep-rooted burdock. In early December, he revisits the burdock pit, now 200 feet long, and digs out the last six feet of it even further, so it is four feet deep with a flat bottom and straight walls. He makes it long enough and wide enough to accommodate all the roots he dug to last us through the winter. Then he goes up to the garage, where all the roots were stored after the harvest. At the time of the harvest, it was cooler in the garage than it would have been down in the pit, but now the pit will be about 35 degrees, which is perfect for most roots.

After setting aside enough vegetables to last all of our families for a month or so, Henry loads the remaining vegetables into burlap bags he gets from the coffee shop in town. One burlap bag holds one crate of vegetables, which is just over a bushel. Depending on the season, he may have 10 to 15 bags of carrots, five of potatoes, and one each of celery root, parsnips, beets, burdock, turnips, daikon, and roseheart radish.

He takes all the bags down to the field and puts them into the pit, the first bags standing upright, and the others flat on top of the standing bags. He then makes a chart mapping out what's in the bottom level and what's on top. When he's done, he covers everything with three to four inches of loose dirt to keep the mice out. Either they can't smell very well, or they don't want to dig down that far, because they never seem to bother the storage roots in the pit—whereas they feast on the ones in the garage. On top of the dirt, Henry

Roasted Root Vegetables

6 large storage carrots, peeled and trimmed

6 turnips, peeled

4–6 potatoes, scrubbed and cut lengthwise in half

1–2 large parsnips, peeled, trimmed, and cut diagonally into 1-inch-thick slices

1–2 medium onions, trimmed, peeled, and quartered

1–2 celery root, trimmed and halved, with the halves cut crosswise into 1-inch-thick slices

1 whole head garlic, separated into cloves, unpeeled

2–3 teaspoons dried rosemary, sage, or thyme

Salt, to taste

Freshly ground black pepper, to taste

Extra-virgin olive oil, for drizzling

Preheat the oven to 400°F.

Place all the vegetables and herbs in a large baking dish. Season well with salt and black pepper. Drizzle generously with olive oil, and toss with your hands to coat evenly.

Bake at 400°F, stirring the vegetables occasionally, until they are tender and golden brown, about 45 minutes. Serve in the baking dish or transfer to a platter to accompany a main course of roasted meat.

mounds up a big fluffy pile of hay or straw to keep the cold out. He then covers everything with a tarp to shed water.

In all the years Henry's been doing this, he's never had any vegetables freeze—even though sometimes weeks have gone by where the mercury never crept above zero. Of course, on those days, or weeks, of below-zero temperatures, he cannot open the pit, even if we are running out of vegetables. He has to wait for a fairly warm day, because otherwise frigid air will flow down into the warm pit and freeze the vegetables. But if we time the pit opening just right, the vegetables stay around 35 to 40 degrees, no matter the air temperature, because heat radiates up from deeper levels of the soil and stays in the pit. Henry opens it about once a month, digging deep into the actual, to bring us fresh roots all winter long.

WEEK 13. **Calves Birthed**

A FINE SNOW BLOWS AGAINST THE WEST WINDOWS, MELTS on contact, and trickles down like tears that mesh and meld, creating a sparkly liquid lace that puts the Czech lace curtains to shame. We have arrived with little fanfare at the month named after Janus, the god with one face looking forward and one looking back. The trickling tracery takes me back to other winds, other snows.

Long ago, walking home from grade school, I learned how the wind could take away my restlessness and discontent. In high school, I even made it take away my headaches and heartaches. Today, Janus carries me back to a day exactly eight years ago. On that cold and snowy day, I discovered that if you walk far enough out into a snow-swept, stubble-covered cornfield and then lie flat on your stomach and wait, the wind will sculpt landscapes around you. That night, I saw the breath of Michelangelo's pink-robed patriarch. The deity had gotten tired of floating on the ceiling of the Sistine Chapel and was now busy sculpting mountain ranges all around me, letting me float away on a white sea of peak and plateau, escarpment and overhang, crevice and abyss.

Only our grandparents' catalpa grove breaks the flat landscape of the farm where my sister Jill and her family now live and work.

Earlier that day, I had plowed through drifts higher than the tires on my low-slung Chevy Cavalier to get to the Lutheran nursing home where my grandmother and grandfather had been ever since my grandfather fell and broke his hip. That was when Grandma decided to move with him to the nursing home. She had looked after enough dying people in her life, she said, and refused "to be a bother" to any of her relatives.

I had driven to the nursing home from the family farm where Grandma and Grandpa had lived for more than 60 years, where my littlest sister, Jill, now lives with her husband and four girls. They were away, and I had been looking after the animals. I had battled the biting wind to do the morning chores: letting out the geese and chickens and guinea fowl; breaking the ice on their watering pans; and feeding the goats, Coco and Rechenka, and the cats, stray and tame. I fed them in the barn my grandfather's father had built in 1912, the barn he took such good care of that it stands as sturdily today as it did nearly 100 years ago.

Amazed that I had managed to drive from the farm to the nursing home without getting stuck in a drift, I stomped the snow off my boots in the entryway and went to Grandpa's room. My aunt was there, reading in the only chair. I quietly sat on his bed. His breathing was labored. Even with a stream of oxygen fed through a tube to his nose, he struggled for air. He was in a loose fetal position, eyelids down, eyes not quite shut. Every breath, a jagged gurgle.

I took his hand, soft as a baby's, and told him about the weather. "Almost a foot of snow," I said, "and the biggest drifts are around the watering tank, as usual."

"He doesn't hear you," my aunt said. I was sure he did, and I quickly changed the topic to get away from the watering tank, which, although it had revived the hired man who had fallen from the barn roof, had also been the watery grave where Grandpa's mother had drowned herself when Grandpa was 12.

Every person's life has its share of hardships and tragedies, but I think Grandpa had more than his fair share. He was the youngest of his siblings and was effectively orphaned after his father died of a ruptured appendix, stomach cancer, or some equally painful abdominal disease. The story goes that his wife, Grandpa's mother, refused to let him see a doctor during his illness, as she believed prayer was more powerful than medicine. Some say it was her remorse that led her to the horse tank a few years later.

"They say it will get even colder," I said to Grandpa. And then I told him about the family, about my father, his son, and our farm animals. I told him about one of old Frosty's many offspring, who would calve in a matter of days. It was the same story my father had told Grandpa a few weeks ago, and Dad said it had made him smile.

"She's so big," I said. "She might have twins again. You know, that would make this the third year in a row this one's had twins. Did you ever have a cow give birth to twins three times?"

As I rambled on, his breathing slowed.

"He's breathing easier now," my aunt said. "It's the morphine."

I moved from stroking Grandpa's hand to his whole arm, and then up to his shoulder and chest, my mouth closer to his ear. "Wouldn't that be something," I whispered, "if she has twins three years in a row? She is so big. Dad thinks she will."

I kept talking and stroking as my aunt lifted up the bedsheets and pinched his blue toes. They turned white and stayed that way. My aunt was crying now, blowing her nose, but she existed only at the periphery of my senses. I concentrated on my grandfather.

"It will be okay." I was whispering now, bending close, my lips brushing his ear. "Everything is okay."

His face, even after years in the sun, was unlined. As I kept whispering, his expression softened and his breathing relaxed. He was a young man now, taking a nap after a long morning in the fields and after a full lunch—or dinner, rather, as they called the noontime meal: a proper farm dinner of fried chicken, potato salad, creamed corn, hardboiled eggs, buttermilk biscuits, and lemonade. His breathing was very slow, with long spaces between each breath. He was calm. Time was infinitely slow.

My aunt blew her nose again and rushed out to get Grandma.

I watched as Grandpa took one great breath and let it go. When it was gone, he opened his blue eyes like astral flowers, and gazed calmly ahead.

The sun was down, and the moon not yet up, by the time I returned to the farm. Christmas lights twinkled in the window of the room where Grandpa was born exactly 94 and one half years ago. As I stood outside watching the tiny lights blink, I remembered Grandma telling how our father was born in that very same room on another snowy night 73 years ago. Now Jill and her family use that room as their kitchen, to prepare food grown on the same land that fed my father and his father and grandfather.

The warm house beckoned, but there were animals to tend to, so I turned into the bitter wind and then entered the shelter of the barn. I gave the goats and cats their food and water and closed up the barn for the night.

Afterward, my feet took me not into the house but out along the Danforth slab, the narrow, flat country road my grandfather had traveled on foot, in horse-drawn buggies, in the Klondike buggy, in a Model T, and in countless Chevys. (Republicans, it was well known, drove Chevys, while Democrats drove Fords.) I passed the catalpa grove, where half the trees lay dead, waiting for the next life like incandescent saints, earthly and prayerful.

On either side of the road, the open field beckoned. I turned off the road, stumbled through a deep snow-filled ditch, and trekked across the field, watching the full moon rise. When it was overhead, I lay on my stomach and watched the snowy mountain ranges form. Then I turned on my back in the center of the vast snow-swept field with no beginning, middle, or end. I watched the moonlight soften the snow, as if its source of light had exploded centuries ago and was only now finally fading. The shadow of my body faded too. Nestled between mountain ranges, I gazed beyond them and listened to the wind sing lullabies.

A few days later, the cow birthed twin calves.

Maple Syrup

IV. SAP MOON

WEEK 14. **Hog Heaven**

THE SECOND DAY OF FEBRUARY. DAYBREAK. JUST ABOVE freezing. Light rain overnight, then misty needles of snow, which have matured now into full flakes.

It is still dark, but I have been up for hours, anxious about the day's activities. My houseful of guests—Joel and three chefs from Chicago—are slow risers. Granted, the young chefs, Jared Van Camp, Chris Pandel, and Greg Biggers, have put in a full day and night, serving hundreds of guests before driving three hours south and arriving here after midnight. But nothing I say about the urgency of our appointment today makes them move any faster.

While chefs' professional lives are all about putting food on the table, the only form of meat most of them know are single-portion,

Jared Van Camp makes fresh sausage at Henry and Hiroko's house while Greg Biggers looks on. Chris Pandel is busy making lazy pierogies in the background.

flash-frozen ribeyes, duck breasts, pork chops. That's why they're here in the rolling hills of the Mackinaw River Valley of central Illinois, far from their stainless-steel kitchens and paved parking lots. That's why I arranged this appointment with Dennis and Emily Wettstein, who run one of our neighboring organic farms. That's why we have a date set for sunrise: an appointment for premeditated murder.

From the very dawn of domesticated swine, an ancient Aristotelian tragedy has been enacted all over the world with remarkable fidelity to the original script. It begins with the farrowing of piglets in blossom time, then with their fattening in forests and on pasture through summer and fall. Then, after having had his every physical need looked after, our porcine hero experiences a sudden reversal of fortune. The fact that this is a time-honored tradition, a tale we all know the ending of, does not make it any easier.

Since childhood, I've always helped with the butchering. Even before helping out as a child, I remember Grandma Henrietta talking about it. After Grandpa's farm accident, which crushed his leg and laid him up for years, she had figured out how to do his chores, including the butchering of chickens. Instead of using the stump and hatchet, though, she told me with a measure of pride, she had simply snatched the sleepy birds out of their shed before dawn, tied lengths of string around their legs, and hung them upside down from the clothesline. From there, it was a simple stroll with a sharp knife drawn across their throats and, very soon, plenty of delicious chicken in the freezer.

Perhaps because this image is so vivid in my mind (though I never saw it), I never wanted to be outside while my father killed our chickens. Once the birds had flown over their River Styx, however, I didn't mind the plucking. And I actually liked the gutting—making the careful incisions around the cloaca, peeling back the triangular flap of skin, reaching my hand in slowly and carefully, running my fingernails between the entrails and the main body cavity, loosening everything so that I could pull all the viscera out in one steaming, intact clump.

Although we did all our bird butchering at home, my family always brought our cattle, sheep, and pigs to the Eureka Locker, the local family-run butcher shop. Until a few decades ago, it was easy for anyone with a few acres to raise cattle or pigs for their family and neighbors and bring them a few miles to a meat locker for professional butchering and cold storage. I have a dim memory of the original locker in the center of Eureka, with its old wood floors and old-world feel. But as livestock production and processing became consolidated, and rules and regulations were written by and for large industry, the small-town meat lockers went out of business. (Wood floors, for example, are not up to code.) Without access to processing, farmers stopped raising livestock and tore up their pastures, even on highly erodible land, to do what the government and universities encouraged them to do through subsidies and infrastructure: plant corn and soybeans.

Soon after I moved back to Congerville, a group of farmers and I tried to save a meat locker in the neighboring town of Washington. When I asked the 80-some-year-old owner why he didn't pass the business on to his children instead of closing down, he shook his head and said, "My children are retired."

We were lucky that a local butcher's son chose to go into the business and had enough money to build a new Eureka Locker at the edge of town. We generally bring our hogs and cattle there, to be returned to us a week later in neat squares wrapped in white paper with "Brockman" stamped on them. Our neighbors do the same, and other farmers come from hundreds of miles away to this slaughterhouse, currently the only one in the state of Illinois to do USDA-certified organic processing. The Eureka Locker is a valuable resource in our local food system and in our state, but the chefs are here and slowly rousing themselves to experience the dying art of home butchering firsthand. And so am I. This day will be my first experience butchering a pig.

Pigs are remarkable creatures. It is not idle anthropomorphizing to say that pigs are a lot like us; it is purposeful and precise anthropomorphizing. Because of the many human/porcine structural and functional similarities, pigs play a crucial role in modern medicine. Their heart valves are sewn in to replace our defective ones. Their skin is used to cover our burn wounds.

In some ways, the pig is far superior to us. His snout, for example, functions as an olfactory organ, arm, hand, and spade, all in one. His ears are like radar dishes, and his vocalizations are eerily human. The screams I heard in an industrial confined animal feeding operation (CAFO) in France (it is nearly impossible to visit CAFOs in the U.S.) spoke of terror as clearly as the grunts of my Dad's hogs speak of utter contentment when he scratches them behind the ears.

On a recent visit to a neighbor's farm, I watched a sow wake from her nap when she heard whimpers from her week-old piglets. She sidled her left side up against the fence and herded the whole dozen of her offspring to her open side with encouraging grunts. When they were all safely within sight on her right side, she lowered herself to her knees, and with infinite slowness, she rolled her left side against the fence until she was lying on the ground. As the piglets clambered aboard and each found its specific teat, the one it had latched on to the first time it suckled, the mother sow's grunts and moans turned erotic.

Today the hogs we'll butcher are two heritage Red Wattle pigs, along with a Red Duroc and a White Duroc. They have been living on

pasture and eating organic grains at the Wettstein Organic Farm for the past nine months.

The Wettstein farm is only seven miles from my house, but the overnight snowfall has conspired with my sleepy guests to prevent us from arriving there at sunrise, as planned. I feel bad; out of respect for the sacrificer, my neighbor Denny, as well as out of respect for the soon-to-be-sacrificed, we should have been on time.

Driving down the Wettsteins' long lane, we see the car of the fourth chef in the project, Chris Koetke of Kendall College. As soon as we pile out of our car, we see Chris. Then we hear the short, sharp pop of a gun, muffled by the snow and wet air. One down. There is no time to waste, because we have planned to use every part of these pigs, including the blood, which must not have time to coagulate. We pull on hats and gloves and move in swiftly to help.

Jared, the one chef who grew up in central Illinois and has a passing knowledge of farm life, moves in swiftly with the white five-gallon bucket he brought from his restaurant to collect the precious blood already soaking the snow. The other chefs hang in the background, unsure of their roles.

Denny speaks softly and directly. "Bring the bucket. Widen the cut." Bill Davison, a neighbor and organic vegetable farmer who is an experienced hunter, goes into the pig's chest again with his knife—straight into the heart, which pumps out the remaining blood while

Chris Pandel's Grandmother's Lazy Pierogies with Fresh Italian Sausage

For the Lazy Pierogies

    1 pound ricotta, pressed to squeeze out most of the water

    1 whole egg

    1 egg yolk

    2 tablespoons kosher salt

    1 tablespoon freshly ground black pepper

    2 cups all-purpose flour

    4–6 quarts salted boiling water

Place the ricotta, egg, egg yolk, salt, and pepper in a mixing bowl and stir with your hands until well combined. Slowly sprinkle in the flour until a dough is formed and the flour is absorbed. (If the dough is still wet, add more flour until it is no longer sticky—the amount will depend on the wetness of the ricotta.)

Once the dough is formed, cover the bowl in plastic wrap and put it in the refrigerator for 1 to 4 hours.

Once the dough is chilled, use your hands and pluck half-ounce pieces of dough and roll them in your hands to form long, fat dumplings—about 2 to 3 inches long and almost an inch in diameter at their widest point. Place the dumplings on a floured baking sheet.

After you have rolled all the dumplings, add them in batches to the well-salted boiling water and allow them to simmer for 12 to 15 minutes. They will double in size and become very tender.

Note: If you wish to eat them immediately, melt some butter in a pan, adding half of an onion that has been minced. Add the dumplings, coating them with the butter and onion. Finish with some freshly ground black pepper. If you want to cool the pierogies for another day's dinner, drain them, toss them in a few tablespoons of vegetable oil so they won't stick, and lay them on a baking sheet to be placed in the refrigerator.

For the Fresh Italian Sausage

This sausage may be put into a casing, or it can be used for meatballs, pastas, or sausage patties.

4 pounds pork butt, cut into 1-inch cubes

1 pound fat back, cut into 1-inch cubes

1½ ounces kosher salt

2 tablespoons granulated sugar

2 teaspoons minced garlic

2 tablespoons fennel seed, toasted

2 teaspoons black pepper, coarsely ground

2 tablespoons sweet Spanish paprika

¾ cup ice water

¼ cup red wine vinegar, iced

Toss all the ingredients, except for the water and vinegar, in a large mixing bowl until they are thoroughly mixed. Marinate overnight.

Grind through the medium die of a meat grinder. After removing the mixture from the grinder, emulsify in the bowl of a stand mixer fitted with the paddle attachment. Use all of the vinegar, and then add water as needed. If the consistency is right, you may not need the water at all—just use what you need to make a soft sausage that holds together well in the form of a patty. Form into balls or patties, or simply sauté as loose sausage meat.

---

the animal's legs continue to move. After the blood stops, the men hoist the first pig up into the waiting pickup. The bed is filled with 6 inches of snow, and she lands as if on a feather bed. She is dead—a bullet to the head, a knife to the heart—but her legs are still slowly treading the air.

When we turn back to the barn, Denny has his .22 angled down, following a point in the middle of the next pig's forehead, above her eyes and between her ears. I was worried that this pig would be terribly upset after the first killing, but there is no evidence of any anxiety. She sniffs curiously at the blood but is not bothered by it. She cannot know that her entry ticket into life was the assuredness that she would ultimately be killed and eaten. It is the same for all of us, though our demise may not come so swiftly, and our eating will be more slowly, and by lower life forms.

Denny waits for her to stand still, for the height and angle of her head to be just so. Then I hear the sharp pop again. She totters for a moment and then slumps to her side. Denny takes two swift steps forward and crouches beside her—one knee on the side of her head, near the jowl, just beneath the ear—and plunges his knife into her chest. I watch her eyes. A pale flickering. Gone.

Her four legs tread the air, not wildly, but swiftly and steadily, as the lifeblood drains into the white bucket Jared has brought over again. When the blood slows down to a trickle, we all help heave her 250 pounds up into the truck. To fit her in the pickup, we roll the first hog from her side to her back. Her legs are still at last. The hind ones point up to the heavens, while her front legs are neatly bent as if in prayer. There is a tinge of holiness palpable in the air, filling me with humility and awe. The two pigs rest calmly in the snowbank of finitude.

"And now you know," Euripides wrote in his tragedy *Hecuba*, "And now you know: Life is held on loan. The price of life is death."

The killing takes only an hour. The rest of the day is filled with the aftermath—the hard work of scalding, scraping, gutting, and cutting. The sun has almost set when everyone converges on the warmth and light of Henry and Hiroko's kitchen. There the chefs make six kinds of sausages with the fresh meat, as well as side dishes from Henry's stash of root vegetables.

As I watch them work, I think of the poet William Carlos Williams reminding us that everything we eat is holy because it all comes from the earth, the creation, the "body of the Lord." And it suddenly seems clear that Christianity, and perhaps all religion, emerged from animal sacrifice, from the humble awareness that life comes from life, that the only way to life everlasting is through death, and that we partake each day of the body and the blood, because that is how the world works.

WEEK 15. **Ice Storm Provides**

I F YOU START TO THINK ABOUT HOW MANY PLANTS AND ANIMALS have lived and died since life appeared on earth, you end up either going crazy trying to get your head around infinity or praising the earth's greatest recyclers, fungi and bacteria. These lowly beings are the primary means by which a fingernail, a feather, a hog's bristle, our own bodies become soil and, eventually, host new life.

Much of the recycling work is done by the threadlike mycelia that make up the bulk of any fungus. One cubic inch of soil has eight miles of mycelia. If you are standing on earth rich in organic matter, the area under your foot hosts 300 miles of mycelia. As soon as you move on, they leap up into your footprint to grab any nutritious debris (fallen leaves, cow pies) you may have left behind.

"It's sentient," the mycologist Paul Stamets says of a fungus. "It knows you are there." Stamets found what might be the largest organism in the world, a 2,400-acre site in eastern Oregon that hosted a contiguous growth of mycelium before logging roads cut through it. In his 2005 book *Mycelium Running: How Mushrooms Can Help Save the World*, Stamets writes: "Estimated at 1,665 football fields in size and 2,200 years old, this one fungus has killed the forest above it several times over, and in so doing has built deeper soil layers that allow the growth of ever-larger stands of trees."

I have had a lifelong love affair with trees, and so, unawares, I have also loved the fungi that make their existence possible. If you walk down the gravel lane that goes from the apprentices' trailer to the bottom field, you pass three sentry oaks, each about 200 years old. They are not so much guards as guardians—watchful, graceful beings who shelter us under their leaves in summer and their limbs in winter. The lane goes alongside the three white oaks and then bottoms out and makes a sharp turn to the north. At that point, near the base of the hill, an old burr oak stood for centuries.

But one year, a February ice storm toppled it. Perhaps the slowly eroding hillside had undercut it, or perhaps disease had weakened it,

or perhaps the weight of ice threw it off balance just enough to reach its literal tipping point. It was an unexpected end to a grand tree. We wasted no time mourning its demise, however, and quickly accepted it as a gift. We decided that, in death, it would host new life—shiitake mushrooms to be precise.

We immediately ordered "spawn" from a supplier—not spawn of the devil, but spawn of shiitake. Spawn is made of threadlike mycelia—the vegetative part of a fungus. The mushrooms themselves are fruiting bodies, the means by which a fungus produces spores to sexually reproduce itself. But the bulk of a fungus is the mass of branching threadlike hyphae that make up the mycelia.

While we were awaiting delivery of the shiitake spawn, we got out our chainsaws and went to cut branches from the old oak while standing on the spongy soil and its miles of mycelia, which undoubtedly knew we were there, and found plenty of bits of bark and sawdust to grab once we were gone. Perhaps the fungi even knew what we were after: branches about seven inches in diameter that would become the food source for their exotic foreign cousin.

Once we removed branches of the right size, we cut them into logs about three feet long. To inoculate nonnative fungi such as shiitake into a tree, you need fresh logs from a live tree, or from a very recently downed one like this. If you try to inoculate old, dead wood with shiitake or other mushroom mycelia, it will not take because native fungi will have already colonized the log. Since we are loathe to cut a living oak, the ice storm gave us this opportunity to harvest oak branches for shiitake.

Sautéed Shiitake Toasts

As with all fresh foods, the best thing to do with them is to get out of the way, preparing them as simply as possible. You can give the fruiting bodies of the great recyclers the respect they deserve by frying them in butter and eating them on toast.

6–8 fresh shiitake mushrooms

2 tablespoons butter

12–16 rounds of sourdough baguette, or country bread, toasted

Brush any soil or debris off the mushrooms.

Heat the butter in a sauté pan.

Take the stem off each mushroom and slice the mushroom into strips. Stir them into the hot butter. Cook until limp. Serve on the toast rounds.

In Japanese, *ta-ke* means mushroom, and whatever precedes that word usually describes the type of tree the mushroom grows on—matsutake grow on pine (*matsu*), and shiitake grow on oak (*shii*). Shiitake will grow on other trees as well, but the flavors are better on oak, and the dense oak logs will bear mushrooms for five to seven years, longer than lighter woods. So we cut the oak logs and hauled them into my basement and called friends and neighbors to let them know that a drilling and inoculating party would happen shortly.

On the day the spawn arrived, mixed in with damp sawdust, everyone came over with their drills, and we set up a shiitake assembly line. Henry and Bill Davison, who had recently orchestrated the scraping, gutting, and dismantling of the hogs, set logs atop sawhorses in my basement and drilled holes every six inches in parallel rows in a diamond pattern all over the log. Through trial and error, we figured out how to stuff the loose, damp, spawn-infused sawdust into the holes. Once each hole was packed full of the sawdust/spawn, we sealed it with hot wax to prevent the spawn from drying out and dying, and also to prevent the vigorous native fungi from taking over during the time it would take the shiitake mycelia to fully colonize the log.

The whole inoculation process took the better part of two days, and the end of each day was celebrated with a few beers. (But not before all the drills were put away, since one of the farm rules is, "Never drink and drill.") Once we were done, we had some 60 logs primed and ready to bear shiitake mushrooms for the next five years or more. It takes the mycelia about four to six months to colonize the log, and after that you start to get mushrooms.

While the ground was still frozen and easy to traverse, we hauled the logs—now an all-you-can-eat buffet for the shiitake mycelia—down the hill from my house into what would be deep shade come summer. We returned home with visions of mushrooms dancing in our heads—their delicate brown skin cracking to reveal creamy white flesh and releasing deep, woodsy, earthy flavors.

Delicious as mushrooms are, however, they are just the tip of the proverbial iceberg when it comes to the benefits of fungi to humans and to the earth. Mycologists have found that over 90 percent of the plants they look at have mycorrhizal associations ("myco" for the fungus, "rhiza" for the root) in which the fungi act in partnership with the roots of plants to extend their reach into the soil, enhancing their uptake of water and nutrients. In this mutually beneficial relationship, fungi extract food (carbohydrates, such as glucose) from the plant roots, in effect photosynthesizing vicariously. In return, the plant gets access to the huge network of mycelium, and its hundreds of miles of surface area that can absorb water and mineral nutrients from the soil. The enhanced access to water means the plants are more drought-resistant, and the enhanced nutrition means they are often healthier.

Now and then, Henry pays a local ag company to test his soil. It always comes back that he is low in phosphorus, and the company tells him how much phosphorus he needs to buy and apply to his fields. But there is no sign of phosphorus deficiency in any of his plants, and Henry knows they are getting plenty of it, thanks to the mycorrhizae.

In a conventional field, however, there are few mycorrhizae to be found. Agricultural chemicals, particularly fungicides, kill fungi and upset the interconnections and synergies between the soil, fungi, and plants. Ag companies then sell "solutions" to the problems they have caused. It is similar to the problems people face when they start taking prescription drugs. Soon the number of drugs spirals out of control, because for each one you take, you need a few more to counteract the side effects, and things often go from bad to worse. Similarly, if you spray a fungicide, you kill the mycorrhizae that used to supply your plants with nutrients and water, so now you need to apply more nutrients, and you need to pay for GMO seed that's engineered to be drought-resistant. The farmers and their fields get poorer in the process, while the companies get richer. And so the damaging cycle continues, while the agribusiness companies' coffers increase.

For these and many other reasons, Henry tends to the invisible fungi in his fields, providing them with organic matter and disturbing them as little as possible. By leaving one of his ten-acre bottom-land fields fallow for two years, he gives his mycorrhizae a chance to grow and branch and network undisturbed. During this time, they form associations with many different kinds of plants, both in the field and in the forests surrounding it, forming a giant underground network connecting the whole habitat. Perhaps fungi are not only the earth's greatest recyclers but the earth's greatest networkers as well.

WEEK 16. **Wood Work**

FEBRUARY IS FICKLE. THE ICE STORM THAT PROVIDED US WITH shiitake oak logs melted completely a few days later when a warm front brought a couple of days in the sixties. But now the snow is coming down again, thick as ever, and I'm back to feeding the woodstove. A small stick is burning with fury in the front of the firebox, while the larger logs seem waterlogged and barely burn at all. They glow red, and slowly turn into charcoal, but raise no flame.

The small stick is a piece of hedge. Dad never puts hedge in his woodstove, and cautions us not to either, since it burns as hot as coal. Our stoves are meant for wood burning, not coal burning. But it is a small stick, so I take my chances, and watch as it burns brightly and spits out mini-fireworks of sparks.

Hedge is from hedge trees, also known as Osage Orange. They are the only trees we do not normally use to heat our homes. Gathering wood is a winter task, a big part of our lives from December through March. Henry and Dad make mental notes each summer of which trees have come down in the woods, and where and when. Then, during the cold months, they'll say one week, "Let's go get that black walnut down the back hill that came down two years ago." Or another week, "We better get that elm that came down three years ago next to the barn pasture before it starts to rot."

Henry waits for a day that's not too muddy or too cold, preferably on a weekend when the kids can help out. Then he puts the word out that we're going to get wood, and whoever is available comes to help. We generally have two people running the chain saws, and the others carrying logs up to the truck. For many years, the two chainsaws have been Henry's and Dad's, but with Dad now suffering from more frequent bouts of nausea, dizziness, and delirium, our neighbors Bob and Renée have begun to help out.

I always relish the moment when the echoes of the chainsaws die away and silence returns to the winter woods. Then everyone joins in to pick up the last logs and break up the last twigs and

small branches, which we put into feed sacks for kindling. When the trucks are completely loaded, we bring the wood to whomever's house that particular load is for and unload it onto the woodpile. People without much upper body strength (that would be me) help stack the smaller pieces of wood, while stronger folks split the larger logs—sometimes with an axe or maul, other times starting with a sledgehammer and wedges.

But hedge never comes under the sledgehammer or axe. In many ways, it's more like stone than wood. If you try to take a chainsaw to it, sparks fly and the chain will be made as dull as a butter knife in no time. The tree is native to a small area of the Red River Valley in southern Oklahoma and northern Texas, and the strong wood was valued by the Osage tribe, who made unbreakable bows with it. They and other tribes actively spread the tree for that purpose, but it was the white settlers who spread it even further for their own purposes—first as living fences, and then as fenceposts.

Before barbed wire was invented in 1875, many thousands of miles of young Osage Orange trees were planted near each other and then pruned to promote bushy growth. If done correctly, the resulting fence was praised as being "horse-high, bull-strong, and

Zoe carries a log up to the top of the hill for Asa to split. Wood is the main source of winter heat for our homes, and this family activity takes place every few weeks throughout the winter.

hog-tight." After barbed wire made living hedge fences obsolete, the trees were put to another fencing use—as nearly indestructible fence posts.

Grandpa regularly pruned his hedge trees to make them grow straight for this purpose. Then he would save the little branches to burn in the heater under the cows' water tank to keep the water from freezing in the winter. After Grandpa's accident ended his active farming career, his tenant removed all the fences so he could plow, as national farm policy recommended, "fencerow to fencerow." The tenant also pulled out all the hedge posts, as they got in the way of his machinery and were no longer needed to keep livestock. At that point, in the early 1960s, Grandpa's hedge fenceposts were already 50 years old, with no rot evident. Dad kept them in the barn for years, and then set them as the corner posts for the cow pastures when we moved to The Land in the early 1970s. They are still there, solid as concrete, almost 40 years later.

All farmers and ranchers of a certain age know that hedge wood is so hard you can't drive a nail into it, and so dense it will never rot from the inside. Nor will it succumb to termites or other insects. Slowly, over many decades, my dad says, the posts will begin to rot from the outside, but extremely slowly. Scientists have found antifungal compounds in the heartwood that protect it from normal decay, and the outer sapwood is so thin that even small-diameter posts have a high proportion of heartwood. A hedge fencepost, it is said, will still be standing tall when the farmer who set it is laid in his grave.

Now that most farmers no longer keep livestock, and those that do pack them into confined animal feeding operations or CAFOs, Osage Orange fenceposts and fencerows, and the tree itself, have rapidly disappeared. Only scattered remnants of the thousands of miles of living fence remain.

The piece of wood in my stove comes from a gnarled old specimen outside my house. Under a full moon, its branches remind me of the grasping fingers of a wicked witch or evil stepmother in a tale by the Brothers Grimm. The few hedge trees on my property were once part of a hedgerow lining the old settlers' road that curved around my hillside a hundred years ago. Now we use the sturdy old hedge tree to anchor the clothesline, and so had cut a few branches that were in the way of a straight run. That is the wood that dances merrily as it is consumed in my stove.

WEEK 17. Hoophouse Dreams

WE ARE STILL STOKING OUR WOODSTOVES BECAUSE AL-though the days are getting longer, the ice and snow are lingering. The frozen earth is broken by thaws that leave mud gouged deep by winter boots, truck tires, cow hooves. Over-night, all imprints are transformed into artful black sculptures, the comings and goings of the previous day frozen in time and space like stop-action photographs.

But it is only the frozen things that are at rest as we reach the end of February. We are not stills, but swiftly moving pictures. Henry is almost Chaplinesque as he moves about the barn, pastures, fields, and hoophouses, doing all the things that must be done before the grow-ing season is upon us. For although it is still cold, day length does not lie, and the longer days say that warmth is on its way.

What Henry is most intent on right now is creating a bit of balmy weather just a short ways down the lane. This is where his three hoophouses stand, patiently awaiting their springtime role as the birthplace, incubator, and playpen for thousands of vege-table starts. Because the last frost can hit central Illinois as late as May, and the first frost can kill crops as soon as mid-September, we only have about four months of outdoor growing time for cold-sensitive crops.

But with hoophouses, we can grow things (like the long-season *Brassica*) that we wouldn't be able to seed in the field because they need warm soil to germinate, but cool weather to grow and produce. In other words, there would be no broccoli, because by the time the soil is warm enough for the seed to germinate, the young plant would be stressed out in the heat of July and August, and we would be lucky

In mid-April, Henry hand-digs the earth in the hoophouse that will host his customers' favorite heirloom tomatoes. They will bear here from late June through early November.

to get any heads of broccoli at all, since broccoli needs relatively cool weather. But we can seed broccoli and many other crops in the warm hoophouse, and then put the half-grown transplants in the ground in April and May. If all goes well, we can then harvest full-size lettuce and broccoli in late May. What the hoophouse and transplants do is allow us to raise crops that we would otherwise be unable to with the hot summers and possibilities of late spring and early fall frosts here in central Illinois.

After the hoophouses have completed their first act as a plant nursery, Henry gives them a second act for the rest of the season—a Mediterranean getaway. This is where some of the heirloom tomatoes, Japanese cucumbers, and colored peppers will live. They didn't evolve to thrive on a normal Illinois summer of high humidity, waterlogged soil after thunderstorms, and cool days and nights at either end of the season, but we can create the conditions they evolved to thrive on—dry soil, dry air, intense sunlight, and high heat—in the hoophouses.

A hoophouse is a simple series of large convex hoops made of metal or plastic covered with special hoophouse plastic. This plastic skin is stretched tight and fastened to baseboards. Hoophouses are low tech, low cost, and extremely effective for germinating seeds and then potting out and growing the seedlings in soil blocks. Hoophouses are also very sturdy structures. Henry's have survived thunderstorms, hailstorms, snowstorms, and even a tornado that destroyed a small manufacturing company about five miles north of us.

But a couple of years ago, we had the perfect ice storm. The precipitation came down from the clouds as rain, but then it hit frigid air near the ground just in time to freeze on whatever it fell upon. It hit and froze in layers until an inch of ice glazed every surface, including the plastic covering of Henry's hoophouses. All was well until we got six inches of wet snow. At some point, the hundreds of pounds of ice and snow were just too much, and the curved dome of the hoophouse collapsed, the convex covering going suddenly and disastrously concave.

There was nothing to do then but wait for the ice to melt (and for the insurers to deny coverage), and then dismantle the twisted metal, dispose of the torn plastic, order the new metal parts and the big new roll of plastic, and wait for spring. As spring blew in, Henry reconstructed the wood and metal parts.

Then he put out the word that Sunday would be the day to cover the frame with the huge sheet of plastic. By the time the family assembled, from grandparents down to the youngest child, the morning calm had given way to warm spring breezes. So Henry decided to simply tack the plastic down along the sides, hold it with cleats, and use very long extension cords as ropes to wrap around the whole structure to keep the plastic in place until the next day.

Generally, the wind calms down at night, and so we got up just after dawn and gathered around the new hoophouse skeleton. Henry studied the loose plastic as it gently billowed up and down in the breeze, a slow-breathing, supine oracle. We debated our options. In the end, though we were all ready, Henry decided that, in the words of Hamlet, "If it be now, 'tis not to come; if it be not to come, it will be now; if it be not now, yet it will come: the readiness is all." And it was the wind that was ready, not us. Though light, it was gathering strength, making it difficult for us to stretch the plastic taut. And if it's not taut, it will billow and catch the wind and pull away from its moorings at some inopportune time, such as when the seedlings are up but the night is cold.

So we pried off the cleats from the day before and untied the long cords. Then a row of us—Henry, Hiroko, their kids, and the grand-parents—held the long south side of the plastic sheet up at shoulder height and waited some 20 or 30 seconds until the next light breeze filled it like a sail. Then we released our hold, and the wind gently lifted it up and over the curving frame. It slid down the other side, graceful as a dying ballerina. We folded it lengthwise and rolled it up, tied it, and let it wait for the next calm day, realizing that sometimes the best way forward is retreat.

This year, the hoophouses all made it through the winter without any structural damage, but there's a lot of prep to do before the first seeds can be planted in them. In February, Henry starts cleaning out all three hoophouses by removing old mulch and pulling out all the stakes and trellising that held up the heirloom tomatoes, colored pep-pers, and cucumbers last season. Then he hand-digs and turns over the soil, making it loose and flat. He then stretches extra hoophouse plastic over the ends of the tunnel, and puts in a small door at each end so little heat will be lost in his comings and goings. Finally, he sets up the heat tape on the benches and worktables where the germina-tion trays will be, and verdant life can begin.

Before a single seed is planted, though, Henry makes two pilgrim-ages. The first is down to the bottom field for a truckload of black dirt, which will be used as part of the mix for the soil blocks, as well as for a warm, fertile blanket over the direct-seeded alliums and brassica in another hoophouse. The second pilgrimage is to the upper field for a truckload of compost. This will also become part of the mix for the soil blocks, in which individual tiny seedlings from the germination trays will grow until they are ready to be transplanted to the field once the danger of frost has passed.

Because the hoophouses cannot be moved to new ground or left fallow, their soil must always be enriched with organic matter and nitrogen. Rich black soil and composted manure is the perfect mix. The best black dirt on the whole farm is on the south side of the hill that goes up to the apprentices' trailer. It's where the big oak came down in the ice storm a few years back. Near the remains of that fallen giant—now food for shiitake mycelia—is a large patch of loose, sandy, dark-black earth full of humus from all the fungi and bacteria working to break down tree leaves and bark and branches over the years. As the hill curves from south to east, the black dirt turns to the clay that is generally found on forested hills. Henry brings the tractor down and uses the front loader to lift the rich, dark earth into the bed of the pickup, and Matt hauls it up to the hoophouses.

This pepper seedling has just been transplanted from the germination tray to its very own soil block, where it will grow until it is transplanted out into the field in mid-May.

Then Henry drives the tractor over to the compost pile at the north end of the upper field. Matt returns with the empty pickup, and they pile its bed high with composted straw and manure, mainly gathered from Dad's cattle the previous winter and now crumbly, odor free, black, and rich—like good soil, only better. In the spring, summer, and winter, the cows effectively fertilize the ground by doing their business randomly all over their pastures, where it is rained upon and broken down. But in winter, the cattle are brought up to the shelter of the barn, where they congregate around the hay feeders to eat. What goes in comes out in the tight area where they stand, and it generally freezes and remains in a state of suspended animation all winter.

So throughout the winter, we pile up the frozen cow patties, mixed with hay and straw the cows have dragged out from the feeders, and let the rich mixture compost over the next year. While many people do not like to see the words "manure" and "vegetables" in the same sentence, or think about them in the same thought, composting kills pathogenic bacteria and breaks down the plant and animal matter in the compost to a crumbly, clean, fertile substance that looks and feels and smells like the fresh, good soil it will soon be mixed with. And while there are strict regulations governing the composting and use of manure in the USDA's National Organic Program, there were, until the recent contamination crises, no such regulations for conventional producers.

After the bed of the pickup is full, Henry returns to the hoophouses and shovels the compost out of the pickup and into the three-sided bin just outside the first hoophouse. Inside this hoophouse is where he will plant the very first seeds of the season, the slow-growing celery and celery root, and it is where those first seedlings will be "blocked out" into freestanding soil blocks. The question is, "When?" and the answer is, "At the moment when Henry feels the weather has changed, and spring is on its way." If he jumps the gun, he will end up having to burn a kerosene heater, which defeats the purpose of a passive solar hoophouse. But more importantly, planting earlier doesn't give you a head start if the weather doesn't provide you with the warmth and daylight the crops need to germinate and grow.

"Sure, you can plant in mid-February," Henry says, "but the seeds will just sit there until it heats up in late February, so you might as well plant in late February or early March and save yourself some grief." And so we wait, until Henry's sixth sense tells us the time is right.

Windmill

v. WINDY MOON

WEEK 18. **Invisible Corner Turned**

MY SIBLINGS AND I GREW UP WITHOUT A TELEVISION. THAT meant we didn't have a clue about most of what our classmates talked about at school. It also meant we committed to memory a large number of songs and stories we would play over and over again on our one piece of home entertainment technology, the record player. On rainy days, or evenings, or during "nap time"—which seemed mainly for the benefit of our father, a lifelong proponent of the afternoon nap—the six of us would lie down around the small brown square of the portable record player, heads close in and bodies splayed outward like spokes of a wheel. We did this so often we can now, in our forties and fifties, embarrass our children, nieces, and nephews, by launching into a lusty rendition of "The Ballad of Sir Isaac Newton," or "The Sun Is a Mass of Incandescent Gas" at the drop of a hat. These are from the timeless "Space Songs" edition of "Ballads for the Age of Science" that our mother had bought for us, and that we listened to incessantly.

Another of the records we memorized in its entirety was the soundtrack from *Winnie the Pooh and the Blustery Day*. This contains perhaps the best March weather song ever written, with wind that lashes "lustily," as trees thrash "thrustily," and leaves rustle "gustily."

Perhaps it was exactly this sort of blustery March wind that blew Henry and Hiroko together some 20 years ago. They were married on the outskirts of Nagoya, Japan in the month of the Windy Moon, on the 15th to be precise. This day reminds me of that one, with its bright sunshine and chill breeze.

I hunch my shoulders and lean into the wind as I make my way to the hoophouse where Henry is working. I open the small wooden-framed door and lift the plastic veil that hangs over the doorway. Warm, moist air that smells of newly turned earth invades my lungs. I breathe deeply and feel my hunched shoulders relax, and my muscles soften. I've entered a time warp and it's suddenly, blessedly, summer.

Although Henry seems completely focused on his work, I know that he is continually monitoring slight variations in temperature, ready to open or close doors and vents as needed to keep the hoophouse in the balmy eighties. Now, though, Henry is at his station—bending over the workbench, germination trays in front of him, and seed packets at the ready.

It has always seemed to me that there should be some sort of fanfare as the first seeds of a new season go into the soil. But this sacred mundane act generally happens in silence. Henry places the 72-hole germination trays over the heat tape on his worktable and fills them with a mixture of black dirt and perlite up to about a quarter-inch from the top. He doesn't need compost in the mix because the seeds contain within them all the nutrients and energy they need to germinate, the same way an egg contains within it everything a chick needs to develop, hatch, and then live for three days after hatching with no

need for food or water. By the time the seedlings would need to start getting nutrients from the soil, Henry will have blocked them out into the compost-rich soil blocks where they will grow until it's warm and dry enough to put them out in the field.

Once the germination trays are ready, Henry thickly sows his first crops. He generally sows four to six times as many seeds as he wants plants. This provides a margin of error against poor germination and other random disasters, like mice getting in at night and digging up a high-protein snack. Also, this gives Henry the opportunity to select the strongest and the fittest seedlings to block out—a little unnatural selection. As he works, Henry sketches out the rectangle of each germination tray on a page of his pocket-size looseleaf notebook. He records each variety as he plants it so he can track it all the way from seeding to blocking to transplanting to harvesting to post-harvest analyzing.

When the seeds have been sown, Henry covers them—barely—with a light soil mix. He firms it up on top of the seeds so they won't float away when he waters them, which he does with a fine misting

Planted in late April, these blocked-out tomatoes, peppers, and eggplants are almost ready for transplanting down into the field.

spray. A good wetting down at this stage gives the seeds enough moisture to germinate. Watering during the germination stage is a bad idea because it tends to cause the dreaded "damping-off" disease, where apparently thriving seedlings suddenly slump over and perish in a sort of sudden seedling death syndrome.

At the end of each hoophouse planting day, Henry gathers together all of the trays that have been planted, covered, tamped down, and watered. He stacks them on the heat tape on the workbench and then covers the mini-tower of trays, plus the heat tape at the bottom, with a layer of hoophouse plastic. This ensures that even though the nights can still get well below freezing, the germinating seeds will stay nice and toasty in their hoophouse within a hoophouse. As we glance back before leaving for the day, we can feel the verdant vibrations of thousands of plants starting to swell with life there in that tiny patch of hoophouse real estate—a ten- by three-foot bench.

WEEK 19. **Hoophouse Sprouts**

HOUR AFTER HOUR, DAY AFTER DAY, THE FIRST HOOPHOUSE continues to be the site of intense sowing of the many seeds that have been coming in the mail and via UPS ever since January—tomatoes, eggplant, peppers, celery, celery root, dry flowers, edible Johnny Jump Ups, violas and gem marigolds, papalo, epazote, lettuce, radicchio, endive, dandelion, parsley, fennel, basil, shiso, and more.

As soon as the seedlings in the germination trays are an inch or so out of the soil (with roots many times longer down below), Henry begins to "block them out." To do this, he mixes compost, soil, sand, vermiculite, and lots of peat moss (the glue that holds the soil block together), wets it down a little, and uses a soil blocker to press the soil into tight blocks that look like peat pots full of soil—without the peat pot.

He then carefully extracts, one by one, the strongest seedlings from the germination trays and uses the end of a ballpoint pen to press the root down into the center of a soil block. All year long, Henry saves out-of-ink pens for exactly this purpose. It's not easy to twirl the long, wispy, hair-like root of a seedling around a defunct ballpoint pen and place it swiftly and firmly into its own little soil block. The year I tried, it seemed that Henry planted ten to my every one, with speed and precision, while I tried desperately not to break the root or damage the tender stem. It made me think that, if I ever needed delicate surgery, I'd like Henry to do it, even if all he had to use were a ballpoint pen!

He does the small subtle movements again and again, hour after hour, day after day—sometimes with help from Hiroko and the kids, or from Matt and the apprentices, but much of the time alone with NPR, and the seedlings, and the rhythms of the work. Farmwork takes

In April the March-planted beet seeds send up their first red-veined leaves. Henry layers beets, carrots, lettuces, and Japanese turnips in amongst the peppers and tomatoes in his greenhouses, to be ready for the very first market in mid-May.

strong minds as well as strong bodies. There is a contemplative calmness to repetitive actions, whether it's blocking out seedlings, weeding
carrots, or picking beans. Some of the apprentices never get to that
meditative state, and they leave the farm after a few weeks. I don't
get there that often, with my mind fluttering to other worries and
responsibilities. But Henry and Matt and the others seem to flow into
it, and do what needs to be done efficiently and calmly, even though
to most of the world it looks like mind-numbing repetition. My dad
says that when he watches Henry work with such calm purpose and
efficiency, he sees his own father. He always remarks that the similar-
ity is uncanny.

At the same time the seeding and blocking are going on full force
in the first hoophouse, Henry prepares the second hoophouse for direct seeding of alliums (the onion family) and brassica (the cabbage

family). The second house is aligned with the first, and seems almost an extension of it—except that there is a 10-foot gap between the two. Henry uses 40 feet of the 16- by 72-foot hoophouse for direct-seeded transplants.

Direct-seeding means placing the seeds directly into the earth, not into a germination tray or soil block or peat pot or other container. When the crops are large enough to be transplanted to the field, they are simply dug out of the hoophouse soil and put directly, "bare root," in the field. Most crop families cannot handle that kind of stress, but the alliums and brassica have strong, fast-growing roots that can quickly reestablish the plant in a new environment.

To get the ground under the hoophouse ready for direct seeding of the allium and brassica plants, Henry scoops a series of eight-inch-wide troughs that run from the center aisle to the outside edge, where the curved side of the hoophouse meets the baseboard at ground level. Then he mixes compost with the hoophouse soil, puts it into the troughs, and levels them out. On top of the soil–compost mixture, he spreads about an inch of the black dirt he brought up from the bottomland. This creates an extremely fertile bed for planting.

He lays out all his varieties, maps them out in his notebook, and then thickly sows a broad band of seeds across each eight-inch filled trough, and sprinkles another quarter inch of black dirt on top of them. Then he puts two- by six-inch boards in between each eight-inch swath of planted seeds. These boards are for us to stand on as we work with the plants, so we don't compact the soil. They also physically stop any weeds from coming up in between the rows of seedlings. Then Henry tamps the soil down and waters the seeds.

Finally, he tucks them in by laying hoophouse plastic directly on top of the ground, creating another hoophouse inside a hoophouse so the soil temperature will rise to around 80 degrees for quick germination. The black soil is important, not only for fertility but also for getting the soil up to temperature. The seeds are enclosed in a black blanket that will warm up much faster and to a higher temperature than the surrounding lighter brown soil when the sun hits it and the dark color absorbs the rays.

Looking back, Henry admires the pattern of the parallel boards and, in between them, the 28 thickly seeded rows of different alliums, including onions, leeks, and scallions. He can see in his mind's eye the different sizes, shapes, colors, and flavors that each of the varieties will become. I think of some of their names and can't resist reciting a few of them aloud: White Wing, Redwing, Superstar, Red Baron, Gladstone, Walla Walla, Red Marble, Bianco di Maggion, Bleu de Solaize, Bandit, and Feast.

About a week after direct-seeding the alliums, Henry follows the same procedure on the other side of the center aisle, planting 32 varieties of brassica, including many kales, broccolis, kohlrabi, cabbage, brussels sprouts, and collards. Within days, the second hoophouse is hosting tens of thousands of sprouts. A few weeks later, Henry will plant extra lettuce starts in the remaining 32 feet of this hoophouse, ensuring that we will have some nice lettuce heads at the very first farmers' markets. Around the same time, he'll plant colored pepper starts here as well, in between the still-small lettuce heads. Once the lettuces are harvested for the first CSAs and markets, this hoophouse will be dedicated to colored peppers for the rest of the season. And when we're done with the seedlings in the first hoophouse, it will be dedicated to producing Japanese cucumbers for the remainder of the year.

Henry's third hoophouse is the largest of all, running 72 feet long, like the second, but wider by 4 feet and also taller. It will become home for some of the eight most popular varieties of heirloom tomatoes: the red and yellow Brandywines, Rose de Berne, Cherokee Purple, Striped German, and the Zebras—Green, Red, and Black. These tomato plants start their lives like all the others, when Henry sows the seeds in germination trays in the first hoophouse in late February or early March. In mid-March, he puts them into individual soil blocks, and then he places over 250 of them into their hoophouse homes by mid-April—a full month before the remaining 1,000 or so tomato starts can be safely planted out in the field.

In that same hoophouse, before the tomatoes grow too tall and start to shade things below, Henry layers on an early crop of carrots, beets, Japanese turnips, and radishes. The radishes will be ready to eat in about three weeks, and the carrots, beets, and turnips shortly after that—to the delight of our first customers, and the chagrin of some of our competitors at the market.

Our neighbor across the aisle at the Evanston Farmers' Market farms north and west of Chicago. Every year he stops by Henry's stand to chat about how the winter went and to look over what Henry's brought up for the first market. Seeing carrots and beets and lettuces in mid-May, he shakes his head in disbelief and says, "Henry, you devil from the south!"

Henry smiles, knowing it's not a matter of devilry but of hard work, hoophouse plastic, double planting, and the efficient use of time and space.

WEEK 20. Ramps Up

WHILE WE ARE TENDING TO OUR FIRST WISPY SEEDLINGS, Mother Nature is way ahead of us with fully formed ramps, ready for the frying pan. But this first wild green of spring was a complete unknown to me until I returned to Illinois. Then, as part of my work with the Land Connection, I made the acquaintance of Kris and Marty Travis, the stewards of Spence Farm, who live and work about an hour due west of Henry's Farm.

Marty told us about the ramps growing in his cousin's woodlot, and said he could use some help digging them. So a ragtag group of about six of us joined the Spence Farm folks for what would become, in a few years' time, a highly sought-after invitation to join in the annual Ramp Dig.

A few days earlier, the weatherman had forecast cold rain, but the day of that first dig dawned clear and the mercury soared. We brought spades and boots, and drove half a mile or so down the road from the big cream-colored Spence farmhouse to a 20-acre, 75-year-old grove of timber. By the time we entered the woods, around 11 a.m., the air in the low-lying woodland was steamy and the black soil wet, spongy,

and lushly carpeted in bright green ramps with burgundy stems. As soon as we began digging, our nostrils filled with the musky, pungent scent of earth and the unmistakable garlic–onion smell of ramps, which the wild foods evangelist Euell Gibbons called "the sweetest and the best of the wild onions." According to *The Encyclopedia of American Food and Drink*, the work "ramp" comes from "rams" or "ramson," Elizabethan words for wild garlic.

Digging ramps is not easy. The wet soil sucks at your spade, and the dense network of tree roots stymies your best efforts to pop loose clusters of ramps. Marty showed us how to work in pairs, with one person gradually loosening the ramps with a spade while another gently pulls them up, wipes off as much mud as possible, and places them in a plastic-lined box. The hours passed quickly, and I had just barely entered the zen of ramp-digging when our hosts called us back to the farmhouse to start cleaning the ramps, and ourselves, in preparation for a midday springtime feast.

Washing ramps is even more arduous than digging them. You swish them in a bucket of water and then work on them one by one, stripping away the loose balloon of slick skin surrounding the pencil-thin stalk, and washing away all the mud grasped by the tenacious roots.

While we were washing, Marty explained that Spence Farm was settled by his great-great-great-great-grandfather in 1830, and that it is the oldest family farm in Livingston County, Illinois. It began as 160 acres (purchased for $1.25 per acre), but by the late 1800s, the farm had grown to nearly 1,000 acres and 36 farm buildings. Horses were bred there and sold as far away as England, and the farm produced sheep, hogs, cows, chickens, and tons of maple syrup from more than 600 trees.

By the 1970s, however, the farm had dwindled back to the original 160 acres. The Spence family nearly lost the farm, but today Kris and Marty are resurrecting it as a diverse sustainable farm and a place where people can learn about the future of farming—crop and animal diversity, heirloom crops and heritage breeds, woodland management, and building restoration—through education and tours put on by their newly formed Spence Farm Foundation.

Marty admitted that his first interaction with ramps had been trying to kill them. They carpeted his cousin's forest floor each spring in such profusion that they crowded out the wildflowers. So Marty took a weed-whacker to them, but that only seemed to make them stronger. Next, he tried dousing them with Round-Up herbicide. That knocked them back, but only until the next season, when they returned unfazed.

Finally, Marty started asking around about these persistent and pungent "weeds," and discovered that chefs were willing to pay upwards of $10 a pound for this delicacy. When he began calling chefs in Champaign and Chicago, everyone he called put in an order. This is when he decided to hire a workforce, which we were part of that first year, and go into the ramp business from mid-March to mid-April.

It is fitting that most of the Spence Farm ramps go to Chicago restaurants, since ramps and Chicago have an intimate connection that has been all but forgotten. According to research by John Swenson, the native Menomini people called the broad-leaved wild ramps *pikwute sikakushia* (skunk plant), and they referred to the area near the southern shore of Lake Michigan, where the ramps grew abundantly, as *Cicaga Wuni* or *shikako* (skunk place) or—yes—Chicago.

As we left our washing to go into the house for a farm lunch, Marty explained that the reason most native Illinoisans have never seen a single one of these delicious native plants is that their habitat, boggy forestland, all but disappeared as Illinois's rich forests were cut and wetlands drained to make the land productive. The forest that had originally covered this area had been cut over a century ago, and then planted in row crops for the next 40 years. But the low spot where we had just dug the ramps was always mucky, so around 75 years ago, his cousin's family had let it revert to woodland.

Ramp and Goat Cheese Pasta

Today, ramp hunters head into Illinois woodlands in late March and early April, before the trees even begin to bud, to gather this native plant for the first fresh greens of the season. Both the foliage and the bulbs, whether raw or cooked, can be used on pizza or sandwiches, in salads and soups, and in omelets, quiches, and other egg dishes. At the same time the ramps are coming into season, baby goats are being born, which means it's also the start of the fresh chevre season. What better way to welcome the new season of earthly delights than with a ramp and goat cheese pasta?

1 pound linguine, spaghetti, or other pasta

15–20 fresh ramps, both stems and leaves

4 tablespoons olive oil

1 clove garlic, thinly sliced

¼ cup fresh chevre (or more, to taste)

Pecorino–Romano cheese, freshly grated, to taste

Olive oil (optional)

Put a large pot of salted water on to boil and begin cooking the pasta as directed.

Clean the ramps, removing the translucent husks over the bulbs (if they are freshly dug) and the roots. Slice the stems into ½- to 1-inch lengths, and coarsely chop the greens. Reserve the greens.

Heat the olive oil in a large sauté pan until just smoking, and then remove the pan from the flame. Add the ramp stems to the oil and toss them well, until they are coated with the oil.

Return the pan to the heat and sear the ramps until they are blistered, brown, and soft. Reduce the heat and add the garlic to the pan, tossing until it is toasted to a light brown.

Drain the pasta as soon as it is al dente, and then add it to the pan along with the ramp greens. Toss until the leaves are wilted. Stir in the chevre. Transfer to serving plates, and grate the fresh Pecorino–Romano over the top. Finish with a drizzle of olive oil, if desired.

Although the first year's Ramp Dig yielded less than a thousand pounds, Marty calculated that he had made more money on a tenth of an acre of "wasteland" than neighbor farmers were making on 100 acres of the best soil in the world.

WEEK 21. SPRING EQUINOX: Patchwork Emerges

WE HAVE REACHED ONE OF THE TWO MOMENTS EACH YEAR when 12 hours of daylight are perfectly balanced with 12 hours of night. While many cultures celebrate the equinox, Henry hears it as a starting gun: the beginning of a race, unfolding at an ever-quickening pace, until we reach June 21, the longest day of the year. Henry writes,

> I may not be a solar-powered being, but during the growing season I am definitely a solar-activated being. To keep up with the plants on my 10 acres, I have to match my lifestyle to theirs. Starting at the Spring Equinox, I rise a little earlier each morning and go to bed a little later each night until the summer solstice, when the birds sing me awake at a quarter after four in the morning and nightfall doesn't chase me home until after nine in the evening.

Now, while his workdays are still a relatively leisurely 7 a.m. to 7 p.m., Henry multitasks—working on the seedlings in the hoophouse while also plotting this year's field layout. He remembers what grew in each part of the field last year, knows what cover crop is currently there, and imagines what will grow best there this year. His spring imaginings are all about the art of crop rotation, the first rule of which is to never plant the same crop in the same place two years in a row. To do so is asking for trouble—problems with fertility, insects, disease, weeds, and soil health.

Unlike conventional fields throughout the Midwest, which are all barren at this time of the year, Henry's fields are a beautiful patchwork quilt in shades of green and black. Each shade denotes a different cover crop. The patches of blue-green stippled with pale, soft green are the wheat and hairy vetch cover crop he sowed last fall. The black patches are the late-season beds of fall greens and roots. There crops formed a canopy that shaded out late-germinating weeds.

The dark green patches are where the late crops of lettuce, beets, and other noncanopy crops stood. Henry allowed weeds to grow there, so now these beds are covered with field pennycress, a "wonderful weed," according to Henry. It is wonderful because it survives the winter, holds the soil against wind and water erosion, and is edible. It also grows rapidly, reaching 18 inches by mid-April and providing a rich green manure to till under prior to planting. On top of all that, it releases phytochemicals that inhibit nematodes, the nearly microscopic wormlike organisms that attack plant roots, decreasing the plants' vigor and causing tough, misshapen root crops. So this weed, a bad thing to a conventional farmer who would kill it with chemicals, provides Henry with fertilizer, pest control, erosion control, and spring salads, too.

Each weed, cover crop, and vegetable crop has multiple roles to play in the plot Henry is masterminding as he uses defunct pens to poke one delicate root after another into its own soil block. He envisions the patch of earth in the corner of the bottom field, now covered in a feathery hairy vetch cover crop. This is a legume, and as such, with the help of nitrogen-fixing bacteria, it takes nitrogen out of the air and puts it into the soil. Since corn needs a lot of nitrogen, Henry will plant it here after he tills the vetch under. In this way, he imagines patch after patch, crop after crop.

In between hoophouse work, if the weather permits and the soil is dry enough, Henry begins to prepare the field for the first tilling. The preparations include cleaning up any stakes, baskets, or crates that were left in the field at the end of the season and filling in the deep burdock hole and the now-empty storage pit that held all the vegetables we enjoyed all winter. Once everything is nice and clean

and smooth, Henry waits until the soil is dry enough, and then starts tilling under the cover crops and forming beds as needed for planting.

Timing is crucial. The longer he can wait before tilling, the more the cover crops can grow and create nutrients and biomass to feed the soil. But if he waits too long, there won't be time for the turned-in green manure to break down and release the nutrients that will feed the vegetables that feed us. Undecayed cover crops can inhibit seed germination, tie up water and nutrients, and make it impossible to create the smooth seedbed you need for good soil-to-seed contact. So Henry keeps a floating till-down plan in his mind, always watching the temperature and the forecast and adjusting the plan accordingly.

As soon as the soil is dry enough and the cover crop is decomposed enough, Henry begins planting seeds weekly directly into the field, starting with lettuce; spinach; kohlrabi; Japanese turnips; mustard, collard, and turnip greens; radish; arugula; and choi. This weekly planting will continue clear through September, weather permitting, with Henry fitting it in and around the other undertakings: transplanting, weeding, mulching, and harvesting.

Now is also the time to sow oats and clover in last year's vegetable field, which will now be fallow for its two years of rest and

Our friends Laura and Miles take a walk through the fallow field of orchard grass, alfalfa, and clover after our annual Potluck and Tour.

rejuvenation. Fallow does not mean that nothing is happening, or that the field is unproductive. The oats will grow quickly and be ready to harvest for hay in late May. After that, the slower-growing clover will begin to take over, pumping nitrogen into the soil as it grows and preventing erosion.

While Henry is down in the field doing the first tilling, he checks on the garlic. The blanket of straw mulch has done its job protecting the cloves from frost heaves and keeping them cool through the first false spring days. Most of the garlic is now poking its stiff, strong blades through the blanket of mulch, but there are a few that need a little help. Henry and the kids pair up, one person on either side of a bed, and crawl down the paths between the rows. The garlic cloves are spaced five inches apart, so wherever there is a gap, they swiftly scratch away just enough mulch to allow the garlic beneath to see the sun. The hidden garlic shoots are golden, like the straw, rather than green, since they haven't been able to make chlorophyll without sunlight. Now that they can see the sun, they reach for it and will turn dark green within a few days.

WEEK 22. **New Life Borne**

MARCH IS A SCHIZOPHRENIC MONTH, UP IN THE SIXTIES one day and down in the twenties the next. It seems like the cows wait for the coldest, windiest days to drop their calves. I have been watching the black heifer's udder and vulva loosen over the past week of warmth. As a last blast of Arctic air comes down, I know she is close, because her udder is filling and she is standing alone in the far corner of the pasture.

This evening, I am over at Mom and Dad's place to do the evening chores with Zoe's new dog, a needy rescue she named Koko, short for *kokoro,* which means "heart" or "spirit" in Japanese. Koko makes a beeline for that back hill, but I think nothing of it, as the big black heifer is contentedly eating hay up near the barn. I begin filling the water buckets, and then I realize that Koko isn't just running around following scents as usual. She is chasing a new black calf. I drop my water buckets and yell at her to stop, but this only makes her chase the calf further away. The calf is lively, probably born in the afternoon, and must have already suckled, judging by her energy level. But Koko, a city dog, won't heed my ever more foul-mouthed demands for her to stop chasing the calf and come to me. The mother is indifferent too—perhaps because it is her first experience being a mom, or perhaps because there is tasty hay in front of her.

The calf is so black, and night is falling so fast, that I quickly lose sight of her. I run back to the pickup and yank opened its creaky door. This is the one sound Koko never ignores, as she loves riding in cars and trucks. She immediately jumps in, and I slam the door shut. I then run to the house and ask Mom for flashlights and tell Dad what had happened. His health has been up and down all spring, but on a generally southern trajectory. Weak as he is, though, he immediately puts on his overalls and comes out to help.

We begin searching around the barn and through the pasture, but can't find the newborn anywhere. As I walk along the fence, I imagine the calf squeezing under it and wandering out onto the road. Dad says that's unlikely. More likely, he says, Koko chased the calf down into the bottom pasture, where we had separated out two yearling bulls. They are gentle creatures around us, but have been known to butt and even kill, inadvertently or not, newborn calves.

I tell Dad to wait up near the barn in case the calf returns to her clueless mother, while I go down to the lower pasture. Holding two flashlights in front of me like headlights, I scan the pasture as I move slowly down the hill, where small trees and brush provide shelter from the winds. Finally, I see the two young bulls near the brush at the very bottom. I approach them and see that they are standing with their heads angled down toward a particular spot. I follow their gaze and there, deep in the underbrush, I catch the glint of the shiny eyes of the black calf. I shoo the bulls off, and they canter away.

I get on my hands and knees and crawl into the underbrush, talking softly. The calf seems tired and does not resist as I half-carry, half-drag her out. Then I gather her up in my arms, one arm folding her front

legs under her chest and the other folding her back legs under her rump. This is easy to do with a lamb, but hard with a 100-pound calf. She struggles to get away, and I struggle to hold her tightly yet not injure her. About a quarter of the way up the hill, I realize that years of sitting in meetings and in front of computers have seriously compromised my upper-body strength. I am panting and losing my grip when I stumble over my long scarf and nearly fall. I manage to set the calf down clumsily, but as soon as her feet touch the ground, she tries to run. I lunge forward and grab her tightly.

I catch my breath, and feel terrible asking, but I have no choice. I yell up to Dad asking him to come down and help. He is unsteady on his feet, and nearly blind in the dark, but he slowly makes his way down. I ask if he can take the back end of the calf while I take the front. We position ourselves side by side, lean over the calf, and take a few breaths. "On three," he says, and we lift and steady ourselves shoulder to shoulder. The weight is more manageable now, but the squirming creature is even more unwieldy with two people trying to carry her. Slow step by slow step, we begin walking her up the hill in unison, an awkward promenade.

Halfway to the barn, we are out of breath and need to stop and rest. The poor calf seems to be sweating and as exhausted by the ordeal as we are. On three, we stand up again, but I step on my long scarf and it jerks me back down. Weak as I am, I see how much weaker Dad was, and how much this task is taking out of him. He should not be out doing this sort of work, but there is no way I can do this job on my own, and there is no way Dad will abandon a calf. So we once again lift on three. Step by shaky step, we get all the way to the barn, set the calf down, and shoo her inside. Her mother glances over her shoulder coyly, and then turns back to the hay and keeps munching.

Dad and I make a soft straw bed for the calf and bend her legs to make her lie down in it. We stand for a while, catching our breath and marveling over the complete lack of motherly instincts exhibited by this cow. We recall how Frosty and her daughters would not even let us within spitting distance of their calves—Frosty was especially prone to charging anyone who dared get between her and her calf. We laugh, remembering the time Frosty suddenly charged my sister Beth, who couldn't have been more than 13 at the time. Beth took off for the gate, but old Frosty was too close on her heels for her to stop to open it. With an adrenaline-fired leap, she cleared that five-foot-high gate as if it weren't even there.

In the morning, the calf seems none the worse for the adventures of her first 24 hours in this world, and Dad and I have aching muscles and full hearts.

Spring Grass

VI. GRASS MOON

WEEK 23. **Wind Sprints**

IMAGINE IF A MARATHONER HAD TO SPRINT THE WHOLE 26 MILES and 385 yards. That's pretty much what the main growing season is like on Henry's Farm. But in April, we're still in spring training, and we use the Transplant Wind Sprints to get in shape.

Wind sprints, you may recall, are those slightly sadistic athletic drills a particular junior high coach had you do. You remember the one. He'd blow a whistle and then you had to run flat out—up and back, up and back across the gymnasium or football field—go, go, go! Then he'd blow the whistle and you could catch your breath (wind sprints are all about getting winded) by walking around the gym or field slowly, until the whistle blew and you had to go all-out all over again.

The transplant season is kind of like that, but with showers replacing the whistles. April showers bring May flowers, but they won't bring May, June, July, August, September, October, and November vegetables unless we have windows of dry soil to get seeds and starts into the ground. At this time of year, those windows are tiny but crucial. Since the days are still relatively short and the temperatures are relatively cool, it takes a long time for the soil to dry out between showers. It's not unusual to go two or more weeks in April without one day dry enough to work the soil. Henry remembers one year when we didn't have a single day dry enough for transplanting from mid-April to mid-May. That year, we ended up doing all of the transplants—except for the very first lettuces—during one very intense week in late May. That week was not a wind sprint, but more like a sprinted half-marathon, as we put tens of thousands of bare-root alliums and brassica into the ground—plus all the basil, tomatoes, eggplant, peppers, celery root, parsley, and late lettuces.

"Spring," Henry says, "is all about waiting for dry soil."

Of course, "waiting" on Henry's Farm means doing lots of other tasks—many in the hoophouses, others in the barn, and others down in the field. We mulch the perennial sorrel and chives, sharpen and oil tools, clean out the barn, order twist-ties and bags and other market supplies ... but when Coach Henry says the soil is dry enough to plant, then it's time to go, go, go! Because every day of dry soil could very well be our one and only chance to get a particular crop in, the wind sprints are intense dawn-to-dusk workdays when every available hand is called into action. Henry doesn't usually get the season's apprentices until May or June, so he rounds up Matt, who has been creating art all winter, plus as many family members as possible—ranging from elderly grandparents to siblings to young children.

The first wind sprint of the planting season begins in early March, with the potatoes and onion sets. Since these are roots and tubers that will be planted with no delicate green parts above ground, we don't have to be as careful about the temperature or the next day's rainfall as we need to be with bare-root transplants. There is a festive air as we all come together in the fields again for the first time since the garlic planting last fall. With no foliage to absorb the sun's rays, the fields are glaringly bright. And the trees' bare branches are alive with springtime birds. Their songs echo over the field, portions of which Henry has just turned into an all-you-can-eat smorgasbord for them. We place our knees, feet, and hands in the freshly tilled soil, surrounded by sweet air and hillsides just starting to shimmer with the first buds of brown and gold edging into gray and green.

Onion sets are tiny onion bulbs, less than an inch in diameter, and they are one of the fastest and most fun things to plant. Henry is planting these to be harvested early as green onions and doesn't want them to begin forming bulbs, so we plant them as deeply and as close together as possible. We grab a big handful and jab each little onion down as deep as the soil has been loosened by the tiller, about four inches down, and about two inches apart. Kazami plants with an intensity and accuracy that puts the rest of us (except for Henry) to shame. He looks like a planting machine, placing each onion in the soil in exactly the right place and at the right depth ... *bam, bam, bam, bam* ... his hands a blur.

If we have enough people helping, all 1,200 of the onion sets will be in the ground in the space of a few hours. It seems like a great accomplishment, but it's nothing compared with the garlic of last November, when 20,000 cloves were planted. But it is early spring, and we are not the lean, mean planting machines we were then, so we slap the dirt off our hands and straighten up and look back with pride at the rows of onions we have just completed.

The nice thing about wind sprints is that after you're done, you can walk around slowly for a while to recover. So after the onions and potatoes are in the ground, we spend the next few days back in the hoophouse, which is now fairly bursting with seedlings of every description. As Henry continues to plant thickly in the germination trays, we try to keep up by delicately extracting individual seedlings from the trays to block out.

After many long days of effort at the worktables in the hoophouse, the blocks of miniature lettuce, radicchio, dandelion, flowers, celery root, celery, eggplant, peppers, and parsley cover nearly every square inch of soil and benches in the hoophouse. But now it's time to block out the tomatoes and basil as well, and so Henry somehow manages to fit another 24 trays of blocked-out tomato seedlings in the hoophouse. While the cold-tolerant crops are nearly ready to be transplanted into the field, the peppers, eggplant, tomatoes, basil, and sweet potatoes have another month or so left in the hoophouse. We need to make sure the danger of frost is past—sometime in mid-May—before they will start their new lives down in the bottomland.

Our hoophouse work is broken up by more wind sprints whenever the weather allows. One dry day, we plant, by hand or by push planter, the first regular shell, sugar snap, and snow peas. The dry, wrinkled, gray-green peas look like little pieces of gravel, but our mouths are already watering in anticipation of the first sweet peas of the season in June.

Once we pass the last hard-freeze date of April 10, the more strenuous wind sprints are upon us. The first big round of transplanting starts with over 30 trays full of dozens of lettuces of every description, along with radicchio and dandelion greens. Each of those 30 trays has 72 soil blocks, so for the greens alone, we need to insert more than 2,000 individual plants into the ground. To keep track of all of the varieties,

Henry regularly consults his tattered field notebook before giving us instructions. Mom and Dad are often the runners, getting the correct trays from the pickup and then walking along the row, dropping a plug every foot or so—making it handy and efficient for the planters, who are on their hands and knees, to quickly scoop out a hole in the freshly tilled soil, place the plant in, and press down, firming it up and scooping a shallow bowl around it to catch water, before moving on to the next plant, and the next and the next. We bend and kneel and scoop and plant, scoop and plant.

These windsprint days begin to feel more like a distance race as we begin the brassica bare-root transplanting. Henry digs up all the brassica—broccoli and cabbage, kohlrabi and brussels sprouts, cauliflower and more—from the floor of the second long hoophouse. He gently shakes most of the soil from their roots, then immediately places them in big five-gallon buckets with six to eight inches of water in them so the roots will not dry out. We load bucket after bucket of plants into the back of the pickup and haul everything down to the field.

Mother and daughter take a brief break, waiting for Henry and the tractor to prepare another bed for transplanting.

We start with the brassica rather than the alliums because brassica will get too big and leggy to transplant if they stay in the hoophouse too long, while onions never reach that point. For any bare-root transplanting, Henry needs to make sure not only that the soil is dry enough but also that there is a high likelihood of rain in the 24 hours following the transplanting, so those fragile bare roots will be able to take hold and begin bringing water up into the plant.

Henry's practice of direct-seeding in the soil of the hoophouse and then planting the bare-rooted starts is fairly unusual, but in his experience, the pros outweigh the cons. The main advantage is that it saves a lot of time and space. You prepare the troughs, thickly seed them, cover them, and you're done. The plants do the rest. Henry has also found that the plants, particularly the brassica, grow more quickly and strongly in the earth than they do in soil blocks. And if you use weed-free soil and weed-free compost, little or no weeding will be necessary. Then when it's warm enough to transplant them, it's a quick and easy task to dig them up, place them into the big five-gallon buckets, and then take tens of thousands of plants to the field all at once.

The disadvantage of direct-seeding is that there is no soil around the roots when you go to transplant them. This means timing is crucial. You don't dig them up until you're sure you have the time and manpower to get them into the ground. And you don't dig them up until you are pretty certain that it will rain shortly after they are transplanted. For many years, Henry hedged his bets by putting some of the cabbage and broccoli in soil blocks and the remainder as bare-root transplants. The first few weeks after transplanting, the bare-rooted plants looked terrible. They wilted down and lost their leaves, and it seemed that they were about to give up the ghost. But over the next few weeks, they not only recovered but equaled and then surpassed the ones that had been transplanted in soil blocks. The bare-root transplants eventually sent out roots that ranged wide and deep, and the plants grew bigger and stronger than their coddled counterparts.

When all the brassica are finally in the ground, we begin on the thousands of bare-root scallions, onions, leeks, and shallots. The weather at this time of year can be wildly variable. Sometimes it is cold and wet, and we work in layers of long underwear, shirts, and jackets. But last year, it was suddenly hot and windy, a deadly combination for the tender plants just emerging from the protection of the hoophouse. Out in the cruel world, the just-transplanted bare-root alliums and brassica wilted flat against the ground. They looked pathetic, and for the first time ever, Henry and the apprentices hauled water down from the well on the hill to give a drink to every single one of the 10,000 transplants. We left them that evening, each in their own circle of moist soil, as flattened and as lifeless-looking as pulled weeds in the hot sun. But when I returned to the field in the morning, I felt I had witnessed the miracle of Lazarus. The starts were upright, turgid, alive, and growing, revealing nature in all her powers of resurrection.

WEEK 24. **A Good Egg**

"DID YOU THANK THE HENS?" THIS IS THE QUESTION that still echoes in my mind every time I go out to gather eggs from my chickens or ducks. And whether I do it out loud, as I did as a child at my grandmother's prompting, or internally, as I do today, I always thank the hens.

As early as I can remember, eggs were always special, associated with holiday breakfasts or birthday cakes. The only time I remember eating eggs with abandon was the one week each summer that we got to spend at Grandma Henrietta and Grandpa Fred's farm. There we had them every single morning. I usually stayed at the farm with my cousin Ann, and gathering the eggs with her each day was not so much a chore as a mission. Each day, eggs appeared in the straw-filled nesting boxes, sometimes still warm to the touch. Their size and shape seemed custom-made to cradle perfectly in a child's hand. Upon returning to the house, we'd show the basket to Grandma, and she would *ooohh* and *aaahh* over it, just as impressed as we were. Then she'd ask us if we had thanked the hens. The time or two we forgot, she had us go back out to do it.

And it wasn't just my grandmother who knew that eggs were an unimpeachable good, something to be grateful for. My sister-in-law Hiroko tells us that during World War II in Japan, eggs were so precious that only pregnant women or the sick and elderly were allowed to eat them.

Few people stop to think how precious an egg is, and fewer still think to thank the modern battery hen, whose eggs roll off onto a conveyor belt as soon as they are laid. During my confirmation into the Lutheran church, I was told there was not only sin as a general concept, but that it came in two varieties—sins of omission and sins of commission. I still remember my inward groan when I learned that you were pretty much damned if you did and damned if you didn't.

But if there are both sins of omission and commission, we who eat eggs from industrial sources are no doubt guilty of both. We are party to the sins of commission, the debeaking of the baby chicks immediately after hatching; the close confinement with thousands of other hens, without room to stretch their legs or flap their wings; and the whole life of the bird lived without sunlight, green grass, or fresh air, without the ability to chase a cricket, take a dust bath, or fly up to a roost at night. But on top of all that is the sin of omission: no one ever thanks these hens for their eggs.

Because these chickens live in such unhealthy and stressful conditions, they are often unhealthy themselves, and you can see this in their pale, watery eggs. A good egg is laid by a mentally and physically healthy hen. What this translates into is free-running chickens that eat high-quality, unmedicated feed, plus all the insects and plants they want, with the odd bit of meat thrown in when they capture a mouse or other small creature. (Yes, chickens are omnivores, too.) The hen's quality of life is of the utmost importance when it comes to the quality of the egg, for only a happy hen produces an egg with a viscous white and a high, plump yolk. Unlike the pale, watery yolks we are used to in supermarket eggs, these yolks are brilliant orange, even red. In fact, egg yolk is *rossi* (red) in Italian.

A free-range hen who pecks and scratches and eats a huge variety of nutritious bugs, insects, and plants, gives us eggs high in omega-3 fatty acids. Since this was reported a few years ago, some commercial egg producers have been adding algae to their chicken feed to boost the omega-3s in their eggs. This may help out on the omega-3 front, but not on the larger problem, which is treating hens as if they were inanimate egg-producing machines. And what you get out of a hen treated like a machine is

a dull shadow of the real thing. What you get out of a hen treated like a hen is an egg that tastes like the ones that prompted Henry James to write:

In April we indulge in the sudden abundance of milk and eggs, as the goats give birth to kids (one of a rare set of quadruplets is shown here), and the hens enjoy the fresh new grass, weeds, and insects.

> I had an excellent repast—the best repast possible—which consisted simply of boiled eggs and bread and butter. It was the quality of these simple ingredients that made the occasion memorable. The eggs were so good that I am ashamed to say how many of them I consumed ... It might seem that an egg which has succeeded in being fresh has done all that can be reasonably expected of it.

James's euphoria is unmistakable. Once you have eaten an egg like this, you will never turn back.

Now that you have your fine egg, what to do with it? My favorite thing to do is fry it lightly in butter and have it on toast. But I can't argue with Vladimir Nabokov when he writes about how to boil a perfect egg. I stumbled across this recipe in 1999 while perusing "Nabokov under Glass," an exhibit of Nabokov's writings and writerly paraphernalia at the New York Public Library. There on a single sheet, handwritten in pencil, I found and copied this recipe.

The recipe title is a play on words. In the Paris markets Nabokov frequented after leaving Russia and before settling in the U.S., egg sellers don't sell you eggs until they know what you are going to do with them and when. It's not just nosiness. It's information needed in order to know which eggs to sell you. Two-week-old eggs are for baking, week-old ones are for omelettes, and the very freshest eggs are for *oeuf à la coque* (soft-boiled eggs), which Nabokov renamed "Eggs à la Nabocoque."

Eggs à la Nabocoque

Boil water in a saucepan (bubbles mean it is boiling!). Take two eggs (for one person) out of the refrigerator. Hold them under the hot tap water to make them ready for what awaits them.

Place each in a pan, one after the other, and let them slip soundlessly into the (boiling) water. Consult your wristwatch. Stand over them with a spoon preventing them (they are apt to roll) from knocking against the damned side of the pan.

If, however, an egg cracks in the water (now bubbling like mad) and starts to disgorge a cloud of white stuff like a medium in an old-fashioned seance, fish it out and throw it away. Take another and be more careful.

After 200 seconds have passed, or, say, 240 (taking interruptions into account), start scooping the eggs out. Place them, round end up, in two egg cups. With a small spoon tap-tap in a circle and then pry open the lid of the shell. Have some salt and buttered bread (white) ready. Eat.

V.N.
November 18, 1972

A notation in ink was made at the top:
Maxime de la Falaise McKendry for a cooking book

And a later notation under it:
Never acknowledged by Maxime

WEEK 25. **Bees Buzz**

A HABIT OF GRATITUDE IS SECOND NATURE WHEN YOU GROW up with a grandmother who insists that you thank the hens for their eggs. So it is not surprising that I feel the same gratitude toward bees.

I got my first hive of bees a year or two after we moved out to The Land. I can't remember exactly how or why. Maybe it was just that I needed a 4-H project. Or maybe it was the memory of that long row of blindingly white hives along the catalpa grove at Grandpa and Grandma's place all those years. I had a slight fear of them as a child, but still liked to sidle up, barely breathing, and watch the bees take off and land on the runway at the base of each hive.

But it wasn't until I got my own hives that my fascination deepened into love. I remember my early beekeeping days with hallucinatory clarity. I would go out to tend them in the mid to late morning, when most of the bees would be out foraging. I remember the hot summer morning air, the rank smell of the weeds that I tramped down near the hive, the beads of sweat escaping from the band of my hat and slipping into my eyes. I especially remember the moment of inserting the hive tool under the hive cover.

Prying open the cover of a hive of bees is more exciting than watching Indiana Jones enter an Egyptian tomb. Opening the hive opens the senses. You have to first break the sticky propolis the bees make from tree resins and saps to seal the hive. That first scent, as you break the seal, is tangy and enlivening, and it creates a heightened awareness. Suddenly, you inhale all the distilled essences of summer in the bees' glue, beeswax, musky brood, and sweet and spicy honey.

The buzz of hundreds of thousands of bees adds to the otherworldly feel by creating an intense concentration that is calming. You lift off the cover and set it gently next to the hive, every movement slow and deliberate—a sort of bee tai chi. You listen to the calm buzzing, alert for the high-pitched warning whine of an angry bee about to launch a suicide attack. The few times I got stung, I always felt worse

Nearly every fruit and vegetable we grow requires pollinators in order to set fruit. In a healthy ecosystem there are many wild pollinators, but as a backup, Teresa keeps bees to pollinate her fruits.

for the bee than I felt for myself, knowing that the worker bee had disemboweled herself as she pulled away from my flesh.

When I kept bees in the early 1970s, it was a simple matter of giving them enough space to raise brood and enough space to store honey. That, and the sun and rain and wide array of blooming plants— from maple, elm, and willow in April to goldenrod and aster in October—were all they needed. I never had to check for varroa mites, tracheal mites, nosema, or foul brood. The bees were healthy, and the ecosystem they supported, and were supported by, was relatively healthy.

All that has changed. When I first moved back to Congerville and put a hive in the yard outside my house, it seemed fine through the summer and into the fall. I left the bees with plenty of honey to last the winter, and then on the first warm spring day I suited up to check on them. But as I approached the hive, I heard not a sound. I took out my hive tool and pried up the cover. There was no greeting, no buzzing, no breathing.

As I investigated further, lifting off the honey super and looking down into the brood chamber, what came to mind was the video footage I had seen after the agrichemical factory explosion in Bhopal, India. Thousands upon thousands of bee bodies were piled up between the frames—frames that should have contained eggs, larvae, brood in all stages of development, all gearing up for the first big gathering of pollen and nectar.

Instead there was the silence of death. I felt terrible and wondered what I had done wrong, thinking some negligence on my part had led to this tragedy. But when I asked Henry and Teresa about it, they said the same thing had happened to the hives they started keeping after they returned to Illinois in the 1990s following their various travels.

Thirty years earlier, they, like I, had done very little with their hives and never had a colony die. But in recent years, honeybee populations have plummeted. Bee researchers call bees "the canary in the coal mine."

Our image of honeybees is a lot like our bucolic images of farm animals—and just as far from the truth. We picture fields of clover, blossoming orchards, wildflowers beneath the trees, and happy bees industriously gathering nectar and pollen to take back to the hive. But today, most bees are captive, stressed out, and malnourished. They are trucked from state to state and fed junk food—high-fructose corn syrup and soy protein—instead of the honey and pollen they evolved to eat. And their cheap junk food, like ours, is derived from genetically modified plants, including corn that has been engineered to contain Bt, an *insect*icide. When they arrive at their destination, they are released to pollinate a single crop in vast, chemically treated fields. Already severely compromised, their exposure to a toxic cocktail of insecticides only weakens them further.

There are many ongoing studies into why honeybee colonies are collapsing. From a common sense point of view, though, I would say that the toxic load they carry from the biocides they are exposed to, combined with their stressful lives and poor nutrition, has left them susceptible to any number of ailments. Colony collapse disorder undoubtedly has many contributing causes, but what it comes down to is that bees have come up against an agricultural system so alien from the natural world that they can no longer coexist with it. And this means it is not just a bee crisis, but a pollination crisis, and a food crisis. That's why the term "agricultural collapse disorder" makes a lot more sense than "colony collapse disorder."

In the spring, Teresa and I choose a bright sunny day to check on her overwintered hives. We don our white coveralls, elbow-length canvas gloves, and veils that fit over a straw hat. On a sunny morning, the bees are in a good mood, focused on their foraging and not on the curious humans. We crack open the hive, and that same intoxicating aroma from my early beekeeping days invades my brain. I feel my breathing and my heartbeat slow as my eyes and ears become more keen. A happy low hum rises up, and a smile of relief floods my face. My eyes meet Teresa's over the hive, and I read the same relief there.

We proceed to lift off the almost-empty honey supers and look down into the brood chamber. There we slowly pry up each frame, Teresa with her hive tool on one side of it, and me with mine on the other. Then she grasps it, turns it on its side, and examines the broad surface of the comb, looking for the queen and seeing what is in the brood cells.

Although we did not find the queen that day, we saw evidence of her work. Some frames were full of cells, each with a tiny white egg deposited in the bottom, lying there like a pearly grain of rice. Others frames were full of larvae, some tiny, others fat and shiny, nearly bursting out of their cells. On other frames, we saw the capped pupal stage. And we watched a new bee, soft and fuzzy, with crinkled-up antennae, emerge from a cell.

WEEK 26. **Drakes Mount**

Like my great-grandparents and grandparents before me, I entered—in a very minor way—the waterfowl business. Shortly after I moved to Congerville, I acquired six snow white Pekins (two drakes and four ducks), three heavy-bodied Appleyards (a rare breed from England, good for both meat and eggs, that look something like a mallard on steroids—all three females), and two elegant dusty gray-blue Swedish Blues (one duck, one drake). My drakes were rather idle and decorative, while my seven girls soon proved themselves to be marvelous layers, providing me with one amazingly rich egg apiece each day, like clockwork.

There is nothing quite so satisfying as a fresh duck egg. I assume Laurie Colwin was writing about chicken eggs, but her wise words in *More Home Cooking* are even more applicable to duck eggs: "In my opinion, the perfect form of egg is sunny side up, very gently cooked and covered until a pink, filmy veil forms over the yolk. These eggs should be served with very lightly buttered toast ... Both eggs and toast get the merest sprinkle of salt and nothing else. You do not eat these for breakfast: You eat them for dinner, when you are fully awake."

The problem with the peaceable kingdom of my little barnyard was not the ducks or their eggs. It was the particularly rabid form of sexual maturity the drakes were entering. For weeks, I chalked up their behavior to "boys will be boys," and went on with my life. As we edged into late April, a premature heat wave caused my house to open up like a hothouse flower. It soon came to resemble the midwestern version of a traditional Japanese farmhouse in summer, with all the windows, doors, and sliding doors ajar. Soon, I could no longer bear the fever-pitched barnyard activities. The open doors and windows of my house let in breezes and birdsong, along with the first houseflies. The breezes and birdsong I welcomed, the bugs I could live with, but the predominant and continual sounds of rampant duck sex wafting into my summer house were getting on my nerves.

As Lord Chesterfield famously said of human sex, "The pleasure is momentary and the position ridiculous." This is true in spades for duck sex, which may be the most ungainly and ridiculous in the entire animal kingdom. The drake chases down the object of his desire and clamps his viselike bill onto the feathers on the back of her head, pinning her to the ground. He then clambers atop and attempts to gain solid purchase by clomping with his big webbed feet where her wings attach to her back—right, left, right, left, right, left. Finally, when he feels steady enough, he swings his tail feathers up and over to one side, lurches his body to follow, and aims his phallus toward her vagina, hoping to penetrate its labyrinthine twists and turns before gravity takes over and he tumbles off onto his side, quacking and snorting.

After what was at most a microsecond of penetration (if in fact he got lucky), the drake rights himself, his phallus dragging along the ground. Meanwhile, the poor girl gets up, shakes her feathers out, and scrambles to get a sip of water or a bite of food before the next drake, who's been waiting in the wings, climbs aboard and starts stomping on her all over again. There is a definite pecking order to this whole process, and sometimes the drakes further down the line are so impatient, they attempt to climb on while the more dominant one is already aboard, forming an unseemly duck-sex pyramid.

Most other bird species lack phalluses. Their mating consists of a brief "cloacal kiss," which not only sounds, but actually is, much nicer than what was happening between my ducks and drakes. Waterfowl are among the 3 percent of all living bird species that retain the grooved phallus found in their reptilian ancestors. Male waterfowl are especially unusual in that their phalluses vary greatly among different species, ranging from a half-inch to more than 15 inches long. These also display a remarkable level of diversity in texture and design, ranging from smooth and straight, to corkscrewed and covered in spines and grooves.

Scientists speculate that male waterfowl evolved longer and more intricate phalluses to give them a competitive edge over those not as well endowed when it came to fertilizing females. The behavioral ecologist Patricia Brennan found that the vaginas of female waterfowl are just as ornate, with many twists and turns and dead ends—all countermeasures that seem designed to exclude the phallus.

And so the battle of the duck genitalia raged in my backyard until I found myself jumping up throughout the day and running out of the house with a broom, yelling at the drakes and chasing them away from the ducks. By the time I returned to the house, they were up to their old tricks again. Finally, I stood out in the duck yard and shook my head at them. "Sorry, fellas," I said, "not in my backyard."

That evening I called up Henry, who brought over the hatchet and did the deed. I have never gotten used to killing, and I'm sure Henry hasn't either. I don't know that it's something one ever gets used to, which is probably a good thing. Traditionally, killing seems to fall to the menfolk, while most everything that happens after is done by the women. The plucking and gutting were something Grandma excelled at, and even when I was a child, the process never bothered me. It's a challenge to get all the pinfeathers out, and the smooth, boat-shaped body that is revealed is a thing of beauty.

While I was working my hand around the body cavity of the first drake we had killed, using my fingernails to break through the light membranes holding all the insides inside, I felt something unusual near the opening—not intestine, not heart, not liver, not gizzard ... a tumor, perhaps? When I pulled the viscera out onto the table, I held one of the unknown objects in my hand. It was an organ of some sort—kidney-shaped, but not kidney-colored—a delicate ivory with a webbing of tiny blood vessels feeding it. I cradled it in the palm of my hand where it nestled comfortably, like a miniature boudin blanc. Suddenly, it dawned on me, and I turned to my brother and held it out for him to see. "*This*," I said, in the tone of a prosecuting attorney holding the murder weapon, "was the problem."

Chef Paul Kahan concentrates on removing the skin from the neck of a just-killed and just-plucked duck at the Brockman farms.

Indeed it was. Those poor drakes had testicles that would not have been oversized on a rottweiler. No wonder they had been behaving so badly; they had been at the mercy of their raging hormones. But much stronger than the pang of guilt I felt was my pride in liberating my girls from molestation. I felt something like what Nicholas Kristof must have felt when he detailed in the *New York Times* how he had bought the freedom of a Thai sex slave.

Of course neither my actions nor Kristof's actions were as uncomplicated as they might have seemed at first. After some weeks of living unmolested, eating and drinking without fear of being grabbed by the back of the neck and mounted, I observed some strange behavior around the big watering bowl: the girls were mounting the girls.

This, however, was not the problem at hand. After we slaughtered the drakes, I had to figure out what to do with their testicles. When you've raised an animal from infancy to adulthood, fed and watered it each and every day, made sure that it was safe from varmints each night, and let it out to enjoy each new morning, once you've seen it through to its end, you are loathe to throw away any part of it. Even experienced chefs suddenly feel compelled to use every last piece of an animal after they've seen it through the passage from life to death.

One of those chefs was Chicago's Paul Kahan. He and his staff had come down to the farm to participate in the home butchering of 50 ducks I had raised (that would be used as part of a fundraising dinner for The Land Connection at Paul's Blackbird Restaurant). When I saw Paul carefully excising the skin and underlying fat from the ducks' necks, I asked him what he was doing, and he told me he was going to use it to make duck cracklings to sprinkle on a green salad, a popular way to use duck and goose skin in the Auvergne region of France.

This evening, though, I was not as concerned about what to do with the skin, as what to do with the testicles. So, as a delaying tactic, I rinsed them and put them in the refrigerator. The next day, I called my friend Mari, who called her culinary school friends, who finally got back to me with a suggestion: wrap them in bacon and pan-sear them. Now that I think about it, I wonder if a culinary student was putting me on, since even a cricket or horsefly is probably pretty good once it is wrapped in bacon and pan-seared. In fact, the pan-seared duck testicles were a quick and easy dish, and the bacon was a very good idea, as it turned out that the balls themselves had little taste. They had a light texture that reminded me of sweetbreads or a very light foie gras that melts in your mouth as you bite into it. Later, when I read up on testicles as a foodstuff, I found out that they are more akin to brains. And "pan-seared and wrapped in bacon" seems as good a fate as any when balls become brains.

Pan-Fried Duck Cracklings

Remove scraps of skin and underlying fat from any part of a duck carcass. Cut the scraps into small chunks and cook them in a heavy-bottomed pan on low heat for about 30 to 40 minutes. When the pieces are golden and crisp, remove with a slotted spoon, and place on paper towels to drain. You can crumble onto a green salad immediately, or store in the refrigerator. If stored, gently reheat cracklings prior to serving on top of a soup or salad.

Sweet Potato Planting

VII. PLANTING MOON

WEEK 27. The Enchanted Planting

NOTHING, NOT EVEN RAMPANT DUCK SEX, CAN SERIOUSLY dampen the delights of the Illinois spring. The wind ruffles the rhubarb leaves, revealing their bright red petioles. The asparagus shoots up so fast, you have to harvest it twice a day. By day, the indigo bunting passes over Henry's fields in brief bursts of sapphire flight. By night, the tiny tree frogs sing a song that never goes out of favor.

Here in our protected corner of the Corn Belt, spring is not silent. We are blasted awake before dawn by the mating songs of our avian friends, and before long, the woods surrounding our homes and fields are a vast maternity ward. For the past few weeks, I had a titmouse nesting in the canvas awning outside my window, one robin with a tidy nest tucked in a forked branch of the big oak outside the kitchen, and another robin with her sloppy nest spilling down the ledge of the high window of the chicken coop. This morning was the first time the mother robin was not sitting impassively on her nest on the chicken-coop ledge when I walked down the lane, so I went over and reached up, expecting to touch a small, smooth, dry egg, and instead touched something soft and wet—new life!

For mother birds and organic farmers, May comes laden with hope and uncertainty. We are in the thick of planting season, putting thousands of warm-weather transplants and tens of thousands of seeds into the ground, investing each with an irrationally exuberant hope of compounded returns. One small wrinkled kernel of sweet corn will yield a corn stalk with two ears of corn, each containing over 500 new kernels. One sweet potato slip will grow into a vine stretching six feet across the ground in every direction and yielding as many as 10 large tubers in the fall. One tiny tomato seed, in a good year, will yield 50 pounds of fruit.

But our hopes are surrounded by uncertainties: Will it rain enough? Or too much? Will the spring be too cold and damp for the summer crops? Will the summer be too hot for the lettuces and greens? Will the apprentices be able to persevere through whole days of weeding? Will Henry's sciatica return? Will Walnut Creek flood? Will the fields be damaged by high winds or a freak hailstorm? Will the first frost come too soon?

Luckily, we're too busy to spend much time dwelling on endless what ifs. There is precious little time to do anything but concentrate on the demands of the moment—and each moment is demanding. Our Miami, Kickapoo, and Illiniwek antecedents on this land didn't call it the Planting Moon for nothing. The wind sprints are over, but the successive seeding continues for most of the other crops that have been planted weekly or biweekly, weather permitting, since April. The planting of the spinach, peas, parsnips, parsley, salsify, and burdock are done for the year, while daikon, kohlrabi, and Chinese cabbage won't be planted again until August for the fall crop. That still leaves radish, arugula, lettuce, choi, mizuna, mustard and turnip greens, Japanese turnips, dill, cilantro, dandelion, beets, carrots, chard, fen-

A pair of dandelion seeds watch the earth-shaking spectacle of a cucumber sprout shouldering its way into the world.

nel, leek, and scallions. In addition to these, in May we plant all of the sweet corn, flour corn, and popcorn, and begin planting beans, soybeans, cucumbers, summer squash, basil, the warm-weather spinaches, amaranth, nasturtiums, and okra. This is also the month for planting winter squash, pumpkins, watermelons, and muskmelons. At the same time, waves of the warm-weather transplants come down from the hoophouse: 500 bell, hot, and ethnic peppers; 500 Mediterranean and Asian eggplants; and 1,000 tomato plants. Then there are 1,000 or so celery root transplants, and about half that many basil plants. And we mustn't forget the 1,000 sweet potato slips.

At this time of year, we truly are "slaves to a springtime passion for the earth." I was surprised to learn that those words, from a beautiful sonnet called "Putting in the Seed" written in 1920, are by none other than that old New Englander, Robert Frost. For the oft-anthologized Frost, nature is a mirror and a metaphor, a way of revealing emotions. In his youth, as his biographers have recounted, Frost was as fleshly as any of us. "Putting in the Seed" ends with the couplet,

> The sturdy seedling with arched body comes
> Shouldering its way and shedding the earth crumbs.

Anyone who has watched a seed sprout knows that the final image of the arched body of the seedling shouldering its way through the earth is precise as well as suggestive, making accuracy itself erotic.

I never get over the enchantment of planting. There is such magic and wonder in putting in the seed, in sprouting, in growth, that it has inspired poets and preachers for millennia. Indeed, it was a local pastor's sermon about the miracle of "dead seeds" sprouting that turned out to be the inspiration for Dad, and our whole family, to abandon formal church services. Grandma Henrietta was a strong woman and a staunch Lutheran in the Lake Wobegon tradition. Even my Catholic mother had to convert before marrying my father, so Grandma's grandchildren would not be brought up as "idol-worshippers." The conversion was not such a tragedy for my Italian grandmother, who once, when the priest mentioned he had not seen her at confession for a long time, shot back, "What do *I* have to confess!?"

When we moved out to The Land, we began searching for, as Grandma put it, our new "church home." One Sunday, we went to a church in Morton, 10 miles to the west. It was a bright spring day, and the world was a startling shade of green. The pastor had also been spring-struck, and who knows, may even have been out planting seeds around his house. For whatever reason, he had decided to make the miracle of life coming forth from a seed the subject of his sermon. Unfortunately, he insisted on referring to the seed as a "dead seed." I could see my father flinch and twinge at every mention of that dead seed coming to life. The flinching turned to fidgeting, and then to fuming, as the pastor, not wanting to let a little botany get in the way of a good sermon, waxed on about how the brown, dry, lifeless seed, through the miracle of sunshine, water, and the Hand of God, could put forth roots and shoots, leaves and fruit.

After the service, before we even got to the privacy of our van, Dad was sputtering about a pastor so ignorant of basic biology that he did not know the difference between a dead seed and a living seed—that a dead seed would never sprout, with or without water and sunshine. Perhaps the Hand of God could bring a dead seed to life, but not in our present world.

I don't recall any announcement being made on the way home about this being the end of our search for a church home, but from then on, we never again went to church. Perhaps if that pastor had preached from the earthly gospel of Robert Frost, our family might still be Sunday churchgoers. Instead, we have become every-day-*but*-Sunday churchgoers, worshipping by working in the fields and resting on the Sabbath.

WEEK 28. **Asparagus Rising**

LIKE THE FIRST BURST OF BLOSSOMS OR THE FIRST TWITTER of returning songbirds, the rattle of Dad's old pickup truck coming down my lane on a warm May evening is a true herald of spring. Although his steps are slower and he hangs onto the railing more than he used to, neither rain nor age will stop him from his self-appointed rounds as he delivers the season's first asparagus.

Dad goes to the asparagus patch every morning with a paring knife and a pocketful of plastic newspaper-delivery sleeves. If the day is not going to get much warmer than the fifties, he'll skip the evening picking, knowing that the spears will have put on little growth. But if the days are hot and the soil moist, there will be full-grown spears in the evening that were barely out of the ground that morning. Under ideal conditions—warm and moist—asparagus can grow 10 inches in 24 hours, which does seem to qualify as a resurrection. This feat takes place, quite fittingly, around the same time as Easter and Passover. While most of summer's vegetables are still being coddled in the hoophouse, or only just beginning to send their roots down into the still-cold soil, the perennial asparagus is bursting with the very first flavors of the new season.

Perennial vegetables are a godsend, particularly for the early spring markets and CSAs, not to mention our own dinner tables. Unlike most other vegetables, which are annuals, asparagus can be productive for 20 years or more if the plants are well tended. During one of Henry's early years in the vegetable farming business, we spent a cold spring day digging asparagus crowns out of our old family garden patch, where they'd been producing for some 20 years, and transplanting them, along with newly purchased crowns, into his new asparagus beds in the lower and upper fields. An asparagus crown looks less than regal, more like a straggly mophead of light brown roots. In fact, it is compressed underground stem tissue that forms buds from which new shoots—the edible asparagus spears—emerge. In our big asparagus relocation, I saw that many of the crowns had been eaten by mice or voles, and imagine they must have enjoyed the high levels of sugar that nurture the developing spears. If the crowns were too severely damaged, we left them for the mice, since frail crowns produce wimpy asparagus. The larger the crown, the more vigorous the resulting asparagus plant will be.

You have to wait a year or two, ideally three, before you begin harvesting from a newly planted asparagus patch. Actually, "waiting" is not exactly the right word. It is more active than passive. Because asparagus generates virtually no shade to keep the weeds under control, you need to weed the patch season after season, doing your best to ignore the juicy stalks that beg you to try them—just one! Instead, you weed and wait, allowing the plants to build up their strength. Then when that fine day comes and you start harvesting, the plants will be so robust that nothing will harm them, and you will be rewarded with a taste treat made all the more delicious through delayed gratification.

The reward is not only for your tastebuds but also for your eyes. A stalk of asparagus is as dazzling as any iris, with the same delightful combination of bright green and dusky lavender. The purple bracts pull the eye upward, pointing in ever-closer formation toward the tight head, which, if left alone, will mature through the summer into feathery fronds.

Marcel Proust was also struck by the beauty of asparagus. Gifted with magnificent powers of observation and acute sensory memory (and the good fortune to have had many servants and a cork-lined room where he could write all night, undisturbed, fueled by vast amounts of caffeine), he wrote:

but what fascinated me would be the asparagus, tinged with ultramarine and rosy pink which ran from their heads, finely stippled in mauve and azure, through a series of imperceptible changes to their white feet, still stained a little by the soil of their garden-bed: a rainbow-loveliness that was not of this world. I felt that these celestial hues indicated the presence of exquisite creatures who had been pleased to assume vegetable form, who, through the disguise which covered their firm and edible flesh, allowed me to discern in this radiance of earliest dawn, these hinted rainbows, these blue evening shades, that precious quality which I should recognize again when, all night long after a dinner at which I had partaken of them, they played (lyrical and coarse in their jesting as the fairies in Shakespeare's *Dream*) at transforming my humble chamber into a bower of aromatic perfume.

Before we go any further, let me add something more to that chamber[pot] remark. Proust was not the only writer to notice this phenomenon, or to make a point of mentioning it: Gabriel García Márquez does the same in *Love in the Time of Cholera*. I read both references smugly, knowing (from way back, via my father, the geneticist) that this phenomenon of odoriferous urine after eating asparagus was a genetic characteristic. One either did, or did not, metabolize a number of sulfur-containing compounds in asparagus and then did, or did not, have smelly pee. Decades later, I learned that there had been a crucial error in the seemingly straightforward asparagus experiment. The researchers had their subjects eat asparagus and then, a short time later, asked them if their urine smelled, and tallied up the answers. The subjects dutifully reported back "Yes" or "No." But the "Nos"—while being perfectly honest—*also* had odoriferous urine. In fact, we all do after we eat asparagus. The "Nos" couldn't smell it because the genetic trait was not whether they metabolized the smelly compound or not, but whether their nose could detect it or not.

People have been smelling asparagus-perfumed chamberpots (or not) for a very long time. We know that people were eating asparagus long before recorded history—from the simple fact that by the time the histories *were* written, asparagus had already become a favorite food. Ancient Nile-dwellers praised asparagus in their earliest documents, describing how it grew wild along the Nile and how fond they were of it. For millennia, the only asparagus was the wild variety. The

Roasted Asparagus with Olive Oil and Balsamic Vinegar

In most of the country, asparagus season lasts from mid-April to the first of June. The specific date for the end of asparagus season varies from year to year, but it is stated unequivocally in the traditional German rhyme: Kirschen rot, spargel tot, *"Cherries red, asparagus dead." But rest assured that asparagus will be resurrected next spring—and like all short-lived things, it's all the more cherished for its transience.*

> **1 pound fresh asparagus, rinsed and base ends snapped off where they naturally break (usually 1–2 inches up)**
>
> **1–2 tablespoons extra-virgin olive oil**
>
> **Kosher salt and freshly ground pepper, to taste**
>
> **1 tablespoon balsamic vinegar (the best you can afford)**

Preheat the oven to 500°F. In a large, shallow baking sheet, toss the asparagus with the oil, salt, and pepper.

Roast the asparagus, shaking the pan every 2 to 3 minutes, until tender and lightly browned, about 10 minutes.

Remove the pan from the oven and drizzle the balsamic vinegar over the asparagus, shaking the pan to combine well. The best way to eat this is with your fingers, rolling each spear to coat it with the vinegar. (Even Emily Post says this is okay.)

Romans sent their special "asparagus fleets" all around the Mediterranean to find and gather it. At some point, though, the Romans successfully domesticated the plant and were able to cultivate it throughout their empire.

You can do a lot with asparagus, but when it is in season, it is best to do very little—and to do it quickly. Emperor Augustus, when he wanted something done, would proclaim: *Velocium quam asparagi coquantur*—"Let it be done quicker than you would cook asparagus." When I hear my Dad's old Toyota pickup rattle down my lane, I grab a pot and put a little water in it and light the flame. The water is boiling by the time I've rinsed the asparagus and snapped off the base of each spear. (They snap naturally at the point where it is tender, so you don't have to worry about stingy, tough ends, and you don't need to peel the spears at all.) In about two minutes, I scoop the spears out of the boiling water, drizzle them with olive oil and a little balsamic vinegar, and indulge in the taste of springtime.

WEEK 29. **First Harvest**

T HIS MAY BE THE PLANTING MOON, AND HEAVEN KNOWS there is plenty of planting to do in May, but there is much more that must be done, and done now: thinning (lettuce and fruit—peaches, apples, pears), trellising (peas, hoophouse cucumbers, and hoophouse tomatoes), hilling (mounding dirt up against the potatoes and leeks), hoophouse sowing (of late tomatoes for fall harvest), hand-weeding (carrots, parsnips, parsley, and onion transplants), mulching (kale and potatoes) and push-hoeing most everything else to uproot the first flush of weeds.

On top of all that, we must get ready for the first market in mid-May. This "getting ready" has its own sub-universe of tasks: washing all the harvest boxes and baskets; washing the market truck inside and out (which includes disinfecting the area where the crates of vegetables will be stacked, just in case any mice took up residence there over the winter); checking and repairing our market tents, tables, and scales; going through the harvest box and cleaning and sharpening the harvest knives; getting all the twist-ties ready, along with the quart and pint boxes; and preparing the wash area for the first harvest.

The children have their own market prep tasks as well. Asa attends high school at the Illinois Math and Science Academy, and he lives

in the dormitories there in Aurora. He will be home and working on the farm over the summer, but for now, the market tasks fall to Zoe and Kazami. After they come home from school, they go through the hundreds of signs we use to label the vegetables at the market. Each one gives the name of the vegetable ("Dragon Tongue Beans") and a further bit of description or information ("Tender Dutch Heirloom"). The kids sort the laminated signs, washing those that are in good enough shape for another market season, and removing any that are too beat-up to be used again. Those signs get to have a new incarnation, and Zoe (who, Kazami confesses, does have the better handwriting) uses markers to create the new signs, while Kazami does the lamination and then punches holes at the top. At the market, we put clothespins through those holes, and then pin them onto the tops of the upturned vegetable crates, so the customers know what they're looking at, whether it is one of the 20-some varieties of lettuce or an unusual herb like Papalo Quelites.

Finally, we reach the day we've been preparing for ever since Henry placed his seed order just before Christmas: it's time for the first harvest. A normal workday for the apprentices and farmhand begins at 6 a.m., but harvest days always begin at "first light," which Henry defines for new apprentices as "the moment when you can distinguish a yellow leaf from a green leaf." First light varies according to the day of the year and the weather. But you can usually rely on the birds to sing you awake just before first light, and if you hustle, you will make it to the field at the moment when there is enough light for your retinal neurons to distinguish colors.

 As with the days of the planting marathon, harvest days are another time when every hand is needed—from that of a four-year-old niece to a 74-year-old grandparent. Henry directs the action, sending people off in ones or twos. In a good year, when the spring has been warm and not too wet, we start by harvesting the lettuce heads and baby beets we planted in the hoophouse. We do the hoophouse work first thing in the morning, because plants under plastic heat up rapidly, and it is easier on the plants if you harvest them when they are crisp and cool.

What Henry has to offer customers at the season's first market has changed considerably since he began double-planting in the hoophouses. Instead of a meager offering of the perennial chives, sorrel, and asparagus, he now starts selling beets, carrots, Japanese turnips, radishes, arugula, and head lettuces at the first market in mid-May. Even with the hoophouse crops, though, the truck will be less than a third full for the first market, which is good in a way, since we have not yet gotten up to the speed and stamina we will need for the huge harvest days of summer.

Once the hoophouse work is done, we turn to the field of greens. There we harvest spinach, loose lettuce and other greens for mesclun, arugula, sorrel, pea shoots, dandelion, mizuna, lambs' quarters, golden frill, and purple streaks. Henry often sends me off to the sorrel patch for my first harvest job. Normally, he sends Dad off to the cilantro and dill, but since Dad's symptoms are still plaguing him, that task falls to one of the apprentices. Matt is starting in on the chard—green, ruby, and rainbow. When all the greens have been harvested, Matt loads them onto the truck and takes them up to the wash area. We ride or walk up with him, ready to wash and bag the lettuce and spinach.

Harvest days are so intense that there is no time for the usual two-hour midday break for food and a nap. Instead, Hiroko makes a full farm meal, and we all tuck into it, picnic style, after the first big wave of greens harvesting is done. Hiroko's meals vary from week to week and season to season, but they always consists of a main dish (a soup, a curry, or casserole), a number of side dishes featuring many different vegetables, a big rice cooker-full of steamed rice, and an amazing cake of some sort for dessert. Whether it's an apple cake, a lemon–poppy seed cake, brownies, or scones, the baked stuff disappears fast.

As soon as the bagging is done, we're back down in the field for the second wave of harvesting: the radishes, chives (flat-leaved Asian and hollow-stemmed Western), green onions, green garlic, and rhubarb. Although May is the time of planting, many things we bring to the first markets were planted long ago—like the asparagus and rhubarb.

Rhubarb loves rich organic matter, and we oblige by planting it in the bottomland, near the stream. We enrich the soil further each year with a heavy mulch of chicken bedding and composted chicken manure. This causes the rhubarb to grow to gargantuan proportions—the stalks four feet long and two inches in diameter. When Kazami was three or four, he would completely disappear under the umbrella-like leaves when he tried to grasp the stalks at their base. He would be there right beside us one moment, and gone the next. Then we would see some of the elephant ears shaking a short ways away, lightly at first and then more violently, as if we were witnessing some extremely localized seismic activity. Finally, a leaf would thrust itself up above the rest, and at the end of its stalk would be Kazami, the rhubarb mole.

The plants in our rhubarb patch are probably more than 50 years old. They may even be 100. As rhubarb matures, it gets root-bound and the stalks will get smaller and smaller unless you subdivide and replant it. So when we first moved out to The Land, we brought with us some rhubarb root stock from Miss Kraft, our neighbor in town. We planted it down in our family garden area and enjoyed it for many years. When Henry started his farm, he dug the patch up, subdivided the roots, and planted them across the stream, where the patch is to-day. It grows larger every few years, as he further subdivides Miss Kraft's old root stock and mulches it well, ensuring that it produces big new stalks each year.

WEEK 30. **Floating Love Letters**

As we ease out of May and into June, signs of the sun are everywhere: early dawns, late sunsets, the longest work-days, shortest noontime shadows, and briefest nights of the year. We are leading up to the summer solstice, and the plants—vegetables and weeds alike—are growing with peak speed and intensity. If we are not planting these days, then we are weeding.

Weeding is not something you can put off on a sustainable farm. Weeds grow more vigorously than vegetables, and if we don't liberate the domesticated plants, they will be choked out. Now is when we must free the wispy carrots, onions, parsley, and parsnips seedlings from the surrounding weeds that are already four times their size. The tools of liberation are many and varied: Eliot Coleman's colinear hoe (we call them "slicer hoes"), stirrup hoes (we call them "scuffle hoes"), regular hoes (the old-fashioned kind—we use them for hilling, push-ing the soil up against the crop to smother the weeds), Japanese hand hoes (not for sale in this country—Hiroko's mother sends them from Japan), rakes (sometimes used for hilling), push hoes (a wide scuffle hoe mounted on a frame with a wheel), and our fingers and hands (often the best tool of all). Henry is as skilled with a hoe as a surgeon is with a scalpel, but I find that I do much better with hand-weeding.

This used to be a fairly easy task in any number of positions: bending over straddling the row, on one knee alongside the row, or on all fours over the row. These days, none of these positions are good for very long, so I switch back and forth between them, and envy Asa (who just got out of school and is now a crucial hand on harvest days), Zoe, and Kazami, who are so flexible that bending seems as natural and easy as breathing.

Since Zoe is a better weeder than I am, I asked her to tell you about it.

> There are two kinds of weeds: those that give up without a fight and those that launch a full-on battle. Fortunately, the weeds I was combating this sultry morning were not the latter. The earth was still damp from the rains that had poured down days ago. This made for perfect weeding conditions, and I should have been feeling lucky, but the beaming sun of the late morning, combined with the cloud of humidity, made me feel the opposite. I clutched my hand hoe tightly and willed myself to begin my task. Before me lay a bed of teeny-tiny cilantro and dill. Halfway down the bed, Daddy had told me, it would change into arugula. I looked ahead down the long row, but couldn't see where it changed.
>
> Looking farther down the field, I could see my brothers with the farmhands, toiling away on thinning the lettuce with their long slicer hoes. Their backs were bent, heads down, and eyes focused, as their hoes advanced in quick, swift movements. Concentration is necessary, because the lettuces are being thinned as they are being weeded. Thinning means that you leave one healthy-looking lettuce per foot, ensuring that the lettuces that are left will grow big without competition from other lettuce plants or weeds. The difficult part of thinning with a hoe is balancing swiftness with perfection. If you try to be perfect, you begin to slow. If you try to work too fast, you often hack off the one lettuce you were trying to keep. I despise lettuce thinning and weeding for this reason, so given the choice, I work on the herbs.

Trying not to think about how long it would take me to weed these rows, I started on the one before me. The sleek cilantro stems contrasted with the weeds' rough texture, making it easier to distinguish which plants to pull. The baby cilantro plants looked like they were suffocating, crying out for water and sunlight, so pulling out the weeds around them made me feel powerful, like a goddess rescuing them. I had set the hand hoe down in the black soil at the start of the row, untouched. Daddy says you're supposed to use it to weed around the plants, and then pull out the closest weeds with your hands. However, I believe that just weeding with your hands is much faster. Plus, I can be more careful with my hands, and not accidentally slice out the cilantro with my hand hoe. After weeding, I scrape dirt from both sides of the row and hill it up around the cilantro. This gives the plants more support and also smothers any tiny weeds I might have missed.

As I start in on the middle row, I feel the sun slowly moving toward the top of the sky, and the rays bore into my arms. Sweat forms under my sombrero. I quicken my movements, trying to forget all of this. My clothes feel wet from perspiration. I shake my head. I will not think bad thoughts. The moist soil is cool to my touch, so I bury my hands as I weed. I make sure to grab the weeds at the very bottom, digging into the cool soil. My knees make prints as I move forward to more weeds, more freeing, and more dirt. I look ahead to see how much more I have to go. Not good. I look back. I haven't even gone five feet yet, but those five feet are weed free. As I set back to work, I remember how once Grandpa told me never to look forward at how much there is left to do, just look back at how much you've accomplished. Grandpa is so right, I thought.

After a while, I get lost in my thoughts, thinking of tomorrow and my future and my life. The sounds of birds surround me and blend with the sound of my hands clearing the weeds. Sweat pours down my face, and I lift my head up for an occasional breeze. After a while, I notice the sun is directly above me. It gets hotter, and I feel like my hair is on fire. By this time my sombrero has come off, since it was getting too hot. I think of putting it on again. But my hands keep working, and I set myself a goal. If I weed all the way to the arugula, I will put my hat on and go drink some water. It's an ambitious goal, and I am glad when my brothers get done with their lettuce rows and come to help me. Asa starts on the third row, while Kazami starts where the arugula begins and comes toward me. I work harder, rejuvenated by the thought that this job could end soon. I can already feel the water trickling down my throat. I stop thinking random thoughts and fill my mind with commands: pull, push, pull, push, move.

Finally, I meet up with Kazami. Together, we go to the other side of the bed to help Asa finish. With three people, the distance that had looked so hopeless before seems like a piece of cake to cover. Soon we all meet up, and one half of one bed of herbs is officially done. I look at my watch and see that it has

This sturdy shed, graced with wild grape vines, was built by my brother Fred and our father more than 35 years ago as a sheep shed. Now it serves as a tool shed, protecting all the hoes, hand tools, planters, trellising poles, and other equipment from the elements.

taken us an hour. But looking back at the baby cilantro stems waving in the breeze, I am overpowered by a strong feeling of accomplishment. I savor this feeling as I drink some desperately needed water. A voice cuts through my thoughts. I look up to see Daddy calling from the tractor: It's time to start on the other side of the bed. I pick up my hand hoe and follow my brothers through the heavy, humid air.

After a long, hot day of weeding, it's hard not to collapse immediately upon returning home. But for some reason, when I returned from Henry's fields to my house one late May day, I happened to glance at the redbud tree outside my back door. After its frilly purple-pink flower stage in April, I seldom take note of the small, unobtrusive tree. But today I saw, for the first time, at the very end of each leafed-out branch, a single, new, brilliant-red, heart-shaped leaf emerging. How have I lived so long and never noticed the brilliant rubies in the crown of this common tree?

How many other things have I lived among so long and not appreciated? I start to think about them: My father bringing me in to his laboratory to help wash and put away glassware when I was very young. My mother insisting that each of us children were by far the smartest and best-looking kids in our classes at school, and "not just because you're my kids!" And my siblings, each so different from the other, but each of whom I cannot imagine life without.

Perhaps I was suffering from sunstroke, but suddenly everything around me seemed a treasure. My eyes lighted on an herb bouquet from Teresa on my kitchen counter—made with sprigs of perennial sage, tarragon, mint, oregano, and lovage, with spikes of purple-flowered anise hyssop, chive flowers, feverfew flowers and plain hyssop flowers. I noted with new eyes the attention to details of color, shape, aroma, and texture that went into its creation, and I saw how perfectly it reflected Teresa's personality—in exactly the same way as the quilts she makes.

Teresa does quilting as a form of therapy, and every two years, the therapy yields a double-bed-sized quilt, which is more than you can say about the result of most psychotherapy. Mine she started when I moved to Congerville in 2001, and completed in 2003, naming it "In Winter, Thinking of Spring." She made it from hundreds of hand-cut fragments of antique wool skirts and suits gleaned from the local resale shops. Its starburst pattern, its stitching, its placement of color and texture, all speak of her knowledge of me and my tastes, and also of Teresa and her love of beauty.

Soon, it will be too warm for a quilt, but I keep this one on the bed year-round, for its beauty and its reminder, amongst these busy days, that there is order and beauty in the world, whether created by hand-hoeing a long row of cilantro or by stitching together pieces of scrap material. All of these handmade, heartmade connections to family and the earth surround us—many waiting to be noticed for the first time.

Multiflora Rose

VIII. ROSE MOON

WEEK 31. **Breathing Sweetness**

A S WE ENTER JUNE AND GEAR UP TO GREET THE LONGEST DAY of the year, everyone is putting in 12- to 16-hour days, including us humans, the birds, the bees, and all the other insects that are busy keeping out of the way of the birds and keeping up with the flora, ensuring pollination and fruitfulness in our fields.

Sweetness is in the air, too, for we have left the Grass Moon for the Rose Moon. Already, we are delighting in the flowering and fruiting of all members of the huge Rosaceae family. One of our father's favorite *Far Side* cartoons is of the cow teacher instructing her cow pupils, "... and don't forget to stop and eat the roses." All summer long, we do pause briefly to eat members of the rose family: strawberries, blackberries, raspberries, plums, apricots, apples, crab apples, aronia berries, cherries, pears, and peaches. And it's not just these well-known fruits of the Rosaceae family that are edible. The roses themselves form red "hips," small fruits full of vitamin C, while the hawthorn sets its red or yellow "haws." Both can be harvested in the fall and dried to make teas or syrups for winter.

You can see the family resemblance among all the Rosaceae by examining the flowers and the fruits. At the bottom end of haws and hips, and especially on the aronia berries, you'll see the five bumps found at the base of every apple. More significant similarities are found in the blossoms of the strawberry, raspberry, apple, peach, and plum. They look like miniature wild roses—showy open flowers with five equal petals arranged around a central cup bearing one or more fruit-forming pistils and a large number of pollen-bearing stamens. Native bees, honeybees, and other insects move pollen from the male anthers to the female parts to accomplish fertilization, ensuring that fruit will develop.

Because we spray no insecticides, Henry's bottomland is rife with all manner of buzzing insects hovering over all manner of *Rosaceae* that ring the fields at the base of the hills. Their musky perfume wafts over us from May through August, starting with the wild multiflora roses themselves. These roses seem native, but that's just because they've gone wild. They were introduced to the eastern United States from Japan and Korea in the mid-1800s to be used as rootstock for ornamental roses. But starting around 1930, the U.S. Soil Conservation Service encouraged the use of multiflora roses for erosion control and as living fences to confine livestock. Their robust growth and intense fecundity (one plant produces an estimated 1 million seeds per year, which remain viable in the soil for up to 20 years) were eventually recognized as a problem when the "living fence" took on a life of its own and overtook pastures and other farmland. It has now been designated a noxious weed in several states, including neighboring Iowa, but not here in Illinois.

While multiflora roses are generally white, and the wild prairie rose generally pink, domestic roses now come in a complete rainbow of colors. Yet it was not always so. Despite centuries of hybridization, one long-sought-after color range—pure orange to orange-red to fire-engine red—was lacking. Members of the Rosaceae family lacked the genetic ability to produce true orange or scarlet flowers. It wasn't until 1950, when a rose breeder noticed a genetic mutation for the production of the red pigment known as pelargonidin, that we started to see pure orange to fire-engine red roses. Pelargonidin is an anthocyanidin, a plant pigment with antioxidant properties. It is found in red geraniums, as well as in ripe raspberries, strawberries, blueberries, blackberries, and (in great quantities) aronia berries. The advent of the rose named "Independence" brought pelargonidin into the service of rose breeders, and the rainbow of modern rose colors was complete.

In less than 60 years, roses have become synonymous with that fire-engine-red color—about the same length of time it took for farming to become synonymous with chemical-based monoculture. This is how limited our rearview mirror is—and how fast something goes from being new to being thought of as "the way it always was and always will be."

At the beginning of June, the procession of wild berries around Henry's fields begins with the tiny wild strawberries. Soon, we move on to the soft, juicy mulberries. By the middle of the month, the clusters of white black-raspberry blossoms that ringed the fields during the May days we spent planting and transplanting in the field have been transformed into fruits—first tiny, hard, and green, then red, then purple, and finally black and oozing with juice. The berry clusters ripen unevenly, which means that no matter when we walk by during nearly all of June—whether we are planting, transplanting, weeding, mulching, or harvesting—there are always sun-sweetened, purple-black berries to be devoured.

Around the time the wild black raspberries are on the decline, the tart gooseberries growing in the understory of the woods get going. After that, the blackberries ripen, producing flavors that jump around in your mouth, dark with coffee and chocolate, and bright with lemon and strawberry. Finally, we reap the bounty of the wild grapes, whose vines have climbed high in the trees by late August. Luckily,

Teresa's peaches may have a few soft spots and freckles, but her Evanston Farmers' Market customers find them irresistible.

all of Henry and Hiroko's children like climbing, so wild grape juice and jelly are part of the summer abundance. The waning of each particular berry's season overlaps with the rise of the next berry, so we ride through the intense work of summer buoyed on a seamless flow of wild berries that only ends with the birds picking off the grapes beyond our grasp.

But now, at the beginning of June, the domestic strawberries are in full swing. Henry and Hiroko planted a couple of patches alongside the hoophouses, and Teresa has dedicated a good portion of her acreage to June strawberries. While Henry and Hiroko's are for their family's enjoyment, Teresa brings hers to the Evanston Market. There, every Saturday in June, I watch a stream of early risers make a beeline to her stand, drawn by the seductive sweet and spicy scent of the first gold-spangled, ruby-red strawberries of the season. At this stand and at other local farm stands where perfume still pervades the air, the promise of delicious, nutritious fruit still holds, and farmers like Teresa deliver on that promise.

On two acres of her property, Teresa grows about 100 varieties of fruit. Eight of these varieties are strawberries: Jewel, Earli-glo, Northeaster, Honey-oye, Sparkle, Dar-select, Red Chief, and Gloose-cap. Each berry has a unique flavor profile, with Jewel having the classic, sweet strawberry taste; Earli-glo being most customers' favorite, with a nicely balanced sweet and tart profile; and Northeaster being Teresa's and our mother's favorite, so fragrant it is almost more floral than fruity. My favorite, Honey-oye, is a tart and citrus-y wake-up call to your taste buds and your brain.

Teresa chooses every variety of every fruit she grows based solely on its taste, not its transportability or shelf life. Her strawberries, like the raspberries soon to come, are soft-fleshed and meant to be eaten (or frozen) within a few days of picking. These berries are not the largest, nor the longest lasting, nor the most perfectly shaped strawberries at the market. But there is a reason customers are standing six-deep, waiting their turn: when you bite into the soft flesh, juices and flavors ricochet around your mouth and your brain until you are in a delirium of pleasure. "This," I hear people say again and again, "is what strawberries used to taste like!"

And this is indeed how they tasted, before they were bred for color, size, and shelf life, before synthetic chemical fertilizers, before insecticides and herbicides, before the deadly soil fumigant methyl bromide, and its even more toxic replacement, methyl iodide. Contrary to industrial belief, there *are* simple alternatives to controlling these problems in the strawberry patch, as Teresa can attest. She uses organic straw mulch (thus the *straw* in strawberries) to prevent weed seeds in the soil from germinating, and to enhance the diversity of soil micro-organisms, thus promoting beneficial life forms that all but eliminate soil fungus and nematode problems. For any weeds that do make it through the mulch, she uses human labor instead of chemicals.

Growing fruit without chemicals is no picnic, but it is possible with perseverance and the help of many hands. Time and labor are the most expensive—and valuable—inputs on any organic farm. Raising organic food is hard work that leaves few hours for sleep—or anything else. When I ask Teresa why she does it, she pauses from mulching the strawberries, gets up from her hands and knees, and glances up to the apple and pear trees to the north, and to the peach and plum trees to the south—all in full flower, blinding white and delicate pink against the cloudless blue: "It kinda comes down to … well, I've always loved an orchard."

A few minutes later, she adds, "Another reason I always wanted an orchard is for it to be here after I die. Somehow, it will let me live for at least another generation, when my grandchildren tell their children that Great-Grandma Teresa planted the tree that the apple they're eating came from. It is a comfort."

WEEK 32. **Stealing Potatoes**

WHEN HENRY FIRST STARTED GROWING VEGETABLES FOR a living in the early 1990s, he figured there was no point in growing potatoes, since he could not charge enough for them to cover his time and labor. It didn't take long for his customers to prove him wrong. When they ate an honest-to-goodness potato, many had a revelatory new experience. And some relived an old one.

An older Russian woman and her daughter started coming to the stand one year, examining everything in great detail, asking the price of each thing, and then tsk-tsk-ing at the prices. Finally, they bought one or two potatoes. The next week they were back early in the morning, and they were on a mission. The mother pointed at the potatoes and asked a question in Russian. The daughter translated, "How much for the whole bushel?" Henry said he couldn't sell the whole bushel, because other customers would be disappointed, but he gave her a bulk discount on a half-bushel.

Now, she is a regular customer, always buying in bulk. Henry says she has a keen eye, snatching up a half-bushel of sweet peppers right when they are best for pickling, a bushel of carrots right when they are sweetest for storage. She is, in truth, a rather severe old woman, perhaps having seen more to frown about than to smile at in this world of ours. But when she is ordering her grown daughter to "yes, keep filling" the basket with plum tomatoes and Henry tells her daughter, "She knows they are perfect right now for sauce," and her daughter translates it to her, she smiles and reaches up to touch his face and kiss his cheek.

Even though I grew up on homegrown potatoes, it wasn't until Henry started raising heirloom varieties that I realized they have as many subtle flavors as wine. The Carola is creamy and rich, the Butte is light and silky, the Elba is fluffy and aromatic, and the Peruvian Purple is dense and earthy, with a hint of mineral salts. Those differences are accentuated by the rich soil of Henry's Farm, since soil is as important to potatoes as yeast is to bread. In fact, the aroma of perfectly cooked, steaming hot, freshly dug potatoes reminds me of freshly baked bread—both crying out for nothing more than a dab of butter and a pinch of sea salt.

Henry grows more than 20 varieties of potatoes, including productive old favorites like Kennebec and Irish Cobbler, and the newer heirloom varieties (which are in fact older varieties), such as Ozette, LaRatte, All Blue, Huckleberry, German Butterball, Caribe, Rose Gold, Yellow Finn, Elba, Carola, and Yukon Gold. While most growers constantly seek "the best" variety, generally meaning the most productive, Henry seeks only variety and taste.

"It seems like every year, some varieties do great and other do not do so great," he says, "and I haven't really been able to correlate it with anything. Just goes to show that you don't necessarily have to understand the why and the wherefore of how nature works. I know enough to predict that the vagaries of temperature, rainfall, disease pressure, and so on will favor different varieties from year to year, but I don't know enough to predict which varieties will respond to which conditions. And that's fine. I don't need to know."

With variety, Henry's customers get many different colors, textures, and tastes to choose from, and Henry gets an insurance policy. When you look at the world through potato eyes, you quickly learn the lesson of the Irish potato famine—which is diversify, diversify,

diversify! More than 62 percent of the Idaho potato crop today is the Russet Burbank, and the remainder is slight variations on it. This leaves the crop susceptible to pests of all sorts. Instead of following nature's example and diversifying, the industrial growers use tons of fungicides, among the most toxic substances known. They not only kill fungi, but they also kill every living thing in the soil.

This is one reason that even though Henry's Farm is not USDA-certified organic, every year he buys organic seed potatoes from suppliers in Maine and Wisconsin. Although Maine was long ago supplanted by Idaho as the top potato-growing state in the U.S. (and the U.S. has been supplanted by China and India as the main potato-growing nation), Maine still produces the most varieties of seed potatoes. Henry buys 14 of his varieties from Maine, and 8 from Wisconsin, for a total of about 600 pounds of seed potatoes, which turns into some 4,000 pounds of potatoes harvested in a dry, hot year and over 6,000 pounds in a wet, cool year.

As soon as the soil is dry enough to till in late March or early April, we haul the 20- and 50-pound bags, each with a different variety of potato, down to the area of the field Henry has carefully chosen for this year's potato patch. As Henry plows the cover crop of wheat and vetch to ready the bed for planting, we wield paring knives to cut the potatoes into three or more pieces, each with at least one "eye," an indentation where a sprout will grow.

Years ago, when Asa was only five and Dad had just had surgery to reattach a retina, Asa was his "seeing-eye boy" during potato-planting time. Asa would point to an eye on the potato, and Dad would cut off that piece with his small pocket knife. Then Asa would point to the next eye, and Dad would make the next cut ... and so it went until a 50-pound bag of potatoes had been transformed into buckets full of cut potatoes, ready for planting.

Because we always hill and then heavily mulch the potatoes, we don't need to plant them deeply. In fact, it's better to plant them only a few inches deep, so the sun can get them growing as quickly as possible in the cool part of the season. As it gets warmer, we bury the potatoes in extra soil so they stay nice and comfortable during the summer heat. Then when the plants are about 12 to 18 inches tall and the soil has warmed up, Henry and his team mulch the emerging potato plants with about a seven-inch layer of fluffy hay (which gets compacted to a few inches over time) that keeps the ground cool during the hot summer.

Boiled Stolen Potatoes

The aroma of a freshly cooked stolen potato will forever change any notion you may harbor about "boring potatoes," and give you as many reasons to live as there are varieties of potatoes.

1 Dark Red Norland (red skin), 1 Caribe (purple skin), and 1 Irish Cobbler (white skin), recently stolen (or one of each kind of whatever local potatoes are in season)

Wash the potatoes, but do not peel them. A new potato has a paper-thin skin that will rub off during washing, if you want it to, but I recommend keeping as much of the skin on as possible.

Place potatoes in a pan of boiling water and cook until forkable (depends on the size of the potatoes). Put on a plate and cut open. Inhale the steam. Eat.

Before that mulching, the goal is to not have to weed the potatoes at all. To achieve this desired end, Henry watches the weed crop as carefully as he watches his vegetable crop, and he times things such that the first hilling covers up and kills the first sprouting of weeds, and the second hilling catches the second sprouting. Luckily, potatoes grow faster, taller, and sturdier than the weeds in the spring, so we can push up soil several inches in depth against the potato stems and drown out all the weeds without drowning out the potatoes. In so doing, we create a furrow between the two rows, and hilled mounds where the potatoes are planted. Not only does hilling eliminate the weeds, but it also buries the potatoes deeper. You need soil on top of potatoes anyway, either by planting deeper or by hilling, because the new crop of tubers forms *above* the piece of potato you just put in the ground, and potatoes exposed to the sun turn green.

While green eggs and ham may be okay, green hash browns are not. The green you see on a potato that was close to the surface, or kept in a light place on your counter, is chlorophyll, which is harmless. But its presence indicates that the nerve toxin solanine, produced at the same time as chlorophyll, is also present in high quantities. Solanine is part of the potato plant's natural defense against insects, disease, and predators. Levels increase with prolonged exposure to light and heat, and in high enough quantities, solanine can cause nausea, headaches, and neurological problems, which eliminates most of the potatoes' insect pests. Unless you're actually seeking out green potatoes, you're not likely to ever suffer from solanine poisoning. An average adult would have to eat between one and four pounds of completely green potatoes to feel any ill effects. But just to be on the safe side, we never sell green-tinged potatoes.

The flowering of a potato plant indicates that the production of the underground tubers has begun. On Henry's Farm, potatoes are harvested with the generally accepted plunge of a potato fork into the earth. But before the full-scale harvesting begins, Henry gauges the readiness of the potatoes, and the family gets potatoes for supper, by "stealing" them. We sidle up to the plants and pull away a big handful of mulch near the plant. Then we scrabble away at the dirt with our hands, taking whatever potatoes are close to the surface and large enough to eat, before carefully replacing the mulch and scurrying away from the scene of the crime to the shelter of the kitchen, where a preheated oven or boiling pot of water awaits. The beauty of stealing is that the potato vines are unharmed, and so continue to grow and produce potatoes.

When the stolen potatoes are big enough, generally in late June or early July, we start digging in earnest for our CSA and market customers. These are the vaunted "new potatoes," which are simply potatoes dug from a potato vine that is still alive. The resulting tubers have extremely tender skins and tender, delicious flesh. In previous years, Dad was the primary potato-digger. Each week he would team up with one of Henry and Hiroko's kids. Dad would dig with the potato fork, while his helper would quickly scoop up the unearthed potatoes and put them in the waiting crate. This year the apprentices take turns being digger and gatherer. We only dig as many potatoes as Henry will sell at market or distribute to the CSA that week, while the rest keep growing.

Digging potatoes is like discovering secret treasure. When grade-school children come out to the farm on field trips, Teresa likes to dig potatoes with them. She tells them the basics of organic agriculture, and then has them guess the names of a number of different vegetables as the class circumnavigates the field. Then she gives each child a small ziplock bag and has them line up behind the most recently dug potatoes. She grabs the potato fork (always left upright to mark where to start digging the next week), scrapes away the decaying mulch from the row, and then positions the fork close enough to the plant to pop up most of the potatoes, but not so close that you stab them in the process (which, Henry tells his apprentices, is one of the cardinal sins of farming). One foot on the fork, driven by most of your body weight, will put the fork's tines completely underground. Your back then comes into play as you pop the nest of potatoes to the surface. When the potatoes emerge into the daylight, there are exclamations of wonder from the children, who bend down to grab a potato and pop it into their bag. This makes me wonder if even these rural children have ever seen a potato in its natural habitat.

This kneeling down and touching the soil reminds me of Millet's painting, *The Angelus*, which was originally entitled *Prayer for the Potato Crop*. A man and a woman, peasant farmers, stand in a flat, open field as the sky is suffused with the orange and rose hues of sunset. They have stopped mid-work with their tools—potato fork, gunnysacks, and wheelbarrow—around them. There is a seriousness in their faces, which are in shadow, and in their postures as they bow slightly toward the basket of potatoes between them, hands clasped in prayer. The basket of potatoes looks at first glance like a baby's cradle, and there is something about the trinity—man, woman, basket of life— that is deeply moving.

WEEK 33. **Allium Hankerings**

O N JUNE EVENINGS, THE HUMID AIR DIFFUSES THE HORIZ-
ontal searchlight of the setting sun, and the world shimmers
softly. A few diamond sparkles shoot from the drops clinging to the brambles that edge the fallow field as I take a detour on my
way to the chive patch to feast on black raspberries, still warm from
the afternoon sun.

The berries are a treat, but I have a hankering for chive pancakes.
Although I will never be able to make them as well as Hiroko does,
they are still a quick, easy, satisfying supper.

Chives are one of the many members of the allium family, and
the alliums are now at their peak. Each week, we pick crates full of
onions—red, white, yellow, Walla Walla, and the baby red, yellow, and
white cipolline onions—plus shallots (red and yellow), leeks, scallions, and rakkyo.

Although all of the alliums Henry grows have their own distinctive tastes and aromas, they also have a strong family resemblance.
Most people can immediately identify an allium by simply cutting it
and bringing it to their nose.

This is because alliums contain sulfur, which the plant takes from
the soil and turns into sulfurous compounds that are a sort of silent
ammunition. These wait in the plant's cells until an animal comes
along and tries to eat the plant. Then the damaged cells release enzymes that break the sulfur compounds into irritating molecules.
When we slice a raw onion, we are being zapped by a highly evolved
defense mechanism. Cooking transforms these sulfur-based molecules into the savory flavors we love.

Although most alliums need no introduction, rakkyo often fools
people. They look like tiny tear-shaped shallots, but otherwise, they're
nothing like shallots. They have a unique flavor, somewhere between
garlic and onion but milder, and they are very solid, yielding a satisfying crunch when chewed. They are popular in China and Japan and
are best known as a component of *tsukemono*, traditional Japanese

pickled vegetables. The wonderfully crisp texture is good not only pickled but also fresh, in stir fries and salads.

Other than rakkyo, the only allium we need to explain to our customers are the Asian flat-leaved chives, also known as garlic chives. Henry encourages customers to buy the Asian flat-leaved chives if for

---

Asian Chive Pancakes

Asian chives are wonderful in eggs, whether scrambled or in a quiche. And they are good in any stir fry or Asian noodle dish. But I have come to love them most in Hiroko's chive pancakes. The dipping sauce is what puts this dish into the winner's circle, and you can modify it according to your tastes.

For the Dipping Sauce

¼ **cup soy sauce**
3 **tablespoons rice vinegar**
½ **teaspoon sesame oil**
Sugar, hot pepper flakes, minced fresh ginger, or toasted sesame seeds, to taste (optional)

For the Batter

1 **cup all-purpose flour**
¼ **cup rice flour**
¾ **cup cold water**
1 **tablespoon canola oil, plus extra for the pan**
1 **cup garlic chives (about 1 big bunch), sliced into 1-inch lengths**

To prepare the dipping sauce, stir together the liquid ingredients in a bowl, mixing well. Add the extras as desired. Set aside.

In a large bowl, gently mix the flours. Add the water, a little at a time, until you reach the consistency of a thin pancake batter. Add the 1 tablespoon canola oil, and stir until smooth. Wash the chives and cut them into 1-inch pieces. Stir them into the batter, tossing to coat.

Heat a large, nonstick frying pan over medium heat and coat it with oil. When the pan is hot, drop the batter with a ladle to form 4 pancakes, each about ¼ to ½ inch thick. Cook over medium heat about 4 minutes, and then flip and cook about 4 minutes on the other side.

Serve the pancakes hot, with the dipping sauce.

All chives (the standard ones shown here, as well as the Asian and Mongolian chives) send up edible flowers in spring, which make beautiful, delicious garnishes.

no other reason than, as Henry is quick to point out, regular chives are (gasp!) hollow. You are buying thin air surrounded by a thin oniony tube. Henry is even quicker to point out that the regular hollow-leaved chives are "a pain in the butt" to harvest once their peak season is over, because they get yellow and damaged, and it's hard to find enough good ones to make a bunch. Asian chives, on the other hand, are easy to grow, easy to harvest, do well in every season, and taste great, being both much more pungent and sweeter than regular chives.

WEEK 34. SUMMER SOLSTICE:
Hot Winds Blow

AFTER THE HARD RAINS EARLIER IN THE SEASON, THE SPIGOT suddenly turned off. Hot, windy days began to plague the field. Think of an inch, I told a friend. Better yet, draw a one-inch line on a piece of paper. Or just hold your thumb and forefinger an inch apart in the air. Now divide that inch into 10 equal pieces. It's not easy to hold your forefinger that close your thumb. I've tried it.

And it's not easy for plants to survive on that little rain. I've watched them try it, too. But that's the amount of rain we must deal with, more often than not, during a good part of the summer—although generally not this early. After a long, hot, dry, and windy week, a tenth of an inch of rain was, Henry says, "the bare minimum to make a difference."

That difference is that the parched plants already out of the ground got a lifesaving drink, while the seeds still underground may have gotten the moisture they needed to germinate. And we hope it was enough rain to soften and loosen the crust, allowing those seedlings to break through. Sometimes the bare minimum is all we need.

After the mud-luscious month of May and a damp early June, dry earth is now blowing in the hot wind, filling our nostrils with dirt and our hearts with foreboding. A week of mid-nineties weather and continual hot winds is par for the course in the height of the summer, but not in mid-June. Are we developing our own sirocco? Did I hear someone say global warming?

More likely, global "weirding." Rather than a simple across-the-board rise in temperatures, we may be headed for hot flashes, cold snaps, violent storms, intense flooding, and completely unpredictable weather—from hotter heat waves and droughts in some places to colder cold snaps and more violent storms in other places. All of this will make farming a lot harder and will ultimately raise everyone's food bill (not to mention all our other bills as well).

What we're worried about right now is that the wind blowing through is not your usual cooling June breeze, but a hot, Santa Ana–style wind. It blows so fiercely that it shakes all the remaining hollow cicada skeletons from the trees, along with the last echoes of their courtships. It will have a brief and tumultuous life, but not to worry—it's only passing through. It came from somewhere else, and will end up somewhere else, as winds will do, and so it becomes a kind of mutable metaphor for the human condition. We never see exactly where a wind comes from or exactly where it will end. We don't even see the wind itself, but rather its actions, the forces it applies to visible things like grasses and tree branches, large hats and small birds, which bend and shake, bow and quake, and sometimes get blown off the head, off the bough, or off course.

Drought following a period of rain causes the earth to crack, but in a healthy soil with good soil structure, roots reach down to subsoil moisture. Here a Winter Density Baby Romaine thrives even in the dry weather.

We hope the hot wind-tunnel effect doesn't dry out the delicate young plants too much. If they make it safely through the day, we should be fine, as there is a good chance of rain soon. Of course, even

the much-desired silver linings of rain clouds, their rain, have their own dark clouds attached, as rain will give yet another boost to our *bêtes vertes*, the weeds.

At the market last week, Henry gave an early-morning Kabuki-style dramatic interpretation of the weather patterns around the farm to one of our faithful customers. It was a very dry interpretation. (The early birds get not only the best produce, but the best theater.)

We know when rain is near because the farm dogs—Wrinkles, Koko, and Chico—hear the dislocated thump of thunder long before we do. The wind whips up the dust, the sky darkens, and phalanxes of black-bottomed clouds sail in over the horizon. We smell the rain on the breeze, and our hopes rise. Then the clouds hit the high-pressure zone sitting impassively above us and career off, leaving just a few drops on ground that is so hot and dry it hurts—to look at it, to feel it, to watch the thirsty plants wilt in it. Henry worries that it may have been just enough rain to get the weeds in the top layer of the soil to germinate, but not quite enough for the deeper-planted vegetable seeds. Even if some do germinate, the life will quickly burn out of them in the baking soil.

 Life can, and does, burn out quickly sometimes. It happened the day before the frail rain, when the mercury hit 97 degrees. I let my chickens and ducks out of the coop early in the morning as usual and then, as usual, went out at noon to check on them, gather eggs, and give them food and water. I went about my chores and then noticed one of the hens had gotten inside the sunny, fenced-off area that protects my raspberries from the fruit-loving hens. This happens now and then. They get in, and then, being bird-brains (and I mean that in the best possible sense), cannot figure out how to get out. So I did what I usually do—lifted up a section of fence for her to get out.

That's when I noticed something was very wrong. She could barely stand up. And when she moved, she staggered like a drunk. I watched as she gathered all her strength, and made a tottering beeline to the shade of a nearby tree and collapsed. I brought her water, and even dipped her beak in it, but she couldn't drink. I picked her up (you know a chicken is in a bad way when she lets you pick her up and makes no fuss whatsoever) and brought her into the basement and laid her on the cold concrete floor, water within reach. I checked her every five minutes for nearly an hour.

The last time I went down and tried once again to encourage her to drink, she went into convulsions, her wings slapping the concrete, her body rolling this way and that, like a ship in a perfect storm. I held my breath and hoped that she was regaining her strength, and flailing because she was upset to be alone in a strange place. But deep down, I knew I was watching her death throes, that it was too late, and that nothing I could do would undo seven hours trapped under the brutal sun, unable to reach shade or water.

I left her in the basement and went back to work in the fields. Our farming days are so full now that morning skids swiftly into night, even though the days are reaching their maximum length. The best part of the day is when the sun slips softly to the horizon. Then in the space of a single breath, the whole world softens: the air turns cool, the colors muted, the earth breathing deeper and slower, under the comforter of darkness.

At dusk, I returned home and brought the poor hen, cool at last, down to the little stream beyond the shiitake mushroom logs. I pushed my way past the tall weeds and grasses, and then through the multiflora rose bushes, whose thorns slowed the procession until, as I pulled free, the shaken branches released their musky petals over her body.

She was heavy for a hen—maybe five or six pounds—and still full of eggs. At the stream, I thanked her for all the eggs she had laid in her short life. I apologized for her untimely death, for not noticing her situation sooner. I stood on the wooden bridge and tossed her in. She fell gracefully and lay on her side in the almost dried-up stream, looking a bit like Ophelia. The water began to pool in front of the dam her body had made. I thought she might float down our little River Styx. But the water found a way behind her, making a new rivulet around her tail. And that was how I left her—her red comb gentle on the black bank, the water flowing around her soft, feathered body.

WEEK 35. **The Pageantry of Peas**

To MY EYE, THERE IS NOTHING QUITE SO GRACEFUL AS TREL-lised pea plants in full swing. And nothing quite so tasteful as a crunchy sugar snap pea eaten straight off the vine. And nothing so captures the essence of the first part of the growing season as peas.

None other than the esteemed writers Marcel Proust, Thomas Jefferson, and E. B. White have seen fit to discuss peas at length—Proust in *Swann's Way*, Jefferson in his garden notebooks and letters, and E.B. White in his essay "Coon Tree" in *One Man's Meat*, where he laments (more than 50 years ago) the fact that people have lost touch with their food, and just want it "simply and fast."

> The American kitchen has come a long way, and it has a long way to return before it gets to be a good room again ... we will soon get to the point of eating "simply and fast" [according to a speaker White heard at the American Society of Industrial Designers]. He said we would push a button and peas would appear on a paper plate .... It really comes down to what a man wants from a plate of peas, and to what peas have it in their power to give. I'm not much of an eater, but I get a certain amount of nourishment out of a seed catalogue on a winter's evening, and I like to help stretch the hen wire along the rows of young peas on a fine morning in June, and I feel better if I sit around and help with the shelling of peas in July. This is all a part of the pageantry of peas, if you happen to like peas.

Well, we like peas. And we like the pageantry of peas. Henry pores over the seed catalogs each December, doing his best to restrain himself from ordering every single variety. Then, as early as he can work the ground, he plants sugar snap, snow (or Chinese), and good old-fashioned shell (or English) peas.

Peas are in fact one of the oldest cultivated crops. An archaeological dig at Jarmo in northwestern Iraq uncovered peas dated at 7000 BC, making them, along with wheat and barley, the most ancient of cultivated foods. The ancient varieties were shell peas, and most of the harvest was dried so it could be stored and either traded or eaten later.

The fresh green pea is a relative newcomer on the world stage, but in recent centuries, it was the fresh young peas that were valued. Thomas Jefferson, who kept notes on his gardens from 1767 until 1824, often wrote of the many varieties of peas and other vegetables he grew at Monticello, noting in his "Garden Kalendar" which were "killed by bug," which others "came to table," and which ones tasted best. He often made mention of the different varieties of peas he planted, and much is made of the circle of gardeners who had a gentlemanly competition each year as to who would have the first peas of the season. The winner would invite the others to a dinner at which the first peas were given a place of honor. To announce the occasion, little notes were rushed around to the circle of friends: "Come tonight—the peas are ready."

The winner of the early pea competition was almost always a Mr. George Divers. One year, it happened that Jefferson's peas were ready before he received Mr. Divers's invitation. His family urged him to quickly send out notes and begin the dinner preparations. "No, say nothing about it," replied Jefferson, "it will be more agreeable to our friend to think that he never fails."

It is this spirit of generosity that a bounteous season engenders. Growing up on a farm, you know firsthand the pendulum swings between frugality and liberality. You're scraping the cellar for last year's potatoes and turnips when suddenly there is an embarrassment of emerald riches—mounds of spinach and bushels of peas. Anyone who has had a backyard garden knows how suddenly you go from tiny fragile sprouts to a sea of tomatoes, cucumbers, and peppers.

With the mood swings of the weather, and the recent trend of hot and dry springs, peas are never a sure thing. But I remember many seasons in the 1970s that were perfect for peas. One day, when the peas were at their peak, all eight of us spent an entire day picking bushel after bushel of them. I remember lugging them up the hill

from the garden in plastic laundry baskets, but I didn't remember why there was this urgency to get all the peas until Henry reminded me—we had to pick, shell, blanch, and freeze all our peas that day and night, because we were leaving for Canada the next day.

So into the brightly lit kitchen we all went, 16 hands bent over one task. There was nothing to do except talk and laugh and listen, and shell mound after mound after mound of peas. We had contests seeing who could find the pod with the most peas in it. Fred, our older brother, who was the most competitive of the bunch, would always exclaim that he had 13 (no, 14!) peas, and then we'd make him show us—one or two would be tiny embryonic nibs. We'd scoff and laugh and argue and get punchier and punchier. It was work, but it was fun. I'm sure it was midnight before the last pea went into the boiling water, and then the ice bath, and then the freezer bag. But when we finally trundled off to bed, giddy with a sense of accomplishment, we were happy as peas in a pod.

Such pea picking and freezing marathons epitomize the link between food supply and season. If fall and winter teach us to be con-

Peas planted in late March are ready to eat by early June. In the past, cooler springs resulted in bumper crops most years. Now May heats up so quickly that we only get a good pea crop every three to five years.

servative, economical, and restrained, then late spring and summer teach us to be generous, openhanded, and free. The fact that every crop is at its peak for only a short time promotes a spirit of making the best of it while it lasts, and conserving part of it for future use, as good a metaphor for how to live one's life as I have ever stumbled across.

The peak of pea season usually comes in late June and early July, accompanied by the sounds and sights of summer—fireflies rising from the grass just after dusk, the irrepressible morning burble of an irrationally exuberant pair of dun-colored house wrens nesting just off my deck, and the crunchy green pop, followed by the cool liquid split, and then the cascade of pings first loud and ringing in the empty bowl, then more and more muffled as the bowl fills. This was the week all the shell peas seemed to mature at once, and we picked many bushels full and then sat around our various family tables shelling companionably, the elders' fingers the most nimble in their easy familiarity with pea botany. As we sat shelling, Dad told this story about one of his mother's many sayings—probably the one he heard most frequently growing up. He later wrote it up for his "Earth-Science Notes," as part of the *Food & Farm Notes*.

Last Tuesday, as the entire crew was finishing the harvest for Henry's CSA customers, we picked most of the rows of sugar snap peas. As usually happens some of the peas were over-mature (the pods were too old to be edible), because they were overlooked in an earlier picking or because they matured quickly in the heat and dryness. As Marlene and I picked our row, one of us on each side, we threw the peas edible as sugar snaps in a half-bushel basket, but stuffed the over-mature ones in our pockets.

As I straightened up at the end of the row and turned to walk to the other end, I noticed that some pickers, not wanting to give over-mature peas to customers, had thrown them on the ground as they moved down the rows. When I saw them lying there all forlorn, I exclaimed "waste not, want not." And Marlene and I picked them up and put them, along with those in our pockets, in a separate basket.

"Waste Not, Want Not" Pea Soup

(adapted from Deborah Madison's recipe)

For the Stock

1 teaspoon butter

1 teaspoon vegetable oil

1 beef soup bone (optional)

1 bunch scallions, including the greens, chopped

6 branches parsley

1 medium carrot (you may leave the greens on)

8 leaves lettuce (outer leaves are fine), torn

½ teaspoon sea or kosher salt

Freshly ground black pepper, to taste

5 cups water

3 cups clean pea pods (use the peas in the soup recipe at right)

Heat the butter and oil in a large pot. Add the soup bone, if desired, and brown on all sides. Then add the scallions, parsley, carrot, lettuce, salt, and pepper. Wilt over medium heat for a few minutes.

Add the water and pea pods, and bring to a boil. Lower the heat and simmer, uncovered, for 20 minutes. Strain into a bowl.

For the Soup

1 teaspoon unsalted butter

½ cup thinly sliced scallion, spring onion, or young leek, white part only

3 cups stock (from recipe at left) or water, divided

2 cups fresh peas

½ teaspoon salt

½ teaspoon sugar

Freshly ground black pepper, to taste

Snipped chives, chive blossoms, and heavy cream, for garnish

Melt the butter in a stockpot. Add the scallion and sauté for about 1 minute. Add ½ cup of the stock (or water, if you didn't make the stock) so the scallion stews without browning. Cook for about 4 to 5 minutes. Next, add the peas, salt, and sugar. Add the remaining 2½ cups stock (or water) and bring to a boil. Then turn down the heat and simmer for 3 minutes, until the peas are bright green.

You can eat the soup as is, but if you like it smoother, you may transfer it to a blender or use an immersion blender right there in the stockpot. Purée the soup for 1 minute, until smooth. Taste and adjust the salt and pepper as needed.

Serve garnished with snipped chives, chive blossoms, and a drizzle of heavy cream.

On that recent Tuesday, we also picked the last of the shell peas. Because they would not go to customers, all the shell peas went into the same basket. They covered the spectrum from a few barely filled out pods, through those of ideal maturity, to overmature—some even with very dry pods.

I don't know whether you have grown shell peas, but you surely have eaten frozen or (gasp) canned ones. So you know that the pod is not edible (too tough and not sweet), even at their proper maturity. So, later that day and evening, we (mainly Marlene) shelled peas at the kitchen table: a tedious and time consuming, but strangely satisfying, task—especially if you keep in mind the great reward that awaits your taste buds.

After pulling a handful of shell peas from a large pile in the center of the table toward me, I shelled those that were not overmature into a shallow cake pan, and threw the overmature ones into another pile on the table. When we finished shelling the good peas, Marlene froze them for winter delight or cooked them lightly for eating.

And the pile of overmature shell peas still on the table? We shelled all of them too. The resulting peas ranged from just over mature to completely dried out. And the overmature sugar snap peas that we had stuffed in our pockets and rescued from the ground? Those too we shelled and added to the pan of overmature shell peas. And the fate of all of these overmature peas that most people would have discarded? Marlene made an excellent pea soup (with carrots, onions, and beef soup bone) that lasted for days. If we had picked overmature snow (Chinese) peas, we also would have shelled those and used them in the soup, too.

Summer Thunderstorm

IX. THUNDER MOON

WEEK 36. Garlic Ascends

I AM LIGHT-HEADED DURING THESE LONG DAYS OF THE GARLIC harvest—perhaps from the pounding heat, perhaps from the enveloping aroma of garlic, perhaps because we are spinning at the outermost reach of the gravitational tether that binds us to our local star, the sun. In our annual elliptical journey, we're always farthest from the sun in July and closest in January—a reminder that things are not always what they seem, or what we think they should be. Right now, when the heat is peaking and the garlic must be harvested, we are actually some 4 million miles farther from the sun than we will be in the cold of January six months hence. So it is that seasons are not so simple as brute proximity to the source. Rather, it is the tilt of the earth, the North Pole tipping its hat toward the sun in a gentle nod, that gives the Northern Hemisphere its powerful summer and ushers in the weeklong garlic harvest.

Just as we plant the garlic all at once in early November, we likewise harvest it all at once in early July. Well, not quite *all* at once—prior to the main harvest, we pull juicy, tender green garlic each week to sell at the market and put into the CSA shares. But those harvests of a few hundred plants at a time are nothing compared with the 20,000 plants that must be harvested this first week of July.

This is a week when extra hands are most appreciated, so we were happy to see last year's apprentice Courtney, and happier still that she brought her friend Mike along to help. The sheer number of plants to be pulled dictates that everyone works from 6 a.m. to 6 p.m., with a two-hour siesta during the hottest part of the day. Henry works longer, though, using every hour from sunup, which is about 5 a.m. this close to the summer solstice, to sundown, close to 9 p.m. Getting the garlic harvested is one of the few jobs that he lets interfere with his self-imposed non-harvest-day curfew of 8 p.m.

He is driven by twin engines of urgency. First, he needs to get the garlic out of the ground before it dries down too much and the tight bulbs begin to open. An exploding bulb is less marketable and harder to rub clean of its flaky outer skins; plus, dirt gets in the center of an opening bulb, providing a perfect habitat for the microbes that cause dry rot. Second, Henry is painfully aware that each hour we devote to the garlic harvest is another hour for the weeds to grow unharried by hands or hoes. The quicker we are done harvesting, the sooner we can get back to the weeding—and to the planting, trellising, mulching, and myriad other tasks that become more pressing each day.

Each day's garlic harvest utilizes both machine and human power. Henry runs the tractor through the beds, dragging an implement with four arrow-shaped sweeps that dig into the soil between the rows. The sweeps loosen the soil near the bulbs, making it easier for the human hands that follow. At the end of the row, Henry applies the brake to the wheel in the direction he is turning and brings the tractor around in a tight circle. Then he goes through the bed again with the sweeps pointing the other way. As he passes by this second time, we test a few

plants, grasping where the stem meets the ground and pulling gently but steadily straight up, doing our best not to break the delicate stalks of the soft-necked plants. If the garlic comes out easily, Henry and the tractor move to the next bed. If the roots hold tight, he comes through yet again, until the soil billows up and the strong knot of roots at the base of each bulb loosen their tight clutch on the earth.

Once the tractor moves on to the next bed, the adults get down on their knees and begin extracting garlic. Children have the advantage of being able to stand up, grasp the garlic plant near the ground and use the strength of their legs to pull straight up. I envy them as I crawl along on hands and knees, then kneel, toes tucked under and sandals slipping off, hunching slightly to pull each plant. After getting tangled in my sandals one too many times, I ditch them in the nearby bed of chard. As I walk back, I move from solid earth to where Henry has loosened the soil, and drop calf-deep in the earth's embrace.

The recent rain means that the moist soil is easy on our knees and releases the garlic with minimal effort once Henry has loosened it. In

The strong roots of the garlic relinquish their hold on the earth as we pull them up in early July to be hung from the barn rafters to cure.

dry years, the bulbs come out of the earth reluctantly, clasping great clods of brick-like earth. Their long roots function like rebar in concrete, forcing us to use harvest knives to cut the roots and free the bulbs. Sometimes the ground is so dry and hard that the steel sweeps will not bite deep enough, and we have to resort to the digging forks, pounding them into the ground with our feet to get the tines beneath the bulbs and then prying them up from the soil. In a dry year, we always break a fork or two. Luckily, they come with lifetime guarantees, so when someone has time to go back to Farm and Fleet, we replace them.

No matter the weather, the garlic patch is always drier than the rest of the field, because garlic is an impressive scavenger of water. A single bulb can have roots that reach 30 inches down, with a lateral spread of 18 inches in every direction. Even with the moisture conservation provided by the mulch, garlic tends to suck the soil dry in all but the wettest summers. After the harvest is complete, Henry waits for a rain to moisten the dry clods and then works the softened ground with the tiller to make a bed for sowing his favorite summer cover crop, sorghum–Sudan grass.

Cover crops are indispensable to any sustainable farm, functioning as all-in-one herbicide, fertilizer, temperature controller, and soil conditioner. They come in many forms—winter cover crops, summer green manures, catch crops, and forage crops. All serve to build organic matter and soil structure, enhance soil microbial activity, and increase nutrient levels in the soil—especially nitrogen, if the cover crop is a legume. In addition, they suppress weeds, prevent soil erosion, and loosen compacted soil with their roots.

Cover crops also shade the soil and protect it from the sun's heat. In cooler soil, microbial activity is lower, and the organic matter is not destroyed as quickly as it would be otherwise. When exposed to the hot summer sun, our black soils are like a roaring furnace being stoked with the priceless organic matter that is the basis of a healthy soil (which is the basis for healthy, tasty plants, which is the basis for healthy herbivores, including market customers and family members). The shade provided by cover crops dials down the heat, preserving precious organic matter.

Henry chooses from a wide menu of cover crops, depending on when and where he is using them, and for what purpose. He plants sorghum–Sudan grass on the harvested-out garlic bed, because it loves hot, dry conditions and grows very tall very fast, reaching six to ten feet by the end of August. From a distance, it looks like a field of corn without the ears. Such abundant, rapid growth is what makes

Smashed Garlic Potato Therapy

If ever there was a marriage made in heaven, it would be freshly harvested garlic with freshly dug new potatoes, as the first potatoes of the year typically coincide with the garlic harvest.

Henry says, "If you're despairing about the state of the world, if life is getting you down, rest assured that there is a reason to live ... freshly dug new potatoes with garlic."

> **2 pounds small new potatoes, unpeeled (any variety will do, but floury ones like Elba or Butte will smash up more easily than waxy ones, such as Carola or fingerlings)**
> **8 cloves garlic**
> **½ cup olive oil**

Preheat the oven to 400°F.

Bring a large pan of salted water to a boil. Drop the potatoes in and cook for 20 minutes, or until forkable. Drain and then return them to the pan.

Peel the garlic cloves and put them in the pan with the potatoes. Smash the potatoes and garlic cloves with a sturdy wooden spoon or the end of a rolling pin until they are cracked and split.

Pour the oil into a roasting pan and heat the pan in the oven for 10 minutes. Carefully tip the potatoes and garlic into the hot oil and cook for 15 minutes. Turn them and cook for another 15 minutes. They come out sticky and crunchy and irresistible.

sorghum–Sudan grass an excellent smother crop. Henry mows this cover crop each time it reaches waist- to chest-high to stimulate root growth. The thick mass of roots squeezes out weeds, even the dreaded perennial Canada thistle, by robbing them of the moisture they need.

In late August, Henry will till the cover crop under, and the root mass will add to the humus, the most stable, long-term form of soil organic matter. In early September, he will use the former garlic bed to plant the last crops of the year—spring radishes, arugula, mizuna, Japanese turnips, choi, and perhaps spinach for overwintering. By then, the old garlic mulch and new cover crop will be decomposing to provide a boost for the resurgent autumn greens.

Henry grows so many varieties that our customers often turn to us for advice on which tomato, potato, or bean to purchase, so we do regular taste tests and share the results. One morning during the garlic harvest, I found myself in the midst of a taste test of four of the just-harvested varieties: Inchelium Red, Sicilian Silver, New York White, and Russian Red. We used the harvest knives to crack open a few heads of each, and then passed the cloves around in a high-octane, early-morning communion.

The Red Russian was extremely crisp and pungent, with the edgy, hot burn typical of hard-neck varieties. The soft-necked Sicilian Silver was at the other end of the spectrum—juicy, mild, and sweet—perfect, we thought, for crushing or putting through a press to be used in a vinaigrette or mayonnaise. The Inchelium Red was nicely balanced, similar to the New York White, but not as complex. Inchelium Red was rated the best-tasting garlic by the Rodale Institute in 1990. But Henry's vote for best-tasting goes to the soft-necked New York White, which is richer and more complex than the others, and, to Henry's taste, perfectly balanced.

The garlic tasting left us slightly giddy, and we returned to the field invigorated. As we work, I wonder if, before dirt became "dirty," there were any negative connotations associated with life-giving soil. Certainly, Henry wears his dirt as a badge of honor. Barbara Mahany, a writer friend from the Evanston Farmers' Market, once asked Henry what he does to clean his dirt-stained hands. Later, she wrote in the *Chicago Tribune*: "Cradling a bunch of green garlic in hands the color of soot, the swirls of his fingerpads indelibly inked, Brockman defends his digits: 'I don't even think of them as dirty. I don't know what they are, but they're not dirty.'"

Just as some people find dirt to be dirty, some find garlic to be stinky. Such people stay far from the farm during this week, when the earthy smell of garlic permeates hands, hair, clothes, truck, barn, house, cats, dogs, knives, even the very dust—not overpoweringly, as one might imagine, but pleasantly.

We move slowly down the long rows, grasping each plant at its base with both hands and pulling straight up. A few hard shakes gets rid of most of the soil, and we rub away what remains in the roots' embrace. Then we place the plants in neat pyramids and move down the row.

As soon as a section is done, Matt drives the pickup along the row, and we load the garlic in the back. Then Matt drives it over to the hayrack, which is positioned in the shade of the wild mulberry trees near Walnut Creek. He grabs giant armloads of garlic and lays them in piles around the perimeter of the hayrack. When the rack is piled high at the end of the day, Henry will drive it up to the barn, where he and the kids will work sorting and bunching it until, or even after, dark.

The largest bulbs—about 10 percent of the total—are set aside for seed and will be planted in late October or early November. Until then, they hang in a separate section of the barn so we won't inadvertently cut them down to sell. This selecting of the biggest and the best for the next year's crop has been done since the dawn of agriculture, long before Gregor Mendel, the Augustinian monk, scientist, and gardener, figured out the laws of inheritance. Mendel elucidated the mechanism that early farmers knew intuitively: saving the seed from the best plants is a simple way of capitalizing on random genetic variation. In this way, our garlic gets bigger and healthier and better tasting year by year as we select those plants best suited to our soil and climate.

The smallest bulbs are also separated out. If we happen to sell out of the larger bulbs before the market season ends, we will begin selling the small ones. If not, they will be our own winter garlic supply. All the rest of the bulbs will be bunched in groups of 20, and each bunch will be tied to another. Zoe describes the scene she joined upon finishing her goat-milking chores:

I came upon the whole crew of apprentices, family, and friends working steadily on an enormous pile of freshly pulled garlic. The garlic was neatly stacked on a long, wide hayrack. Courtney, Mike, Rebekah, Daniel, and our new apprentice, Jesse, were immersed in counting up medium-sized garlic into mounds of 20, then lining the tops up.

When finished, they would lug their pile of 20 to Daddy and Asa, who had the finger-paining job of using faded orange baling twine to tie the tops together, using loops and knots so tight they were virtually impossible to break. After tying one group of garlic together, they tied another group to that same string, so that in the end, they would have 10 groups of 20 bulbs cascading down, all tied on the same string. Each string of 10 garlic bunches, 200 bulbs in all, was taken by Matt, who hung them from the ceiling of the barn to dry. These strings of garlic will be sold throughout the season as individual heads, as well as garlic braids hand-styled exclusively by Daddy.

Evening after evening, the curtain of garlic grows. It sways in the summer breezes as the sky goes from bright blue to dove gray to slate with burnishings. Who knows what constellations of flavor may unwind from a garlic bulb in the months to come?

WEEK 37. **Ripe and Rotten**

I HAVE BEEN GOBBLING UP THE UGLY AND RAPIDLY DECAYING peaches and apples at the rate of about a dozen a day as I work my way through the bushels of *for-us-es*, which is not yet in Merriam–Webster, but if it were:

> **for-us** (pl. *for-us-es*)—vegetables that are not fit to be sold to the public, but whose defects (stabbed, split, broken, too big, too small, too ugly, or just this side of rottenness) in no way compromise their flavor and nutrition. So they are divided among

the family and workers. Instead of going to market, they are kept "for us."

As I work my way through the for-us-es and wend my way around soft spots and wormy cores, it occurs to me that the worst fruit and vegetables—the tomatoes our mother (and chief tomato sorter) deems too soft to make the relatively short, 150-mile journey to market; the red and yellow peppers with sunburn or soft spots; the peaches and apples with bruises and rot—are absolutely the best-tasting produce of all. I wonder if we have lost the animal instinct, and pure animal pleasure, of seeking out and devouring only that food that calls to us sensually with full aromas, saying, "Eat me! Today, I am ripe, but tomorrow, I rot."

Who can resist such an entreaty? I grab an ugly peach from the bucket I picked from Dad's old tree, the one whose branches are propped up with two-by-fours. It is velvety and yielding, beginning to mold on its upper shoulder. I hold it under a stream of cold water in the sink and use my thumb to slough off the soft, moldy portion and wash it down the drain. With just a few sweeps of my thumb, the bad flesh is gone. I know, because my thumb is reading the peach's own Braille. It says: *flavor-filled flesh starts here; stop now.*

I turn it over to see if there are any other soft spots, and brush a light one away down the drain. Then I plunge in my fingers to separate one half of the fruit from the pit. Often, there's a small worm near the pit, and I scoop it, and any evidence of it, down the drain as well. Some peaches split at the stem end, and the pit splits internally as well, which can attract a particular sort of long, thin, and prehistoric-looking beetle with large rear pincers. I make sure any and all of these folks have vacated the premises before letting all my senses drink in what has been transformed, in a few seconds, from a very bad, to a most excellent, peach.

I bring it to my nose and read its spicy-sweet promise, and then bend forward in a modified Japanese bow, arms akimbo, to dive in. The juice runs down my chin as I slurp away, wanting to bury my whole face in the utter bliss of it. I imagine there is a silly grin on my messy face, and for a moment I remember a similarly gleeful grin on my Italian grandma's face as she climbed back into our family van some 25 years ago, after we had gone to a U-pick peach orchard in Michigan. As soon as the doors were shut, she extracted peach after peach from the huge pockets of her house dress, and with a girlish giggle, she told us how many she had eaten while we were picking. She was proud of herself for getting all those peaches for free—although she did complain on the way home that her stomach didn't feel so good.

As I'm washing the stickiness off my face and hands, I think about standards of beauty and tolerances for imperfections. Most people choose their friends and lovers not solely on their looks, but on the basis of their personality, intelligence, wit, humor, sensitivity, and good taste. If we meet an engaging and intelligent person with a good sense of humor who has a habit of, say, leaving his or her socks on the floor, we generally do not (immediately, anyway) turn the person out on the street. We walk around the socks, or ask the person to pick them up, or pick them up ourselves ... no big deal. What, then, is the big deal with eating around wormholes? Yet most people turn away in disgust from an apple with a worm hole or sooty blotch, or from a peach with a moldy soft spot.

I confess that I have a soft spot for soft spots. Just as they reveal genuine, sensitive human beings, they are a reliable way of showing that a fruit has not been sprayed with poisons, and that it is at its peak of ripeness, of flavor and nutrition, of juiciness and pleasure. The quest for cosmetically perfect fruit has resulted in the loss of vibrant tastes—the sharpness and depths that make great fruit great. Fruits in the supermarket are glossy and perfect on the outside, but insipid on the inside—watery, at best, and permeated with the stale taste of long-refrigerated storage, at worst. They remind me of the shiny apple that glistened evilly in the tale of Snow White. And the bad side of good-looking fruit is indeed the poisons—the chemicals used in its production.

I was in a Chicago grocery store not long ago and saw a sign announcing "Fresh Juicy Peaches." They were from California; it was peach season in California (though not yet in Illinois), and when I lifted them to my nose, I detected a faint peachy aroma. It transported me to the corner of Broadway and 23rd in Manhattan one July day about 15 years ago, when I was on my lunch break. I walked by a fruit cart and turned around in mid-stride, attracted by the amazing aroma of very ripe peaches. I bought one, turned, and took one bite, then slurped it down, turned around, and went back to buy a whole bagful. That evening, I made a peach pie in my tiny apartment kitchen in the West Village, which still stands as my all-time best pie-baking effort. With this taste memory burning in my brain, I bought two of those big California peaches at the grocery store, thinking they might be ready to eat in a day or two.

A couple of days later, I ate one. It was unremarkable. I brought the other down to the farm with me where it sat on my counter for weeks, slowly getting wrinkled as it dried out. "Wrinkled" and "dried out" may fairly apply to some people, but they should never apply to fruit—especially a soft fruit, like a peach. Fruit is supposed to gradually soften and break down into a gooey mess perfect for watering and fertilizing the place where a new fruit tree might grow. The only kind of soft fruit that wrinkles and dries out is one treated with toxic fungicides. Ripe fruit is supposed to be eaten, and if not, it's supposed to rot. If it doesn't rot, something's wrong.

How wrong? The USDA studies cited by the Environmental Working Group report that pesticides were found on 94 percent of all the peaches tested, and that there were 45 different pesticides found on those peaches. I am certain that T. S. Eliot did not have the Environmental Working Group in mind when he wrote, "Do I dare to eat a peach?" but he could have, as published statistics consistently show

Teresa's Simplest Peach Melba

1 imperfect peach

2 scoops vanilla ice cream

2 ounces raspberries

Cut any soft spots or insect damage from a July peach, and then cut it in half and take out the stone.

Place a scoop of vanilla ice cream in each half.

Top with raspberries. Enjoy.

peaches to be the most heavily pesticide-laden fruit or vegetable you can buy. You can research these pesticides on your own, or take the USDA's word for the fact that nearly all 45 have been identified as animal carcinogens; as causing birth defects in animals; as damaging the reproductive system; as interfering with hormones, and thus damaging the brain and nervous system; and as damaging the immune system.

This begs a couple of questions: if the USDA recognizes that these chemicals pose grave dangers, why does the FDA approve of their use on our food? And if we have this knowledge, how can we dare to eat any peach but an organically grown one?

Meanwhile, as the fungicide-laden peach continued to dry out and wrinkle on my counter, Dad's peach trees were dropping their luscious and fragile fruit each day. With Mom and Dad down at Barnes Jewish Hospital in St. Louis to see the specialist who we hope will finally give us a diagnosis, I dropped by their empty house each evening after doing Dad's cow chores. I would pick up a half-dozen dropped peaches, anywhere from lightly bruised to half-rotten, and reposition the three-pronged harvest ladder to reach the ripe ones before gravity had its way with them. Then I would bring them home, examine each, and slurp down the ones in an advanced (but not *too* advanced) state of deterioration.

There are many challenges in growing fruit without chemicals—particularly soft fruits, such as raspberries and peaches, which are susceptible to molds in a wet year and to a host of insects *any* year. This past year, Teresa endured an invasion of Japanese beetles of biblical proportions. Teresa's daughter Gabriela wrote of the trials and tribulations of beetle patrol.

> The greedy little black, green, and copper buggers are eating practically everything this year, reducing the grape leaves to something eerily reminiscent of doilies, stripping the cherries until only the pits are left to hang from the trees, swarming so thick on the apples and peaches that those fruits resemble shiny Christmas ornaments. Writhing, evil Christmas ornaments.

Armed with buckets of soapy water (the soap breaks the surface tension so they can't crawl out), we tramp around trying our best to diminish the ravenous hordes. Sometimes this defense against the relentless invaders seems futile; often when we come back to redo a spot, it seems that there are just as many as there had been a few hours before, when we first scoured it. If there are less, it's easy to suspect that the clouds or the rain or the early morning is what's truly keeping them away. Or maybe their four- to six-week reign of terror is slowly beginning to wind down as they burrow into the ground to spawn a whole new wave of troops for next summer.

Usually Beetle Patrol starts with the peaches and ends with the apples and pears. If there are just one or two, you can pick them out with your hands to toss into the bucket, but if there are more—and there are almost always more—your best bet is to shake the branch over the bucket. Some will manage to fly away, but fewer than if you tried to pick them off one by one. The real hazard of this method, when using it on trees, is that while many will get in your bucket, and one or two will get away, a good number will come showering down on you. This is why you should always make sure your mouth is closed before shaking a branch.

After you've enjoyed the downpour, the next step is to look down at your shirt. There will inevitably be several clinging to the fabric with their little claws, which are strong but not strong enough to keep you from picking them off and sending them to sleep with—well, with other Japanese beetles. It may lack the drama of *The Godfather*, but if we spent time making little concrete overshoes for all these guys, we'd never get anything done.

After peaches are several rows of raspberries and blackberries. Up and down and up and down the aisle, shaking branches over buckets, or knocking the beetles into your hand first if the branch is too far away to get the bucket in. The insects are all busy mating before they retreat underground to reproduce, and after a while, you start to feel like some sort of vengeful morality deity breaking up orgy after orgy. If there isn't already a thick layer of dead beetles in the water, one soon forms, which makes your subsequent victims live slightly longer before drowning. They churn frantically, attempting to climb up the slippery backs of their deceased comrades, or to cling to a bit of leaf or fruit that dropped in there with them, struggling against the inevitable in a way that, after a long patrol, can be almost hypnotic.

We don't bother with the cherries, since their season is past, and I generally get the grapes only if there's some extra time, seeing as three quarters of the entire crop has already had all of its leaves annihilated. A few are starting to grow back, and hopefully that will be enough to get all the essential nutrients to the grapes themselves. I'd say "knock on wood," but that will only lead to more Japanese beetles falling on me.

Frustrating as this method is, so far it's the best option. We do use a nontoxic kaolin clay spray to keep insects off certain plants, but rain washes it away, and it can't be used on soft fruit, like raspberries. Pheromone traps are worse than doing nothing, because they draw in more than they can kill. (We've recently had to ask our neighbors to take them down, as they were actually bringing even more beetles to our field.) And since we're committed to being organic, poisonous chemicals are out of the question. So for now, I guess I'm stuck on Beetle Patrol, fighting back the invaders.

As it turned out, thanks to Gabby and the others on Beetle Patrol, Teresa had her best fruit year ever—in terms of both production and sales. We were able to bring some nearly perfect peaches up to the market, and the customers appreciated them all the more, knowing the heroic measures we had gone through to save them from the ravages of the Japanese beetles. And the damaged fruit that wasn't good enough for market made wonderful jam and fruit smoothies and toppings for oatmeal. I look forward to the day when the discerning customer at a farmers' market insists on nothing less than imperfection and can't wait to get home and grab a paring knife and get going on a less-than-perfect piece of fruit from a local farmer.

WEEK 38. **Fencing Lesson**

THE STORM SPED IN FROM THE WEST, CLOUDS GALLOPING toward us like black-clad horsemen of the apocalypse. The wind swooshed through the trees carrying the smell of rain. Before we could run for cover, fat drops hurtled down from the green–black sky. Henry, dripping wet in his new rain jacket and rain pants, which are "excellent in every way except that they are not waterproof," declared an early lunch break before an afternoon dedicated to liberating more rows from the weeds that grew unmolested during the week of the garlic harvest.

This welcome rain, combined with the heat, ushers in the week when we move from mostly green vegetables to the whole rainbow of bright-colored roots (beets, carrots) and fruits (tomatoes, peppers, eggplant, corn, beans, squash). The pigments in plants are not for our eyes only. They play important roles in plant chemistry and provide visual cues to the insects that pollinate them. The same visual cues lead humans, visually and viscerally, to what's good for them.

There is a reason why we and our primate brethren evolved with the most dazzling color vision in the animal world. The packets of pigment that delight our retinal neurons with dark greens, brilliant oranges and yellows, and deep reds and purples, also delight the other cells of our body with carotenoids and anthocyanidins, powerful antioxidants that protect against cancer and other chronic diseases. The pink and yellow chard and the bright red of the beet attract us, and the truth behind the beauty that Keats spoke of ("Beauty is truth, truth beauty") is the truth of life-enhancing phytochemicals.

Food manufacturers are well aware of the fact that our eyes pull us toward bright colors. Kazami is still cruelly tricked by the neon hues found in ice cream parlors. His instincts—hard-wired before the advent of artificial coloring and flavoring—compel him to pick the bright pinks or oranges or blues. But the brightly colored vegetables thriving in these long days and rich soil are not teasing: they deliver on the pleasure their colors promise.

Yellow and orange are healthy colors for vegetables, but not for people. After months of doctors' appointments and many tests, all inconclusive, my mother had hauled my father back to the doctor and said, "Look at him! He's skeletal, and he's turning orange—do something!"

And so, last week, the specialist in St. Louis found, with a single sonogram, two blockages in Dad's pancreatic and bile ducts. He biopsied them at the same time he did the diagnostic procedure and, having determined they were cancerous, scheduled Dad for the Whipple procedure, a surgery devised by a Dr. Whipple in the 1930s to cure pancreatic cancer. The word "cure" only somewhat ameliorated the words "pancreatic cancer." But in the wide space between the two was the comfort of finally knowing what was ailing Dad. That comfort brought him back into the fields the next day, and each day for the few weeks between diagnosis and surgery. He continued to work alongside us at his usual tasks, bunching the cilantro and dill, stacking crates, organizing boxes and buckets, and driving the truck around the field to gather crates of vegetables each harvest day.

The days passed in a blur of sun and sweat that only abated as the long rays dropped behind the western hill the Wednesday before his scheduled surgery. As the sun was setting, Dad came down to the field in his pickup and called Asa and me to come with him so he could show us the cattle chores and the fencing pail.

We jump in the back of the truck and rumble and bump to the pasture near the upper field. Dad points out what we need to do while he's in the hospital—fill the water tank morning and evening and watch how far down the cows graze the grass, so we know when to move them to the next pasture. As he explains which fence gate is attached to which loop to electrify which pasture, there is a sparkle in his eyes and a spring in his step. He even jokes about his Whipple procedure, which, he says with a grin, is just a matter of "taking out all the offending bits and then reattaching everything and sewing it all back together again."

That is a pretty good description. But what none of us knew was that this brutal rearranging of one's guts is arguably the most difficult surgery to recover from—even more difficult, Dad's doctors told us months later, than open-heart surgery. The whole idea of the surgery is to leave the patient cancer-free. The problem is that he will also be duodenum-free and largely pancreas-free—a condition the human body has never in its millions of years of evolution had to deal with, nor would it ever want to.

But at the time Dad was showing us the fencing pail and explaining the fencing system, we trusted in Dr. Whipple and applied ourselves to the task at hand, learning how to check the fence and "make fence" as necessary. Only later, when we worried that Dad might never leave the hospital, did I remember that day with the three generations of us out in the green pasture—Asa, the spring generation, me the late summer, and Dad the fall. And I remembered the essay Dad had written shortly after his own father, the winter in our seasons of generations, had died. He never published it, but entitled it "Fencing Pail."

> When we moved to "The Land" in 1971, one of my earliest jobs was to "make fence." And once fences are made, the need to "fix fence" quickly follows. These are the expressions that Dad used. Not "build a fence" or "construct a fence," but "make fence." Not "repair a fence" or "maintain a fence," but "fix fence."

Why did he use these expressions? Were they used by his father, who died when Dad was only 12? By his farmer neighbors? I don't know, and now I never will.

For about 20 years—since leaving the farm for college in 1952 until moving to The Land in 1971—I did not make fence or fix fence. Nevertheless, the first time I made fence in 1971, or shortly thereafter, I used a fencing pail—just as Dad did whenever he needed to make fence or fix fence. I do not recall putting together my first fencing pail in 1971, nor do I remember what it looked like. But I do know what was in it—all the things needed to make fence or fix fence that were small enough to fit in that pail.

Dad would go to the old two-door garage, or in later years to the new tool shed, reach under the workbench, and grab his fencing pail—an old five-gallon metal pail. It had not been bought new, but rather was a pail that once held paint or grease.

Soon he would say to me, "Get the fencing pail." When I was very young, I could barely lug it to Dad. He would reach for the pail and throw it up into the two-wheel trailer he pulled with the tractor for a big or back-field fencing job. Or, if it was a small or close job, he would carry the pail as he walked along the fence. Later, I could lift the pail into the trailer myself, and even later, on a small job, I would carry the pail along the fence, but never with the ease and purpose that came with Dad's strength and experience. The fencing pail seemed to be an extension of his body and personality—an integral part of being a farmer.

I would love to see that fencing pail again—dented metal with a wooden handle grip worn smooth by the sweat penetrating through his leather gloves—with the wonder of my young boy's eyes, and see all those things needed to make fence and fix fence. There was always a fencing pliers, claw hammer, regular pliers (and in later years a vise-grips), fencing staples, assorted kinds and sizes of nails, and for electric fences, insulators of various kinds. And as he worked on a fence, he threw into the pail pieces of wire, bent nails, broken insulators—anything discarded that would fit in the pail. The fencing pail was always at Dad's side or close at hand as items needed and used went in and out.

And on a rainy day, Dad would clear off a place on the tool bench, take all the tools out of the fencing pail, oil them if needed, organize all the usable nails and insulators, and finally throw all the wire scraps and bent nails into an old wooden nail keg under the work bench. Then everything else went back into the pail until it was needed again—perhaps that same day, almost certainly soon—until the last time.

Whenever I grab my fencing pail and head out to make fence, or more often to fix fence, I sense Dad's genes and farm experience within me—until I too will reach for that pail the last time.

Finished with his cattle instructions and fencing explanations, Dad looks lovingly at his cattle. He puts everything back into the fencing pail and sets it back on the floor of the passenger side of the cab. Then he places the plastic-handled screwdriver on the driver's side dash, telling us that we should keep it there and check the fence every time we drive by the pasture to make sure it is always hot.

WEEK 39. **Bean by Bean**

THE HARICOTS VERTS ARE MASTERS OF DISGUISE. UNLIKE the yellow wax or royal burgundy beans, they are nearly indistinguishable from the stems of the bean plant. They also tend to hide down low near the base of the plant, hugging the stem and the earth, resisting the searching hand and the easy pluck from plant to basket.

After these wet weeks, some near the soil are starting to soften. Every once in a while, you see the white cotton fuzz of mold beginning. Those beans you toss aside, along with those that have more than a touch of rust, or more than one or two nibbles by a bean beetle. Those not-quite-perfect beans get tossed into the neighboring bed, recently tilled under and seeded with cover crops.

The bright yellow wax beans are the easiest to see and pick, seeming almost luminescent as the sun sinks below the hills surrounding the field.

Only the most perfect beans go into the half-bushel basket that moves with you, half-foot by lurching half-foot, down the row. A dozen or so feet into the row, you realize there are 400 half-feet in a 200-foot row, and that you are spending maybe five minutes picking the beans from every six inches of row. You multiply minutes and measurements and feel the chill air slip in from the hillside.

Not wanting to be picking beans at midnight, you start moving faster. You remember Thoreau's declaration, "I was determined to know beans." With renewed determination to do the same, you concentrate on the way the beans arrange themselves, and the way your fingers can grab the greatest number in one motion from bush to basket. You play games with yourself, saying you're not going to look up to see if Matt, who started at the other end of the row, has gotten any nearer. You simply reach and pluck and toss. Bend the plant to the other side. Reach and pluck and toss. Move the basket to the next plant. Reach and toss. Reach and toss. Somehow the Zen of repetition takes over, the efficient pathways establishing themselves in your brain and down your arm to your fingertips. You listen to the evening calls of the birds, the beginning of the insect chorus muted by the coolness. You gradually notice the first goosebumps on your arms.

And then, suddenly, you almost knock heads with Matt. You slowly unbend your body—ankles, knees, vertebrae, neck, head. Bipedal and erect once again, you notice the perfect half-moon halfway up the deepening sky. The evening brings perspective. You are a dot

Joel's Italian Flat Beans with Sweet Onion, Garlic, and Maple-Glazed Ham

This recipe can be used with any kind of bean but was devised by Joel especially for Henry's Italian flat beans. Wonderful on their own, these beans reach their apotheosis when infused with the smoky, sweet, and salty savors that mellow and mingle in this slurpy, unctuous sauce.

1 pound Italian flat beans, trimmed

1 tablespoon butter

1 tablespoon extra-virgin olive oil

1 thick (¼-inch) slab honey or maple glazed ham, diced into ½-inch pieces

2 tablespoons diced white onion

1 tablespoon coarsely chopped garlic

½ cup chicken stock

Maple syrup, for drizzling

Freshly ground black pepper, to taste

Salt, to taste

Extra-virgin olive oil, for drizzling

Parboil the trimmed beans in salted water for 3 to 4 minutes, or until bright green and just tender. Drain the beans and set aside.

Meanwhile, heat the butter and extra-virgin olive oil in a sauté pan. Add the ham to the pan and sauté until it begins to crisp slightly. Add the onion and sauté gently until it is soft, about 2 to 3 minutes. Add the garlic and sauté for another minute, taking care not to let it burn.

Add the chicken stock, just enough to cover the bottom of the pan. Toss in the drained beans, and sauté everything for an additional minute or two. Add the pepper and salt. Drizzle in a thin stream of maple syrup, about 1 teaspoon. Serve hot or at room temperature. Just before serving, drizzle with a little more extra-virgin olive oil.

At the end of the season, when the beans are more mature, you can adapt this recipe by covering the pan at the end of the cooking time and braising the beans for 15 to 20 minutes.

on the horizon, a small part of something much bigger, much longer than one human life. Standing on the earth, you know that you are a part of the same something that everything came from, and to which you and everything will return, and from which you can never be separated.

You balance the bushel-basket of beans on your head and walk—half weary, half triumphant—to the end of the row.

Green Corn

x. GREEN CORN MOON

WEEK 40. Corn Porn and More

CORN SEX STARTS, AS MOST THINGS DO, WITH MALE AND FE-male parts: the tassel at the top of the stalk and the protokernels along the cob. The two are separated by three or four feet, an insurmountable obstacle unless wind and weather collude. When pollen is about to rain down from the tassel, each protokernel sends up a single silk in anticipation. A few days later, a Rapunzel-like spray of blond silky hair emerges from the tip of the ear precisely when the pollen is ready to drop. Then each sticky and receptive silk catches one single, crucial grain of pollen.

While corn pollination involves just pollen and ovum, actual fertilization is a 24-hour ménage à trois among the female ovum in the

Before beginning the sweet corn harvest, Henry checks the different varieties for ripeness as Daniel and Matt stand by. Corn does not provide a high per square foot return, but Henry grows it anyway because it is a classic summertime treat and links us to our ancestors and to the native Americans who developed it.

protokernel and the two cells of the male pollen grain: the tube cell and the generative cell. Fertilization will be successful only if temperature and timing are right. If it is much over 90 degrees, the pollen grain is not viable and fertilization doesn't occur. You know this is the sad case when the silks at the top of the ear do not change from green to reddish brown, as they do once conception has taken place.

If the temperature is under 90, however, successful fertilization occurs over a period of about 24 hours. During that time, the tube cell forms a tube down the center of the silk that allows its brother twin to slide smoothly down the six- or eight-inch length of the silk to reach the embryo sac at the base of each kernel. On the way down, the nucleus of the generative cell divides into two sperm cells, and these migrate down to the growing end of the tube, which finally meets and fuses with the nucleus in the female protokernel and becomes the embryo. One twin thus becomes the kernel's germ from which a new plant can grow, while the other twin creates the energy-rich endosperm that makes up the bulk of the mature kernel. A few weeks after fertilization, plump golden kernels begin to form, each with a germ of life inside that may become another corn plant.

As we were talking about the complications of corn sex one day, Henry said, "I always thought the parallel between the double sets of twins in Mayan myth and the double pair of paired cells in corn fertilization is really interesting."

"Hmmmm ..." I said, rummaging around in the far recesses of my brain. Back when I worked for textbook publishers in New York, I had put together various literature anthologies for high school students, including a collection of world literature. I had read the *Popul Vuh* at that time, the sacred book of the Quiché Maya of Guatemala, but had only the vaguest memory of the Hero Twins. But as I researched them again, the parallels were striking. They are, most probably, pure coincidence, but it is coincidence made compelling by the fact that in the fifth and last part of the *Popol Vuh*, the Maya descended from people the gods fashioned from corn. And this only after, in the first section of the book, the creators failed miserably in their attempts to produce proper and good human beings from other materials.

It is the second and third sections of the *Popul Vuh* that are devoted to the adventures of the Hero Twins, Hunahú and Xbalanqúe, and of their father and their uncle, Hun-Hunahpú and Vucub Hunahpú, respectively. We pick up the story as the father and uncle are tricked into going to the underworld for a ball-playing contest. They lose, and as a consequence, they are sacrificed and buried in the ball court—except for Hun-Hunahpú's head, which is placed in a tree. When a young goddess heard of this strange fruit and went to see it, the head spat into her hand (one has to wonder a bit about the Spanish priest and his translation from the Mayan language) and made her pregnant. Thus, the Hero Twins were conceived and later went on to have many adventures—during which they figured out they were immortal, and naturally had a lot of fun with that.

Modern botany and ancient creation tale collide because the maize from which the Quiché Maya were created is formed by a generative cell (the Hero Twins' father) and a tube cell (their uncle). The generative cell then divides into two sperm cells (the Hero Twins), and the result is immortality: kernels of corn that may be planted, tended, harvested, and the new kernels planted again, generation after generation.

This eternal verity—that seed can be freely saved to grow more of the same plant—ended abruptly with patented, genetically modified seed. These seeds may not be saved and replanted unless the farmer wants to risk a ruinous lawsuit. And the genetic modification commonly known as the "terminator gene," which causes seed to be sterile, could bring the entire history of plant life on earth to a screeching halt.

If we were to tell the Maya that a kernel of corn may not grow when planted, they would scoff at our naive and ill-informed version of reality. The escapades of the Hero Twins are surely more plausible than a seed designed not to grow. And yet we have arrived in this brave new world and have perhaps killed the immortal twins when the germ of a kernel will not germinate, and life will not go on.

Other Native American groups had twins in their pantheons. In Iroquois mythology, Good Mind helps his grandmother, the Woman Who Fell From the Sky, place useful and beautiful items on the Earth, while his twin, Warty One, creates unpleasant things, such as thorny bushes. These twins are not antagonists, but partners in a quest. In their world, nothing is good or bad; everything has its role.

In our corn field, in addition to corn porn, there is, naturally, corn smut. That's what generations of Illinois corn farmers, including my grandparents, called the fungus *Ustilago maydis,* which can infect newly formed silks and take over the developing kernels. Living off of the sugars in the corn, the fungus grows inside the kernel, causing it to balloon into a gray-black kernel 10 times the size of a normal one, and eventually to explode, literally, out of the top of the ear. The smut can infect the plant through any small cut or nick caused by cultivation, hail, or insects. The Aztecs put this knowledge to good use and scratched their corn plants at soil level with a knife, allowing the spores easy entrance into the plant.

They did this because *huitlacoche,* as they called it—which means "raven's excrement" in the Nahuatl language—was a sought-after delicacy for the smoky, mushroom-like flavor it adds to foods. I had my first huitlacoche in a huge open-air market in Mexico City back in the 1980s. A woman was cooking the fungus with butter over a small charcoal fire. It smelled good, so I gave her a few pesos and she scooped it into a tortilla for me. It was mildly earthy tasting and delicious. While the USDA has spent a lot of time and money trying to eradicate the fungus because it renders an ear of regular field corn worthless for most conventional uses, farmers in Mexico put it in cans and sell it as a delicacy.

The James Beard Foundation held a *huitlacoche* dinner in the late 1980s in an attempt to get more Americans to eat it by calling it "Mexican truffle." The attempt largely failed. But every year Henry brings it to the market, and every year more people buy it, even though an ear of infected corn is double the price of a regular ear of corn. We always separate out the *huitlacoche* ears and label them as such, but there is always at least one customer each year who assumes that corn is corn, begins to select an ear from the *huitlacoche* bin, recoils in horror, and then discreetly pulls Henry aside to show him the fungal growth. "I don't think you want people to see this," they say conspiratorially.

Good Mind or Warty One? Delicacy or smut? If anything, the pornography of corn can teach us this: that sex is best when left to nature, and smut does have its pleasures.

Because August was the time of the immature "green corn," many Native American tribes knew this month as the Green Corn Moon and celebrated this seasonal delight with dancing and feasting at Green Corn festivals. Regular corn was the fully mature dry corn, which was ground into corn meal, or popped, depending on the variety. Green corn is still a summer delight to be celebrated. Many midwesterners have memories of their own "green corn ceremonies"— picking the ears just before sundown and running back to the kitchen to drop them into a pot of water that was already on the boil. On Henry's Farm, our green corn ceremony involves peeling back the husk and eating it raw, right in the field, without so much as a drop of hot water or butter or salt.

Green Corn with Marjoram Butter

Teresa suggests marjoram butter as an excellent pairing for sweet corn, but you can make an herb butter with any herb of your choice. The herbal flavors will be stronger if you make the butter a day or more ahead of time.

½ cup salted butter

2–4 tablespoons fresh marjoram (or other herb)

1 teaspoon fresh squeezed lemon juice

Fresh sweet corn (as many ears as there are people for dinner)

Soften a stick of butter at room temperature, or heat for a few seconds in the microwave. Finely mince the fresh marjoram. Mash the herbs and lemon juice into the butter with the back of a spoon.

Get the freshest corn possible. Strip the ears' husks and silk. Plunge the ears into boiling salted water for 1 or 2 minutes. Eat with the herbed butter. You can be as skimpy or as profligate with the butter as you like. Any leftover herbed butter can be refrigerated and used on vegetables or toast.

If our corn has had good weather for pollination and enough rain for the embryonic kernels to fill out, then by August we are harvesting it twice a week. We always harvest it last so that it will be as fresh and sweet as possible, mere hours old, by the time our customers get it. While most other harvest tasks are done in ones or twos, corn harvesting is most efficient when everyone gathers and works together. Because we are all together—everyone from the kids to the grandparents, plus Matt and all the apprentices—and because we are nearing the end of two long, hot days of harvesting, there is a festive atmosphere. First Henry rips off a few ears, takes a bite to make sure the varieties he is about to harvest are ripe, then passes around the sweet milky ears for the rest of us to finish off. Fueled by this treat, enlivened by the cooling air, and encouraged with the end in sight, we pick up our bushel baskets with a sense of exuberance and anticipation.

This is the rarest of harvest jobs, one where you can stand upright instead of bending over, and walk along normally instead of crawling on hands and knees. And once the picking starts, it is another rare farm activity, a highly aerobic one that brings more air into your lungs and oxygen into your bloodstream. This heightens the other sensory pleasures, starting with the hefty ears that feel absolutely right as your fingers curl around them. Then, grasping one near the base, firm in the palm of your hand, the crisp sound as you snap it downward and it tears away from the sturdy stalk. Then there is the heavy plunk as it hits the bushel basket.

Above all there is the clean smell of the corn plants, which is related to but distinct from the smell of the corn kernels themselves. The aromas that rise up as you walk through the corn rows are a combination of the fresh green of chlorophyll, the sweetness of sugars in the plant, the musky sexy fragrance of the starting-to-decay silks, all combined with the earthy dust of the field that we are stirring up off the broad leaves of the corn as we stride through.

The most experienced pickers are those who can tell as soon as a finger touches an ear whether it is filled out underneath the layers of husk and ready for market, whether it is only partially filled out due to poor pollination and will then be "for-us," or whether it is too immature and needs to stay on the plant another week. Dad and Henry are the most experienced and so always pick. Matt is often a picker as well. The rest of us are bearers, which is about right since you need two or three times as many bearers as pickers. The picker moves through the rows and the bearer trails just behind holding out the bushel basket. The picker's arms are in a continual circular motion as he moves them downward to yank off an ear, and then circles back and upward to toss it into the basket on the way to the next downward motion of yanking the next ear from the next stalk with the next step forward.

Within minutes, the basket fills up. As the corn reaches the top and the wire handles begin to bite into the flesh, the bearer calls out to the next person with an empty basket. As soon as that next person is in place behind the picker (who never stops picking), the person with the full basket carries it out to the end of the row where crates are stacked and transfers the ears into the crate designated for that particular variety.

The air outside the corn rows feels cool on our sweaty bodies, especially in comparison to the stifling heat and humidity under the canopy of closely spaced rows. The bearers rotate in and out of the rows as the pickers work their way down one row and up the next. In this way we rapidly fill baskets, then boxes, then the truck itself with hundreds of pounds of freshly picked corn.

Of course, it should end there. But the day is not over yet. The sun is sinking into the horizon, but seems to stop and hang there as we cross the dwindled creek of summer to haul the load of corn to the wash area. There we carefully pack each ear into the crates that will go to market. We put a milk jug of frozen water in the center of each crate, pack the corn around it, and top it off with ice. This turns each box into a mini icebox—a refrigeration unit—so the crates that finally get loaded on the big truck will radiate cold all the way to the market.

As we grasp each fat ear, we clasp hands with all the other people who have ever done so. We are part of a tradition that travels through Asa to Henry to Dad to Grandpa to the first Europeans who were given this gift by the Kickapoo, Miami, or Iroquois, who inherited it from the Aztec and Maya. The heft of corn contains the collective memory of all of them, extending back thousands of years to the beginning of corn, perhaps to the beginning of creation—which, according to the Maya, were one and the same. On an evening like this, it does not seem far-fetched to think that we are the work of the hands of a god who made people from maize and then brushed over the canvas of the earth in strokes and hues of hard work, laughter, music, good food, family, and friends. It is all here, and all because of corn sex—as complicated and sensuous and tenuous as life itself.

WEEK 41. **Aronia Comes Home**

IT'S HARD TO CONVEY THE TROUNCING THE SUN CAN DELIVER during the bright hours of mid-August, especially in the bottomland. Our dad's colleague Tibor Horvath called it "Death Valley." Because it is sheltered by hills on all sides, it always feels hotter than the upper field, where we can usually catch a few breezes. So while Henry, Courtney, Matt, and the other regulars were sizzling in the bottom field, I was lucky to get a call from Teresa: "I'm out here in the aronia field, and it's ready!"

Although aronia is native to most of North America, it is known mainly as an ornamental and is largely unknown for its deep purple clusters of fruit, commonly called chokeberry. And you just might choke if you grabbed a handful and put them in your mouth expecting a sweet, mild taste, like blueberry or blackberry. A few of Teresa's market customers have tried to sneak a taste, and before she could warn them, they found out that this is not your normal berry. It's not that it tastes *bad*, but rather that the strong, tannic, puckering taste is so unexpected.

While not well known here in the land of its origin, aronia is very popular in Russia, Poland, and Finland, where you can easily find it in a variety of juices, jellies, jams, teas, wines, syrups, food colorings, and pharmaceuticals. Teresa and her family put the berries into oatmeal with or without a sweetener, and mix them into smoothies with strawberries, raspberries, and yogurt, again with or without a sweetener. Teresa is also making juice and jelly and is experimenting with an aronia salsa.

That aronia is delicious any number of ways would have been old news to the Native Americans, who harvested aronia, along with other wild berries, for summer eating. For winter, they would grind the berries into whatever meat was available to make pemmican. Everyday pemmican was made with meat and fat from bison, moose, elk, or deer, along with such fruits as cherries, currants, or blueberries. The bright purple of the aronia gave it a festive look, so this form was used almost exclusively in ceremonial and wedding pemmican.

The dark purple-black color and tannic flavor of aronia are clues to its nutritional and pharmaceutical value. Its high vitamin C content prevented scurvy in the Indian communities. One of aronia's great modern-day appeals is its high antioxidant value, measured in terms of oxygen radical absorbance capacity (ORAC). Aronia berries have an ORAC value of up to 16,000 micromoles per 100 grams. In

A close look at the bottom of the aronia berries reveals the five bumps characteristic of fruits of the rose family. The native North American aronia berries mature in early September. Teresa's two acres of aronia will yield up to 25,000 pounds of aronia when the bushes are fully mature. Let the juicing begin!

contrast, the ORAC value for one Granny Smith apple is about 5,000, and a one-cup serving of blueberries, much touted for their antioxidants, has a value of about 13,000.

Even before I learned all that, though, I was sold on aronia. Teresa had first planted just a few bushes in with the 70-some varieties of fruits she grows. When those bushes began producing about four years ago, our sister Beth was visiting. She's a juicing fiend, so she promptly juiced some and began mixing the aronia juice with sweet apple, pear, beet, and carrot juice. I took a small amount of pure aronia juice back home with me and used it to make a sorbet at a ratio of about 10 percent aronia juice to 90 percent fresh-pressed apple juice. It was the most beautiful and intoxicatingly good thing I have ever made. It had a rosy-violet hue and a wild berry tang with a touch of winey tannin, mellowed by the sweet freshness of the apple juice.

Seeing as there are no major producers of aronia in our area, and no one making aronia juice in the whole U.S., Teresa decided to act. She planted 1,200 bushes on two acres of our dad's upper field and mulched them—and was promptly overwhelmed by the season's regular work on her own farm. Quickly, she found herself unable to weed them as she had planned.

Our father had always been skeptical of the whole aronia project (which is his nature as a scientist), but this did not stop him from helping plant and water all those aronia bushes. And when Teresa became overwhelmed with her own farmwork, he did his best to keep the grass around them mowed down as the season progressed. The main challenge for any market farmer who grows a wide diversity of produce is finding time to keep up with everything. When the market season gets going, Teresa says, "It becomes a sort of triage, where the most important things get done and the rest falls by the wayside."

Dad did his best last season to keep the young bushes clear of the surrounding vegetation, but as his symptoms intensified and he grew weaker, he did less, and the tall grasses growing near the young bushes provided perfect cover for voles. Without fear of predation, they chewed away at the base of the plants, resulting in a fair bit of mortality, which meant that the following spring, Teresa had to re-plant about 250 bushes.

It takes as many as three years for aronia bushes to start bearing, but they can produce indefinitely after that if they are kept pruned, producing as much as 40 pounds of berries per bush each year. Keeping those not-too-far-off 25,000 pounds of aronia berries in mind, Teresa began researching aronia juice. When she found that no one in the U.S. manufactured the juice, she decided to go to Poland to do some on-the-ground research the year before her two acres of aronia were due to bear in full force.

At first, she sought out some of her Polish-speaking market customers to travel with her. But when that didn't work out, she asked me to go along. I had never been to Poland, and the notion of going overseas as a roundabout way of researching local food was inviting. Even though aronia is a native North American bush whose productive fruit-bearing cultivars were developed at the University of Minnesota, it was only in Eastern Europe that commercial production and processing had taken off. It seemed time for these two sisters to bring it back home.

Teresa contacted aronia farmers and processors in northern Poland, so we flew to Gdansk and were soon driving down tree-lined country roads surrounded with rolling hills of pastures, potato fields, and thick forests. We were so enthralled that we drove right by our destination. The town of Gaska was announced by a sign, and two seconds later, the same sign with a slash through it announced we were leaving town. So we turned around and went down the only road that was there—a dirt lane that went back to a thatch-covered house surrounded by aronia fields.

As soon as we had deposited our suitcases, we went walking over the 20 acres of rolling hills of aronia. The shiny green leaves glittered in

Teresa's Aronia Juice

Teresa suggests using aronia berries in one of these quick and easy ways—as a delicious way to get your antioxidants year round.

- *Throw them into a smoothie.*

- *Add them to oatmeal.*

- *Add them to an apple or peach crisp or cobbler.*

- *Or make the juice below.*

To make a delicious juice, boil your aronia berries for 5 minutes in just enough water to barely cover them. Then mash them up and let them cool.

Wet some cheesecloth and line a sieve with it. Let the mashed berries drain, and then squeeze out all the juice you can. Add the juice of one lemon for each quart of berries used.

At this point, you can freeze the juice. Then, during the winter, thaw it out, add water to dilute it, and add sugar or another sweetener to sweeten it.

Adjust the water and sugar amounts to your own taste. Some people prefer it straight up, without water or sugar, but it is rather medicinal that way. I like to drink it hot in the winter, but it is also very good cold.

For a special treat, use seltzer water or 7-Up to dilute it, and you'll have an aronia soda!

the late afternoon light and were beginning to blaze red in places. The full-size bushes were some 10 feet tall. Because of an unusually warm year, the aronia had matured early, so we had missed the harvest we had hoped to observe. But we were glad to see that the machine had missed a number of clusters we could sample, and missing the harvest also meant we had more time with the farmers and processors. We visited two aronia farms where Teresa learned how to prune the bushes and got to see the harvesting machine and learn how it works—although we will most likely hand-harvest ours. In between our visits, we popped into store after store, coming home with five kinds of aronia juice, eight kinds of aronia tea, and some aronia syrup and jam.

When I got to the upper field, I found Teresa's van already parked, with a small tent set up behind it. Under the tent was a table and scale and poly-lined boxes—a few of them already heaped with the purple-black, pea-sized berries. I saw people crouched near each bush—our sister Beth from Mexico and our brother Fred from Washington, who had come to look after Dad, who was still in the hospital. Our Nature Conservancy friends Bob and Renée and a few of Teresa's CSA and Evanston Market customers had also come to help with the harvest.

It was hot, but I had on a straw hat, a long-sleeved white cotton shirt, and long cotton pants to keep the sun at bay. We were lucky not only to be in the upper field, where there were slight breezes, but also to be able to go to a four-foot-tall bush and sit right under it, where the leaves provided enough shade to take the edge off the heat. Once situated, we reached in and around the bush, grabbing whole clusters, often 15 or more berries each, and putting them in the five-gallon pail. Sitting in the grass plucking berries also meant a chance to see all of the vibrant insect life in the field. Spiders and spider webs were everywhere, and every other aronia bush had a bird's nest in it. The fledglings were long gone, but it was comforting to think that our field of aronia was also a maternity ward for the grass-nesting birds, who have mostly lost their habitat due to row-crop agriculture.

The aronia berry is relatively hard and dry, but nevertheless our hands were soon stained deep purple, as small amounts of juice were released when we plucked them from their brilliant red pedicles. Each full bucket weighed about 10 to 15 pounds, and each day we picked some 300 pounds. Our first mini-harvest went on for three days and resulted in almost 1,000 pounds of berries from the young bushes. It felt like quite an accomplishment, until Teresa told us that next year the harvest would be some 7,500 pounds, with the following year probably doubling that as the bushes come to maturity.

Teresa finds herself vacillating between optimism and overwhelming anxiety about an endeavor that is more manufacturing than farming. But she is nothing if not persevering. Already, in just five years, she has transformed what was once a three-acre horse pasture into a beautiful, diverse, and sustainable fruit and herb farm. And her goals for the aronia project are as much for the community as for herself. It will provide delicious and nutritious berries and juice to people who otherwise (unless they are going to Poland) would not have access to them. And it will improve the sustainability of the upper field as well. Because there is no need for chemical inputs, the soil and water around the aronia field will remain clean and healthy for future generations. Moreover, aronia is a perennial plant, eliminating the need for tillage, thus eliminating soil loss and nutrient depletion. Aronia is especially suited to our land here in Woodford County that is too hilly for conventional row crops.

Teresa is also looking toward the sustainability of our small farming community. Woodford County has an agricultural-based economy, and an aronia juicing facility will provide local jobs for farm workers and juice press operators. Should demand increase, there is potential for existing farmers to contract and grow aronia for Teresa, especially on land not suitable for row-cropping, providing increased income and stability to these farmers. Area producers would be able to rent the press for aronia, apple cider, or other products, allowing them to diversify and increase their own farm income and sustainability too. Aronia production and processing will help keep local dollars in the community to cycle through other local businesses.

We pick all afternoon and into the evening. The blissful moment comes at about 8 p.m., when the sun sinks into the horizon. Everyone sighs with relief and welcomes the evening, as soft edged and gentle as the days are hard edged and brutal.

WEEK 42. **Watermelon Heaven**

CAMILLE PISSARRO LOVED PAINTING WINTER SCENES, HE SAID, because only in winter was there true color. In summer, he found the light so intense that all the colors faded out. Yesterday evening, looking west at 7:30 p.m. as we packed the last aronia-filled boxes into Teresa's van, I saw what he meant. The sky was molten metal, still so white-hot it hurt to look at it. The world had been overexposed in these nearly 100-degree days, drained of color and energy.

Mid-August always catches me unprepared for her heat and haze. There is a deathly stillness at noon—no breeze, no birdsong, no motion except for trickling sweat. The only living things that enjoy this weather, it seems, are to be found in the plant world. But then I stand up to swipe the sweat off my forehead and see a hawk riding the thermals, hanging high in the blinding light.

Although the longest day of the year is the summer solstice in mid-June, this is never the hottest day of the year. It takes another month for the earth and air to truly heat up, so by the time we hit the dog days of August, they seem much longer than any June day.

They also seem longer because there is so much to do. In addition to continuous weeding, intermittent mulching, and continued weekly plantings (we are doing our best to get the fall crops in the ground now), we are nearly drowning in produce. There are so many crops reaching the peak of their production that we sometimes almost forget to be thankful for the abundance and instead fear we will never match the crops' output of vegetables with an equal output of time and energy.

"August creates as she slumbers," Joseph Wood Krutch wrote, and it does seem that if you turn away from the field and then turn back, you witness, if not the miracle of the loaves and the fishes, then the miracle of the corns and the squashes. The plants you just got done harvesting a day ago are once again laden with yellow crookneck and green zucchini, with huge Pink Brandywine and tiny Sungold tomatoes, with watermelons and muskmelons, cucumbers and beans,

Some melons crack during the jostling ride to market, and others tumble from the pyramidal displays. These melons, often the very best burstingly ripe ones, become samples for our customers.

okra, peppers, eggplants, and so much more that needs to be picked and washed and packed and sold, with the less-than-perfect "for-us" items gorged on or canned or frozen or otherwise preserved for the winter months. I get out of breath just writing about it.

As more and more vegetables reach their peak of abundance, the number of hours we spend harvesting them increases. There are always at least two days devoted to harvests: Fridays for the Evanston Farmers' Market and Tuesdays for the CSA. For our CSA members in Bloomington, Morton, and Eureka, we begin harvesting at daybreak Tuesday mornings and go as far into the afternoon as we need to. These vegetables are packed up that afternoon and delivered that evening.

It is the Evanston Market harvest days that expand and threaten to consume our every waking hour. In May and early June, we only harvest on Fridays. But there comes a point in mid-June when we need to start harvesting on Thursday as well. First, it's just the late afternoon. Then it creeps to all afternoon, and then from mid-morning on. When the kids go back to school in another week, the B team of adults will have to spend sunup to sundown on both Thursday and Friday to bring in the abundance.

This is our last Thursday harvest with the kids. We start with the root crops, because they are not nearly as delicate as the leafy greens or fruit crops, like tomatoes, summer squash, and cucumbers. Under these hot, dry conditions, we are able to preserve quality by getting them out of the field while they are still holding the moisture they pulled out of the ground overnight—moisture that they will lose as the day heats up and their tops wilt.

Before assigning people to their tasks, Henry consults his harvest notebook to see how many bunches of a particular vegetable were sold at the market last week. He also takes into consideration how much of that item is in the field and ready to harvest, plus what the weather forecast is for the market day. If a rainy day is predicted, he will pick far less because market attendance falls off drastically when the weather is not perfect. Then he decides on the number, and designates teams of workers to go dig or pull and then bunch that number. This morning, we'll harvest more than 150 bunches of beets (red, golden and Chioggia), 200 bunches of carrots (orange, rainbow, purple, white, and yellow), 80 bunches of scallions, and 50 bunches of leeks, along with half a bushel each of eight kinds of potatoes.

As we move down a row, we stack the bunched vegetables in groups of three for easy counting. As we near the number, one person goes to get the wooden crates stacked around the periphery of the field and begins to fill them, recounting as each bunch is carefully placed inside, with all the roots in the same direction, so when they are washed, the muddy water doesn't drip on the greens. As soon as a crate is full of bunched vegetables, we haul it to the side of the field and place it in the shade. When one team finishes their task, they call over to Henry, who tells them what to do next.

When all the roots for that week's market are out of the ground, bunched, and crated, we load the crates in the truck and go up to the wash area. There we unload the crates and stack them in the shade next to the washing tank and wet them down with the cold well water. We cover them with a tarp to keep them cool and wet until dark, when Henry will wash them under the electric lights of the wash area.

By mid-morning, the heat and humidity are almost unbearable. But what you thought was boiling at 11 a.m. is lukewarm by noon. You're forced to recalibrate as the temperature keeps rising. No matter if you are weeding, or digging potatoes, or picking tomatoes, the intensity increases, minute by minute, until sweat rolls down parts of your body you never realized could sweat before—not only your forehead and the back of your neck but also your nose and cheeks and ears; not only your chest and back but also your elbows and knees. You begin to have an acute appreciation of the slightest breeze. And you cherish as never before the blessed physics of evaporation.

Then it's time to start in on the melons. Melons love hot days, and while the heat and humidity are beating down there in the melon patch, it occurs to me that there is some justice in the world, because, miraculously, the blazing summer produces the cooling melon. The hotter the weather, the more the melons grow—which made sense, once I heard they are native to Africa.

For hundreds of years, the origin of the watermelon was unknown, as they had already spread throughout Africa, the Middle East, India, and Asia by the time Europeans "discovered" them. But the question of their origin was settled about a hundred years ago when the missionary-explorer David Livingstone found large tracts of central Africa covered with watermelons growing truly wild. In the dry environment, the roots would gather all the water they could, pull it into the fruit, and then, when the fruit was mature and the seeds viable, the watermelon would burst and the moisture from the fruit would be enough to germinate the seeds. This evolutionary strategy by which a devoted parent sacrifices itself for the survival of its offspring has had the unintended consequence of enlisting we humans in the continuation and expansion of watermelon territory, numbers, and varieties.

Most people assume that all watermelons are red because those are the only varieties found in grocery stores, but there is a wide range of flesh colors, from white to yellow to red to the swirled yellow and rose of the Sorbet Swirl variety. Watermelons were brought to America by early European colonists and were common in Massachusetts as early as 1629. A few decades later, the Florida Indians were growing them, and before long they had made it to the interior of the country through tribes trading the seeds with each other. As Pere Marquette traveled down the Mississippi River to the Arkansas River in 1673, and then back up the Illinois River, he noted that the Indians were growing watermelons, even though the nearest white settlement was still hundreds of miles away.

It is probably safe to say that watermelons have been growing in Illinois ever since. Henry and Teresa are continuing the tradition, to the great delight of family members as well as customers. From the time she was five, my sister Jill's daughter Tess figured out the dates of watermelon season and insisted that her annual week on the farm coincide with the watermelon harvest. We don't mind indulging her addiction, as long as she's out in the field helping, since we need as many hands as possible to get the melons from the field to the truck. This is usually done by means of a bucket brigade of watermelon tossing and catching. Zoe describes the scene on a recent watermelon harvest day:

> I love summer because of all the watermelon I get to eat. I have always loved watermelon. In fact, I have a distant memory of eating a whole watermelon by myself that was two times the size of my head. I don't know if I still have the courage to do that, but I know I'll never get tired of the sugary juice distinct to watermelons.
>
> Picking watermelon is an unusual procedure. Daddy knocks on them to hear if they are ready. As I have not mastered the ability to tell a ripe sound from an unripe one, I resort to seeing if the tendril closest to the watermelon on the plant is shriveled up and dry.
>
> All watermelon varieties have different ways of announcing when they are ripe. Sorbet Swirl is a variety that can be picked

when its tendril is dry, so I pick that kind. Meanwhile, Daddy's over in another row, knocking softly on the delicate Cream of Saskatchewans, so as not to crack them open. He pulls a ripe one off the vine and tosses it gently to Kazami.

"C!" Daddy yells to him, and moves to knock on another watermelon.

Kazami catches the melon, wipes off the dirt, and lightly etches a "C" into the rind with his harvest knife so the market customers can tell it's a Cream of Saskatchewan.

"Courtney!" Kazami shouts, and tosses the newly etched melon over to her. Then he turns and waits for the next melon to be tossed his way.

Meanwhile, Courtney hands the watermelon up to Andy, who is on the truck. Andy puts the precious watermelon carefully into a wooden box. The Cream of Saskatchewan is especially delicate, so we are extremely careful with it.

But as Andy places the Cream into the box, it bursts open.

Daddy laughs, saying, "The Cream will do that."

Kazami pipes up. "And it means one more watermelon for us!!"

Kazami is right about the Cream of Saskatchewans generally ending up "for us." Henry grows this variety because he thinks it may be the best-flavored watermelon of all. But it is also the most insanely delicate, cracking, it seems, as you reach to pick it. Or if it doesn't crack as it's picked, it cracks as you toss it to the person catching it. Or if it doesn't crack as it's tossed or caught, then it cracks as it's being put into a crate. If not then, then as it's being chilled in the wash tank. Or as it's put onto the rack to dry. Or as it's loaded onto the truck. Or if by some miracle, it is still intact when the truck door is finally latched shut before our journey up to Evanston, it will have cracked by the time the door is unlatched at market.

"Basically," Henry says, "it will crack if you look at it funny." To most growers, that would be reason aplenty not to grow Cream of Saskatchewan. But to Henry, it's the sign of a good melon—literally bursting with sweet juices.

X-Melon Salad with Anise Hyssop

When Henry etches an X on a melon, it means it is of questionable quality and therefore for us. Whereas the cracked "for-us" melons are always delicious, the X melons are an unknown. Some are immature, some are rotten, and some are drop-dead delicious—so amazing that when you taste one, Henry says, "you sit down and weep."

3 or more different kinds of melons

1 bunch anise hyssop

Wash the melons and scoop out any soft spots. Then cut the melons into big slices and cut the rind from each slice.

Next, chunk up the melons and place them in a large bowl. Mince a few sprigs of anise hyssop, both leaves and flowers. Toss the leaves with the melons, and then sprinkle the flowers on top. Chill and serve.

Or perhaps Henry is just being crafty. By indulging Kazami and all the workers under the blazing August sun, he is giving us the water and sugar we need to keep working.

One particular melon ended up "for us" in a dramatic way when Kazami's toss went awry and the melon landed on the windshield of the old GMC pickup. It caused a huge crack—not only in the melon, but also across the entire length of the windshield. The GMC is a farm-only truck, so we never fixed the windshield, and it reminds us every year of the delicious and accident-prone Cream of Saskatchewan.

WEEK 43. **Basil Daze**

A S I PACK A FEW BAGS OF "FOR-US" VEGETABLES TO TAKE home for dinner, Henry says, "Let's do basil." It's Thursday evening, approaching dark, so "do" doesn't mean "pick" as it usually would; it means "write about."

Thursday evening is when I write *Food & Farm Notes*, and each week, I ask Henry what we should say in this week's e-mail newsletter about what's happening on the farm and what's coming up to the market or in the CSA share. Now is the time, Henry says, to tell everyone that the heat-loving basil is in its prime. It's time to stock up and make a big batch of pesto and freeze it for a blast of summer in the winter.

And we need to share this information now, because just when the customers are getting used to seeing great big bunches of intoxicating basil every week, *poof,* they are gone—not in a puff of smoke, but in a black slick caused by the first night below 35, which could happen in less than a month, as Dad always reminds us at this time of year.

So the Food Notes are easy. But what about the Farm Notes? I roll back the week in my head, recalling the sights and sounds. Early in the week, I saw three yearling bucks in the middle of the road on my way to Henry's. A few days later I saw that one had been hit by a car and thrown to the side of the road. A giant turkey vulture was perched on its belly, its bald red head and powerful curved beak tearing away at the buck's liver and heart. *Doesn't really go with basil,* I think, *but it's what's happening on the farm.*

So I start to write about *Cathartes aura*—"the golden purifier," I hazard to guess, one who comes down to clean up by removing decaying flesh from bones. (Later, I learn I was right on the Greek word *kathartes,* a cleanser or purifier, as in "cathartic," but wrong on *aura,* which is actually the Latinized word for the name Mexican Indians gave to vultures, *aurouá.*)

As I write, I realize the turkey vulture really does go with basil, in that basil emits a strong smell, and so do carcasses, which is how the big bird finds them. As she soars far above in that distinctive upward V, with her silvery underwings and slight teetering back and forth, she can detect the smell of a dead animal below, even if it's under the forest canopy. Perhaps it's a bit of a stretch to compare the smell of life that comes from basil attracting customers and the smell of death from a rotting carcass attracting a turkey vulture, but that's what writing *Food & Farm Notes* is about—making the connections.

But tonight, I'm anxious about writing, because I'm anxious about tomorrow. It is one of the most abundant harvest days of the year, and we are shorthanded. Dad is still in the hospital and Mom and Fred are still there with him. The kids are starting school and won't join us until they get back home, around 4 p.m. I write as quickly as I can, wait for Teresa to send me her Fruit & Herb Notes, and then send out the e-mail and fall asleep.

I dream of two bluebirds, slightly different, both glorious, both dead. First light comes and goes without my knowing because I am caught in my beautiful deadly dream. By the time I wake, the sky is brilliant blue with a thin band of white clouds in the east. Henry, Hiroko, Matt, and the apprentices are already most of the way through the tender greens by the time I get down to the field. It's been very hot, so there aren't a lot of these greens to pick today.

I check in with Henry and get my assignment: 90 bunches of parsley—70 Italian and 20 regular. Parsley is a quick and easy chore, although there are quite a few yellowed sprigs that need to be pulled out from each bunch today because of the heat. I love to harvest parsley, dill, cilantro, and especially basil, because of their aromas. Henry always saved the dill and cilantro for Dad to harvest because you make them into small bunches with a looser twist-tie, which is easier on Dad's arthritic hands than larger bunches with tighter twist-ties. The week before Dad left for his surgery, I worked alongside him and reveled in the citrusy-spicy cilantro and the cool, blue dill. I believe that anyone suffering from anxiety or depression would find relief, if not an outright cure, by harvesting herbs for a few hours each day. I think of Emily, in Thornton Wilder's *Our Town*, who is asked when she goes up to heaven what she misses most about earth. She answers, "The smell of parsley."

I muse about how forlorn a life without parsley would be as I grasp a big handful of the bushy parsley plant in my left hand, cut the stems a few inches above the ground with my right, substitute a twist-tie for the knife, and quickly wrap it around the stems, making a tight bunch. I place it on the ground while moving to grasp the next handful of parsley. My only complaint about the brilliant pastas Joel makes, I think to myself, is that there is never enough parsley on top. When I suggested this to him, he looked at me like I had just uttered blasphemy, because the sprinkling he puts on top is exactly the amount an Italian would put on, meaning it's exactly right. But I am an American, and the parsley is Henry's, and life is short. So Joel pushed the bowl of extra chopped parsley over to me, and I put it all on. I smile at the memory and move on down the row of parsley, cutting and bunching, cutting and bunching.

When I reach my number, I walk back along the row I've been cutting, gathering up as many bunches as I can and carrying them to the end of the row where the crates are. I arrange them carefully in the box, cut ends to the center and leaf ends outward, recounting as I go along. Then I get the remaining bunches from the row, box them up too, and hustle the crates on over to the shade. The sun wilts greens so quickly at this time of year, even this early in the morning, that it's important to move fast and then move on to the next job. I stand up, stretch my arms back, look around for Henry, and call out, "What's next?"

The first set of Friday harvest tasks, the tender greens, takes anywhere from two to four hours depending upon how many helpers we have and how many tender greens there are to pick. We're a little behind already, having just finished harvesting a few hundred heads of lettuce, plus mesclun, 100 bunches of chard, 90 of parsley, 80 of cilantro, 60 of dill, 40 of dandelion, 35 of sorrel, and 15 of red amaranth. The comfortable part of the day soon slips away, and by 9 a.m., the sun is showing its brutal side. As Matt brings the first wave of the harvest up to the wash area, the rest of us start in on the more heat-tolerant greens, the summer "spinaches"—New Zealand (25 bunches), Malabar (30 bunches), and Egyptian spinach (15 bunches).

Regular spinach is a cool-weather green, available only in the spring and fall. But with his customers' season-long greens needs in mind, Henry plants hot-weather cooking greens from all over the world. None of them are even remotely related to spinach botanically, but they all have a mild, spinachy flavor and can be used in most recipes calling for cooked spinach. Best of all, they keep going strong all summer, no matter how hot it gets. In fact, it seems the hotter it gets, the better they grow.

Malabar spinach has become my favorite hot-weather green. It is a beautiful, tropical, vining plant with a gorgeous red stem and thick, dark green, and broad heart-shaped leaves. The large, meaty leaves are remarkably spinach-like in flavor, and it is ideal for soups, salads and stir-fries. Malabar spinach is named after the coastal region of India along the Arabian Sea, which was the setting for Louis Bromfield's novel *The Rains Came*. The proceeds from the novel enabled Bromfield to buy a beautiful 385-acre farm in Ohio, which he named Malabar Farm. Malabar Farm became not only a working farm but also an education and demonstration farm. It also became a mecca for many of the Bromfields' friends—farmer friends as well as New York friends like James Cagney, Errol Flynn, and Shirley Temple. One of the best-known events at Malabar was the wedding of Humphrey Bogart and Lauren Bacall on May 21, 1945. Bromfield was the best man at the wedding.

As each crate is filled, we walk it to the end of the row and place it in the shade until the truck comes around to haul the next load of full crates to the wash area near the barn.

The days at Malabar were filled with agricultural labor and ideas and many friends and good food. At night, when guests and family went to bed, Bromfield would sit alone and write and listen to the night sounds of frogs, raccoons, and owls. This is, in some ways, the life we have developed in and around Henry's Farm. Although we haven't seen Bogart or Bacall lately, perhaps one of these harvest days they will appear in front of us, a sure sign of sunstroke.

Once the hot-weather spinaches are picked, Matt drives around the sections of the field to load the pickup, making sure not to forget any crates stuck way back in the shade under the old blackberry canes or in the tall grasses. Everyone then piles into the trucks, squeezing in alongside the crates as best we can, and we drive up to the wash area and unload.

Henry begins dunking the greens as Hiroko brings the much-anticipated Harvest Day Lunch from the house to the packing area. This lunch is the highlight of the day and is what keeps all of the harvesters harvesting all day long. Hiroko sets out a big bowl of corn and potato chowder, a large green salad, a spinach pie, a plate of tomatoes and cucumbers, some blue corn chips, a few "for-us" melons, and an apple cake. We grab our plates and load them up. It is, as always, "the best lunch ever."

After taking a few minutes to sit in the shade and eat, we move over to the wash area and begin bagging the small amount of mesclun salad mix Henry has just washed. We are working at a disadvantage this summer because we are without the mesclun quality-control officer, our mother, who is still at the hospital with our father, four weeks after his surgery. Luckily Fred is still there too, trading shifts with her, so someone is always with Dad. But we imagine Mom here, under the awning of the barn, sitting around the crates of bagged mesclun, picking up each bag and eyeing it a little suspiciously. She shakes it to gauge the volume, then moves it up and down a few times to gauge the weight, and then she'll say, "It's a little light. It needs another leaf or two." Or it will be too heavy and she'll scoop out a few leaves. Rare is the bag of mesclun that is "just right!" We try to internalize her ability to detect slight variations and hope the customers don't notice too much disparity in the sizes of the bags of mesclun while Mom is away.

Before Asa left to go back to school, he was in charge of organizing all the produce on the truck. Always good at puzzles, he seems to know, almost by instinct, just how to arrange each item for the most efficient use of space, while at the same time keeping the things together that need to be moist and cool (like the greens) or warm and dry (like tomatoes).

After he stacks all the newly washed and bagged and boxed greens on the truck, he puts an empty crate on top of each stack and puts two 10-pound blocks of ice on top of the crate. These will slowly melt down over the vegetables from now until we unload the truck at the market at 4 a.m. tomorrow. Even greens that go into the truck wilted emerge revived, almost impossibly crisp. Asa (or one of us, now that he's gone) then covers everything with tarps to keep the moist coolness in, and shuts the back door of the truck.

When Henry is done washing, he grabs a quick bite. Then he calls for everyone to get ready to head back down to the field. We fill our water bottles with cold water from the well, and sometimes dunk our hats and shirts in the water to help cool us down now that we are building up to the hottest part of the day.

Back in the field, it's time for the second wave of the harvest, the hardy greens. Henry sends a couple of people to the kale (15 bunches of red, 15 bunches of Italian, 60 bunches of green), one to the collards (15 bunches), and I go with Hiroko to cut and bunch the purslane (30 bunches).

If you don't know purslane by name, you probably know it by sight, and you probably dismiss it as a weed. It is a low-growing succulent plant with crisp reddish stems and paddle-shaped leaves. It comes up in gardens, on the side of the road, and in the cracks of the sidewalk. Originally, it came from India, and it is reputed to have been Gandhi's favorite food. Now it is "cosmopolitan," meaning it grows all around the world, including at Henry's Farm, where it is, according to Henry, "a lovely weed."

Unlike foxtail and other less lovely weeds, it grows low to the ground and so does not compete with the vegetables for sunlight. It also makes a gorgeous carpet underneath the heads of lettuce, and helps keep the ground cool. After Henry harvests the lettuce out of the bed, he tills in the purslane (whatever hasn't been picked and bunched for our customers), and the soil benefits from its moisture, organic matter, and nitrogen.

Once the hardy greens are harvested, everyone goes to get a drink of water, and then Henry calls us all over to the basil patch. I have always been a mid-afternoon slump person. But no matter how low I'm slumping, how much I'm sweating, or how much my head hurts, after a few minutes in the basil patch, I am resurrected. If the volatile oils of basil were visible, we would be completely obscured by a great roiling cloud of sparkling emerald green smoke in the middle of the bottomland. A visitor to the field would have no idea that there in the midst of the dazzling green cloud were half a dozen or more people, all cutting away at vibrant basil plants. Basil has woody stems, so the best way to cut it, we've discovered, is to grasp a bunch of the correct size (often about half of the plant), and bend it toward the ground while placing your harvest knife underneath it and cutting straight up. Then you pull any blooming spikes or yellow leaves out of the bunch and wrap the twist-tie around it and throw it into the growing pile of harvested basil.

All summer long, until school claims him, Kazami is the master basil counter. This has been his job ever since he was four or five years old and may have something to do with his mathematical abilities. He comes behind us with the crates, filling each with 30 or 40 bunches, and keeping count. When we get close to the 275 bunches that Henry has ordered, we start a countdown, with each person calling out a number as they toss a finished bunch to Kazami—"25," Zoe calls, "24," I say, "23," says Matt, "22," says Henry ... and then suddenly 3, 2, 1 ... we are done.

Done, that is, except for the tomatoes, cucumbers, summer squashes, beans, soybeans, corn, okra, peppers (hot, sweet, and colored), and eggplants, which constitute the last wave of the harvest day.

WEEK 44. **Hard Harvest Times**

IT'S THE LAST WAVE OF THE LAST HARVEST DAY IN THE LAST week of August—the time when it takes every ounce of my will-power to keep going. But with our reduced crew, there's no choice but to push on through. Henry sends half the helpers to the upper field and half to the bottomland. Down in the rich soil, we pick all the different kinds of cucumbers, the sun beating down on our backs. Each person carries two pails that weigh 25 pounds each when full to the truck and dumps them into crates according to variety before heading back for more. The plants sense from the shorter days that the end is nigh and put forth a last blast of produce, hoping to perpetuate themselves through the seeds in their fruits.

After the cucumbers, we move to the long rows of staked tomatoes, which tower above us and form caverns of still, humid air. You can feel the heat radiating from the tomato plants on either side—the sun above, and up from the earth and mulch below. Your sweaty hands and arms get itchy from the tiny hairs on the tomato leaves and stems. Your fingers turn green-black, and when you finally get to wash them at the end of the day, the water runs yellow for a long time. If you wipe sweat from your eyes as you're working with the tomato vines, the plant exudates make your eyes sting.

So in sweat and tears, we work in pairs, one person on either side of the row, picking each variety into a different bucket. On the heirlooms and hybrid tomatoes, Henry has us pick anything with color on it, because at this time of year, the tomatoes tend to ripen within 24 to 48 hours, and if we leave them on the plant, they will be overripe when we pick again in a few days for the CSA. On the Romas, or paste tomatoes, we pick by feel, waiting until there is an almost imperceptible give to their skin when grasped. The pear and cherry and currant tomatoes we pick as long as they have some color, because they ripen extremely quickly and tend to split their skins easily. When this happens, we eat them as we pick, for a welcome sweet–tart treat.

Meanwhile, the crew in the upper field is picking the bulk of the summer squashes, including all kinds of zucchinis—gold and green, heirloom, and eight ball, plus patty pan, zephyr, and crookneck. Because these plants are at their peak and produce more full-size squash than we can sell, we pick "baby" and "junior" ones as well. The "baby" ones are anywhere from an inch or two to three or four inches in length, depending on the type. Henry mixes them all up, and we will put them in quart containers to sell when we get back up to the barn this evening. "Juniors" are the four- to six-inch zucchini, and they will also get placed into quart containers. Each type goes into a separate crate now, and the truck is heavy and low to the ground by the time we all converge back at the wash area.

Normally, our mother would be here to meet us, ready to begin the sorting of the tomatoes. In addition to being the mesclun quality-control officer, she is the tomato-sorting authority. Henry thinks there must be some genetic memory that runs through Mom's fingers and nerves, something from her peasant Italian predecessors, that makes her the most astute judge of the quality of vegetables. But she is still down at the hospital in St. Louis, taking care of our father through his postsurgery trials and tribulations. A couple of years ago, our father wrote this essay for his "Earth-Science Notes" section of the *Food & Farm Notes* to explain the tomato-sorting process. It is also an homage to Marlene:

At Henry's annual farm tour about five years ago, a gentleman told me how much he enjoyed the great taste of Henry's muskmelons. Then his eyes flashed with a sudden insight as he said, "But you get the best ones, don't you?" I responded without hesitation, and I think to his surprise: "No, you do."

I will use tomatoes to explain the four levels of quality of Henry's produce. I choose tomatoes because they are arguably the pigs' and chickens' favorite of the many vegetables and fruits they eat. And because I am already mourning the demise of the tomato season, which is almost certain to come with below-freezing temperatures within the coming month.

In their season, we pick tomatoes twice a week into pails, each variety into a separate pail. We then load the pails onto my pickup truck—at the peak of the season, onto both pickups—for transport from the bottom field up the steep lane to Henry's barn. There we unload the pails under the lean-to of the barn. Then the number-one expert on sorting tomatoes takes over—and do not get in her way or question her authority or judgment! Her many decades of experience give her seniority over everyone else. I speak, of course, of the matriarch of the farm crew—Marlene.

She inspects each tomato thoroughly yet quickly by eye, by touch, by smell, and, it seems to the rest of us, by some other mysterious sense. All the while, she arranges those tomatoes that pass muster as being first-rate for customers on a single layer in bread trays lined with straw or hay—arranges them, that is, by variety and by ripeness (some trays of those tomatoes that are at their peak of ripeness; other trays of those that customers will be able to keep for a few days after purchase).

But we (the entire farm crew) never eat any of these wonderful tomatoes that have passed Marlene's rigorous inspection. Nevertheless, we all have plenty of tomatoes to eat all season long. And more than that, because we also freeze and can many of them for winter use. The explanation of where our tomatoes come from is a consequence of Marlene's sorting described above. Each tomato that she deems not good enough for the local CSA or the Evanston Farmers' Market is assigned one of two fates. If it is a little too soft, has some rather small rotten spot, or has some other imperfection, Marlene places it in a tray of "for-us-es." The preparation of "for-us" tomatoes for eating, freezing, and canning requires careful inspection, cutting, and often smelling and tasting, but if done correctly, they taste just as good as those for the market or CSA.

If Marlene decides that a tomato is not good enough even as a "for-us," she throws it into a pail to be fed later to the appreciative chickens and pigs. They get the third level of quality of Henry's produce. Thus, the top three levels of tomato quality: those for the market and CSA, then the "for-us-es," and then the chicken and pig food. The fourth level was left on the ground in the field during picking because they were too rotten to even place in a pail with the other tomatoes. Left in the field, they become food for microorganisms and small macroorganisms—and eventually enrich the soil.

While Mom is away, Hiroko takes over the tomato sorting. As she starts in on the dozens of buckets of just-picked tomatoes and the rest of us work on washing and cooling the cucumbers in the wash tank, Henry goes to the tomato hoophouse to pick the popular heirlooms. He adds those to all the buckets surrounding Hiroko, and we return to the field for the final push to the finish line.

Henry and Zoe perform a pas de deux, harvesting ripe eggplants as the sun begins to sink on a hot July day.

A few pairs of workers put on cotton gloves to protect against the irritating prickles on the stems and leaves of the okra and head on over to the okra patch. Henry takes someone to help pick peppers and eggplants. The rest of us start in on the beans, including the edamame. Matt gets the machete and whacks away at the base of the soybean plants and piles them up in small mountains. If we have time, we start to strip the beans from the woody stalks in the field, but if there's no time, we pack them into crates and bring them to the barn to work on at the end of the day, possibly after sundown. Finally, it's time for the corn. Henry calls everyone over, and the picking and carrying begin—the last harvest task of the day, but by no means the last task.

Once we haul everything back up the hill, Henry sends two people to gather the cucumbers and colored peppers from the hoophouses. We sort them out—again, for market and "for us"—and add them to the ones picked in the field.

There are still many tasks remaining, and Henry orchestrates them as he loads the truck. This is the most intense part of the day for him—the hard physical work of lifting heavy boxes into the truck, the mental work of making sure everything is packed properly and every last millimeter of space is filled—all done while directing each person to a different task, keeping it all in his head and redeploying each person as they finish a task.

We have the kids with us now that it is evening, and Henry keeps all 10 people busy on 10 different jobs that are continually morphing into 10 new ones. I sit under the big locust tree and strip edamame from the plants, while Zoe sorts okra; Daniel works on packing the corn with ice; Kazami boxes and counts melons; Rebekah cleans garlic; Hiroko boxes baby squashes, cherry tomatoes, and tomatillos; and Matt fills bushel baskets, each with a different kind of bean.

The finish line seems to recede (asymptotically, as Dad would say—it has always been one of his favorite words and has become one of mine, although I rarely get to use it except parenthetically) as we approach it, but finally we start to carry boxes and trays over to Henry, who is up in the bed of the truck, making sure everything fits. The last things to go up in the truck are the bread trays loaded with tomatoes. Each person goes to the sorting area and brings the heavy trays over to Henry, who stacks them, one on top of the other, until there are three towers of tomatoes in the back of the truck. When tomatoes are peaking in a good year we can bring to market close to a thousand pounds of heirlooms, and nearly that many hybrids.

But tomatoes won't be around that much longer. This is the time of year Dad always starts to remind us that the first frost could be a mere month away (followed by a glorious Indian summer, we hope). We miss him saying this, and we miss him picking the corn with us, moving through the thick leaves and snaking bindweeds with shaky legs but sure hands. We especially miss him kicking the tires of the truck each Friday night as it's fully loaded and ready to go. One time, almost 10 years ago, he kicked and discovered a flat inner back tire. He'll never forget that occasion, and I'll never forget the strange mix of triumph (validation of the countless tires he'd kicked) and despair (now we have to get the tire fixed). I kick the tires now, since it has fallen into the realm of incantation, a way of ensuring, by this action, that no evil will befall us on the way to Evanston. But I miss the way Dad did it, and his comment as he did so, "Don't you think 'Who's Gonna Kick the Tires When I'm Gone,' is the perfect title for a country-western song?"

Frozen Tomatoes

If there's one thing that redeems the stifling midwestern summer, it is the taste of truly ripe tomatoes. Now is the time to put some up for winter. These days, "putting them up" doesn't necessarily mean getting out the Mason jars and the pressure cooker. Freezing is one of the simplest ways to preserve the goodness of summer tomatoes for the dark days of winter. Or, if you have time, make and freeze tomato sauce.

Tomatoes are one of the few vegetables that you can simply wash, cut into chunks, and slip into a zip-lock freezer bag. Nothing could be easier. It's what we do with all the big buckets of "for-us-es" that are waiting for us after the Friday and Tuesday harvests. After thawing, they can be used in any cooked dish, from soup to sauce.

Frozen Tomato Sauce

For winter, you will definitely want to make a quadruple batch of this sauce, from Lidia's Italian Kitchen *(William Morrow and Co., 1998) by Lidia Mattichio Bastianich, owner of the famed Felidia. (I like to start this out with diced-up onion and garlic, and I also add some basil and/or oregano.)*

Salsa di Pomodoro (Tomato Sauce)

3 pounds ripe plum tomatoes, cored, peeled, and seeded
¼ cup extra-virgin olive oil
1 small onion, finely chopped
¼ cup finely chopped carrots
¼ cup finely chopped celery
4 fresh, or 2 dried, bay leaves
Salt, to taste
Peperoncino (crushed red pepper), to taste

Pass the tomatoes through a food mill fitted with the fine disc attachment, or crush them as fine as possible in a bowl with a wire whisk.

In a medium-size nonreactive saucepan, heat the olive oil over medium heat. Add the onion and simmer until wilted. Add the carrots and celery and cook, stirring occasionally, until golden, about 10 minutes. Add the tomatoes and bay leaves, season lightly with salt and peperoncino, and heat to a simmer. Simmer the sauce over medium-low heat, stirring occasionally until thickened, about 45 minutes. Remove the bay leaves. Check the seasoning and add more salt and peperoncino if necessary. Makes about 3 cups, which is enough to sauce 6 servings of pasta.

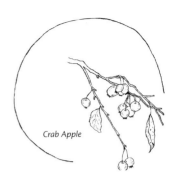

Crab Apple

XI. FRUIT MOON

WEEK 45. **Prodigal Fruits**

AT THE CUSP OF THE SEASONS, HENRY'S FIELDS ARE EQUAL PARTS summer crops (although waning) and autumn crops (now waxing). Many of these are botanical fruits, and they create an embarrassment of riches at the early September markets: mounds of the last melons, tray upon tray of tomatoes, overflowing baskets of eggplants and colored peppers and okra and zucchini, and the full range of cucumbers, from the standard green American ones to the yellow lemon ones, striped Armenians, fat white Sikkims, and West Indian Burr Gherkins.

Under September's Fruit Moon, there is also, naturally, a sudden profusion of tree fruits. I count myself lucky that three of my siblings together have over a hundred fruit-bearing trees, because, as Roald Dahl wrote in *Danny the Champion of the World:* "It is a most marvelous thing to be able to go out and help yourself to your own apples whenever you feel like it. You can do this only in the autumn, of course, when the fruit is ripe, but all the same, how many families are so lucky? Not one in a thousand, I would guess. Our apples were called Cox's Orange Pippins, and I liked the sound of the name almost as much as I liked the apples."

Teresa explained why she planted this variety of apple in her "Fruit & Herb Notes" section of the *Food & Farm Notes*.

My siblings and I have known of the Cox's Orange Pippin, an old English variety of apple, nearly all of our lives because of one of our father's graduate students long ago. Mary Ellen Kennedy was diagnosed with lupus when she was in college and was sick much of her life. But we never thought of her as sick. She was brilliant; she was fun; and all of us children were in love with her. She would spend several days at a time at our house, helping with the gardens, talking biology and politics with our parents, and every time she would come she would have something special for us. One time it was Christmas ornaments to paint, another time a whole collection of classical records from Bach to Telemann, and for several visits in a row it was the books of Roald Dahl, which she read aloud to us.

I remember sitting behind her as she read, braiding her long, thick, dark honey-brown hair, and listening to *Danny the Champion of the World*, the story of a boy and his father and, of all things, pheasant poaching. It was in memory of Mary Ellen (she died many years ago) that I planted Cox's Orange Pippin apples.

"One of the nice things about a Cox's Orange Pippin," my [Danny's] father said, "is that the seeds rattle when it's ripe. Shake it and you can hear them rattling."

We haven't heard the seeds rattle yet—maybe that only happens in England, not in central Illinois. We have, however, eaten the extremely solid, crunchy, tart Orange Pippins, and agree with Danny that they are delicious. They are unbelievably crisp and they have a tart flavor that makes your taste buds tingle and your salivary glands squirt. They are quite beautiful, though not conventionally pretty, with faint orangey-red striping over a yellow background and some russeting for character.

While I was helping Teresa harvest the apples and pears, we got to talking about the big pear orchard our great-grandparents had planted. During my childhood summer weeks on the farm, I loved to climb into the gnarled and broken trees, which, though over 50 years old, still produced pears that would keep through the winter. Grandma Henrietta often told us the story about how during the Depression, she would sell those late-season pears to passersby.

One day an older man stopped by and asked, "Are those Kieffers?" Grandma thought he said "keepers," so she said yes, they were. He repeated, "But are they *good* Kieffers?" And she responded, "Yes, they'll keep all winter." To which he responded, "But are they *Kieffers?*"

Apparently, this exchange went on for quite some time, and they never did reach an understanding. It was only much later, when Grandma learned the name of the variety of pears in the orchard, that she realized what the man was asking.

But the answer remained the same: "Yes, they are good Kieffers, and yes, they are good keepers!"

In Grandma's day, almost every farmhouse had at least a couple of Kieffer pear trees because they are hardy, reliable bearers of fruit that tastes delicious and keeps well into

Because it was delicious and productive, we used an unknown old pear tree growing on Henry and Hiroko's property to graft this new tree. In a good year, it is so heavily laden that branches often crack with the weight of the fruit.

the winter. Today, sometimes the only sign that you're near what was once a farmstead is an ancient Kieffer tree that has stood the stress of floods, droughts, and blights over the decades.

Our grandparents' pear trees were bulldozed nearly 50 years ago, before the land went into corn and soybeans, when the neighbors began farming it after Grandpa's farm accident. Then about eight years ago—almost a century since that first pear orchard was planted—Henry, Teresa, and Jill and her family began to plant that same patch of ground with apple and pear trees. Because they were to be raised without chemicals, they chose older varieties, such as the Cox's Orange Pippin, Sweet Sixteen, Nutting Bumpus, Burgundy, and Black Oxford, as well as new varieties bred especially to be pest resistant, such as Pristine, Williams' Pride, Liberty, and Red-free.

Grandma was in her mid-nineties then, and we drove her from the nursing home out to the farm so she could watch the new orchard being planted. She's still in that nursing home, but Dad is finally coming home. After a month of ups and downs, din and clatter, pokings and proddings, effects and side effects, and side effects of side effects, Dad was released from the hospital. While waiting for Mom, Dad, and Beth to arrive back home, I cooked up a meat loaf of Dad's lean ground beef mixed with Henry's carrots, onions, green peppers, and parsley. I only had a few potatoes in my house—the pink-fleshed Huckleberry, the dense yellow Fingerlings, and the white and fluffy Elbas—but I cut them all into chunks and boiled them up. As the old blue car pulled into the lane, I went out to meet them. Dad was ashen and frail, and he walked slowly and gingerly to the house, too weak to even hold up his head.

When we got him settled in and situated at the table, Dad—who never picks at anything, and whose constant refrain to all of us at every meal was, "Don't pick! If you want something, get a plate and put the food on it!"—this very same Dad reached over to the plate of meatloaf and pinched off a corner and placed it in his mouth and closed his eyes and chewed with utter satisfaction. When I placed the potatoes in front of him, Dad's eyes widened with pleasure as he inhaled the steam and then ate a small piece of the Huckleberry. Then he closed his eyes and slowly chewed.

Henry's Autumn Pear Salad

We often have Asian pears clear through Christmas, and sometimes we have Kieffers into January and February. They keep well in a cool, dark place, like a basement. When the Kieffers are golden yellow and have a sweet, musky aroma, they're ready to eat. Last year, Henry made a warm pear salad with a hint of vanilla, topped with black sesame seeds.

6 pears, peeled, cored, and chopped

½ shallot, minced

1¼ teaspoons diced fresh ginger

1 cup water

½ teaspoon vanilla extract

1½ tablespoons sherry vinegar

1 tablespoon mirin (a Japanese sweet cooking wine)

1 tablespoon soybean oil

½ pound fall greens

Black sesame seeds, for sprinkling

In a 1-quart saucepan, cook the pears with the shallot, ginger, and water over medium heat until soft. Strain and set aside to cool. Once at room temperature, purée one of the pears and strain through a sieve.

Add the vanilla, sherry vinegar, and mirin to the puréed pear and process in a blender or food processor. Slowly add the oil to emulsify. Dice the remaining pears for garnish.

To serve, toss the greens well with the pear mixture. Divide among four serving plates and garnish with the sesame seeds.

After dinner with Dad, Beth and I went home. Beth was shivering already and cranking the heat, but I am invigorated by sweater weather, by the clear chill in the air under what e. e. cummings called the "blue true dream of sky."

The next morning, the most delicious pastel pink and palest lavender suffused the eastern sky. Dad is back with us, I thought. For whatever length of time, he is in a good place where birds herald the sun, which brightens the sky and brings warmth and life to fields and field hands alike. Beauty and silence, morning birdsong and evening cricket song. I had every hope that these, along with fruits of the earth tended by our hands, would heal him.

WEEK 46. **Freeing Roots**

IN SEPTEMBER, SIGNS OF CHANGE ARE EVERYWHERE—IN THE drying leaves of the cornfields, in the air that applies a velvet pressure, and in the held-back heaviness redolent with cold autumn rain that falls to the north of us, but is not yet here. You see it in the wind that whips the oak leaves, loosening them for the fall. You hear it too, if you drive past cornfields with the windows down. Just yesterday, the leaves were soft and breathing; now they are stiff and brittle, rustling and knocking like old bones, waiting for the reaper.

Change also invaded our parents' house. What we thought would be a calm and healing time for our father turned out to be a traumatic month of intense 24-hour care. In our enthusiasm, we jumped the gun with Dad's homecoming meal. We hadn't known that his rearranged guts could not handle anything more than sips of water. With minute-by-minute care, and much trial and error, my mother (a nurse) and my sister Beth (a veterinarian) realized that Dad's salvation, and ours, would be fresh farm eggs. Although the shorter days were causing the hens to lay fewer eggs, we reserved them all for Dad. He existed for many weeks on soufflés and custards, custards and soufflés.

Although we helped my mother out as much as possible, the fields were constantly calling. Each week, more fall crops joined the ranks of the summer crops that needed to be harvested. Burdock was one of them. The burdock we plant is related to, but a different species of, the plant that makes the prickly burrs that stick onto you and your pets as you walk through the fall woods. When Asa was a little boy, not the six-foot-tall strapping young man he is today, he assiduously picked burrs off himself and put them delicately around the wrist openings of my sweater as I harvested autumn greens. They made such beautiful fall bracelets that I wore the sweater that way for months.

I can relate only one other tale of a person who found the seed-burrs of burdock beautiful and useful—the Swiss inventor George de Mestral. He was in the habit of taking long walks through the autumn countryside with his dog, and both would invariably return covered in burrs. During the deburring, de Mestral inspected the prickly bracts closely and noticed hundreds of tiny hooks that would grab onto anything passing by. After experimenting with plastic models that he designed to mimic the burrs' action, de Mestral presented the world with ... Velcro.

Bracelets and Velcro notwithstanding, burdock is still considered nothing but a nuisance by almost everyone in this country. But if you look beyond the burrs, you'll find the secret at the root of the weed: a crisp, earthy-sweet delight. Burdock root definitely falls into the "can't judge a book ... " category of vegetables. At the market, we sometimes wish that burdock were red or yellow and shiny like a colored pepper to attract the human eye. Alas, burdock is dull and brown and looks tough and unappetizing. But it is tender (you can scrape away the thin skin with a light fingernail) and earthy and delicious. It is also low in calories and high in fiber, iron, and inulin, a carbohydrate that is good for diabetics. The humble exterior of the large, dark, woody-looking root belies the sweet, nutty, delicate, crunchy flesh within.

Henry and I first encountered burdock as a food on our separate sojourns in Japan during the 1980s. Although the plant grows throughout Europe and North America, until very recently it had been cultivated only in Japan. It is now cultivated here and there throughout the United States, but its consumption is still more or less confined to those on a macrobiotic diet.

Only now are we rediscovering what many Native Americans also knew about the virtues of burdock. For the Illiniwek, burdock was an important winter food. They dug it in the fall, under the Harvest and Hunter's Moons, and dried it. Then they ate it throughout the long, cold months of winter.

In addition to being used as a food item for millennia, many cultures have used burdock medicinally. Early Chinese physicians treated colds, flu, throat infections, and pneumonia with burdock preparations, and it is considered a powerful source of "yang" energy according to Chinese philosophy and macrobiotic practice— meaning it gives you the energy and strength to do what needs to be done. One of the first times Henry sold burdock, he explained to a customer that it had a lot of yang energy, and when this customer came back the next week she announced that the burdock had given her the energy to clean her closets, a task she had been putting off for years. Nearby customers overheard, and before long, we sold out of burdock.

Perhaps the energy in burdock comes from the energy exerted by those who dig it. The burdock taproot is too long and too firmly lodged to pull up the way you pull onions or carrots. It is a two-person job, and it demands strong backs and arms in highly choreographed teamwork. Another characteristic of yang is heat generation, and the diggers periodically shed layers of clothing as they work to clear the deep hole and extricate the long taproot, which is why Henry likes to time this job for early in the morning, when the world is hoary with frost. As the diggers move down the burdock bed, the hole behind them is very much the size and shape of a grave—albeit a long one.

It isn't much of a stretch to see burdock diggers as grave diggers— perhaps the ones who jest with Hamlet and Horatio. But instead of putting a body into the earth, the burdock diggers are lifting a living plant body up out of the earth—thereby killing it, of course, in order that it can nourish us.

In their choreographed dance, the burdock diggers, Courtney and Mike, face each other over the three rows of burdock in the bed— Courtney standing above with a spade, Mike in the hole with a shovel. The dance commences as Courtney thrusts her spade into the soil to begin forming the trench between two rows of burdock, sinking the spade in a foot at a time. Mike leans to one side as she throws the spadeful of black soil over his shoulder and onto the mound of loose soil behind him. She steps back and takes another cut, lifts and throws. She continues working backward for about six feet, carefully excavat-

ing a 15-inch-wide trench between rows one and two of the
three rows in the bed. When it
becomes difficult to throw the
heavy spadefuls of dirt all the
way over Mike, Courtney steps
over to the other half of the
bed, starting at the beginning
again, but now clearing the
dirt away from between rows
two and three.

At this point Mike begins
his role in the dance of burdock digging. As Courtney sets
to work on her side, he takes
his shovel and scoops the loose
dirt that remains in the trench
she just made on the other side
and tosses it backward over
his shoulder. If they are well-
matched partners in the dance,
Courtney will be finishing up
side two just as Mike finishes
cleaning out side one.

Again, they switch sides,
and Courtney steps down into the just-cleaned-out trench to begin
excavating the next 12 to 15 inches down as Mike goes over to clean
out the loose dirt she just left between rows two and three of the bed.
The smallest roots are loosened as the first layer of soil is dug. Mike
pulls them up, rubs the dirt off them, and throws them in a crate. More
roots are freed as the team digs out the next layer deeper, but the biggest, longest roots don't come free until the third and fourth layers of
soil have been dug up and tossed aside. In a well-partnered burdock-
digging dance, the team carefully but quickly digs down three to four
feet alongside the burdock roots without scraping or breaking them

*Burdock is more
easily dug with a
team of diggers, but
in years past Henry
did it by himself by
the light of the truck
headlights in the
pre-dawn of a fall
harvest day.*

and gently pulls them whole from the earth—and without throwing dirt down each other's shirts or clonking each other on the head with their heavy steel tools.

Mrs. Takayasu's Kimpira Gobo (Stir-Fried Burdock and Carrots)

Traditionally, in Japan, burdock (gobo) is stir-fried—alone or with carrots—in a dish called Kimpira Gobo. It seems that every Japanese household has a slightly different take on this, but here's the recipe from Masako Takayasu, one of our long-time CSA subscribers and great friends.

2 sticks burdock (about ½ pound)

¼ pound carrots

3 Japanese togarashii, Thai hot pepper, or another kind of hot pepper

1 tablespoon sesame oil

1–2 tablespoons olive oil

2 tablespoons sugar

1 tablespoon mirin (optional)

3–4 tablespoons soy sauce

Crushed togorashii pepper, or red pepper flakes, to taste

Sesame seeds, for serving

Wash the burdock and remove its skin by rubbing with the back of a knife or with a vegetable scrubber. Cut it into matchstick-size pieces and soak the pieces in cold water to prevent discoloration. Replace the water two or three times, or until the water remains clear, and then drain the burdock.

Peel the carrots and cut them into pieces the same size and shape as the burdock.

Slice the hot peppers, and after removing their seeds, cut them into thick rings.

Combine the sesame and olive oil in a frying pan and heat it. Add the burdock and carrot to the hot oil and stir-fry over high heat, until the carrots are cooked through. Reduce the heat and add the sugar, mirin, soy sauce, and togorashii or red pepper flakes, to taste. Stir to combine.

Continue to stir over medium heat until the liquid nearly all evaporates. Sprinkle the sesame seeds over the top and serve.

WEEK 47. AUTUMN EQUINOX: Three Dog Night

AS THE FALL GREENS—LETTUCES, RADICCHIO, ASIAN GREENS— come on full force, we redeploy our varmint control team, the dogs. The fall greens and many other vegetables would never make it to market without the help of our faithful canine friends. Joy was our family's first dog, a smart and gentle Lab–Weimaraner mix who was with us from the mid-1960s through the early 1980s. She lived a long and full life, in town and then in the country, but before a farm life entailed Vegetable Guard Duty.

After Joy, there were Pups and Bella and many others, and then the perfect trio: Hime (*hee-may*, which means princess in Japanese), Rinky (previously introduced as Wrinkles, which is short for Rip van Wrinkles), and Chico. Hime, who died tragically, had an irrepressible spirit that manifested itself with big leaps and wet kisses. Rinky has an old and beneficent soul, and she makes the rounds to the workers in the field each day, giving love and taking away our stresses and cares. Chico is our guest worker from south of the border.

Our sister Beth, who lives off and on in Baja, watched one day as a car pulled off to the side of the road, and a writhing bag landed in the ditch before the car sped off. She ran up to see a litter of yellow puppies scattering every which way, having already learned that human contact was a thing to be avoided. Through persistence and coaxing, she gathered them together and took them to the stone hut she built and lives in on the Sea of Cortez.

From the very beginning, Beth knew Chico would be a good farm dog. One of the main jobs of our farm dogs is to bark and chase off any vegetable-loving critters who live in the woods, mainly raccoons and deer. Chico barked at everything, even inanimate objects. If Beth moved her bicycle from one side of the room to the other, Chico would notice and bark at it. If she put a bag or a can on the table, Chico would bark at it.

So Beth found homes for all the other puppies, and then put Chico in the passenger side of her pickup and drove him from Baja to Congerville. At first, we were not persuaded. Chico barked, yes, but he also resisted any human contact. A hand reached out to pet him was seen as a threat, and he would run off to a safe distance and bark. How could he be a farm dog if we couldn't even touch him, let alone bring him down to the field to guard the corn at night?

But over the years, we began to understand him, and he began to trust us and embrace the life, and the work, of a farm dog. A big part of the understanding came through Rinky, who became a mother to Chico. Wherever she would go, there was Chico, too. So when it was Rinky's turn to guard the corn, or the beets, or the radicchio, or the lettuce, Chico would go down and stay near her all night.

Because Chico wasn't tied to the portable dog houses that dot the field, he could not only bark at any marauding raccoon or deer, but actually chase after them and run them out of the garden, lending a bite to the bark if need be. That quality is what prompted our father to declare three years ago, during sweet corn season, that Chico is "the best farm dog ever."

As it turns out, Chico is also the luckiest farm dog ever. All of our dogs have been unremittingly happy and healthy ever since they came to the farm ... until last summer. It all began with Wrinkles having a sore paw that would not respond to any of our ministrations. Then our normally energetic dog became so lethargic that she would not even leave our father's toolshed. That's when Dad began to suspect a systemic fungal infection and took Wrinkles in to see the vet.

Dad's suspicion was correct. She had blastomycosis, caused by the fungal organism *Blastomyces dermatitidis*. The organism is found is the rich soils of the Mississippi River basin and around the Great Lakes. It is sometimes referred to as "the Chicago disease," even though these days Chicago dogs rarely get it because they don't have as much opportunity to dig in the soil as they used to.

Our dogs, however, make great sport of digging deep down into Henry's soil to catch mice and voles. This is also part of their farm work, protecting the carrots and other root crops from the little varmints. Many times, we've seen one or another of them with a nose

deep in the earth, digging furiously, tail wagging with excitement. Unfortunately, Wrinkles's nose was breathing in spores, which eventually colonized her entire body. It was a job-related illness, for which we took full responsibility—including the very expensive treatment, an eight-week course of the antifungal drug Itraconazole.

At first the vet gave us only a two-week supply, as the disease is often fatal, and she didn't want us to pay for the entire course of drugs if we were soon to have a dead dog on our hands. But within days, Wrinkles's energy rebounded, and she appeared to be thoroughly enjoying her expensive drug habit, which came wrapped in the finest grass-fed beef raised by our father.

Then just three days later, with Wrinkles finally back to normal, Chico, who had just finished Wrinkles's seasonal labor of protecting the sweet corn from the ravages of raccoons, was run over by a car on the road outside our parents' lane. Dad figures Chico was still on the job, fulfilling his role in life—keeping the entire property free of vegetable-loving critters.

We're not sure why Chico went over to Henry and Hiroko's place, rather than to Mom and Dad's, which was much closer, but somehow, Chico struggled over the mile or so to where Kazami was playing bas-

Wrinkles and Chico pace the perimeter of the fields, alert for any vegetable-loving intruders. Without them, sweet corn would be devastated by raccoons, and the lettuce family devastated by deer.

ketball under the lights in front of the garage. He saw the battered and bloody yellow dog limp up to him, with his head down and twisted to the side, and immediately called Henry and Hiroko. As soon as they saw Chico, they called Mom and Dad to ask if they knew what had happened. They didn't, but very soon our neighbor called to say his wife had run over the dog when he bolted out from the side of the road right in front of her car. She felt the animal bump-bump under her car and assumed she had killed him. They were relieved, and amazed, to hear that Chico had survived.

First thing the next morning, the grandparents took Chico, stiff and dazed, to the vet. When she told us there were no broken bones, the first thought that our mother, the eternal pessimist, had was, "Oh, no, it's internal injuries, then." But they told the vet to fix him up as best she could. By the time she finished he looked like a Frankenstein dog—ten stitches for the cut on top of his head, a bad abrasion under the cut just above his right eye, eight stitches under his left front leg near his chest, a huge scrape under his tail, and scrapes and cuts on all four legs, from low to high, with Penrose drains inserted at the large wound sites.

For the first time in his entire life, Chico got to come into the house, and Dad made him a bed in the basement. For three days, he refused to eat or drink. Mom now figured he had a brain injury and would not survive. But they continued treating him as the vet had directed—antibiotic ointment for the scraped eye, two kinds of pain medication (which he refused to eat, even when it was wrapped in grass-fed beef liver), regular cleaning of all the wounds with antiseptic and gauze pads, an additional antiseptic to shoot up along the sides of the Penrose drains ... and on the third day, he finally drank a bowl of milk.

A week later, I spent some time on the porch with Chico. He had always been an extremely nervous and wary dog, but that night, he leaned into my hand as I rubbed the nonstitched and nonabraded parts of his wounded body. When I stopped rubbing, he did what Wrinkles always does, but I'd never seen Chico do before—he raised a front leg and gently pawed at me, asking to be petted more. Which I did.

WEEK 48. **Blackened Basil**

T HE END OF SEPTEMBER IS THE SEASON OF CONTRASTS—OF nights in the thirties and days in the eighties, of cold hands and hot peppers, of quickening breath and certain death. This week took us from sweating in the sun on Monday, to freezing under the steel gray skies and whipping wind on Wednesday, to a crisp and bright (but frigid) Thursday. The windy "Windsday" (as Pooh would put it) was the turning point, with the high temperature of 65 occurring at 1 a.m. and then falling steadily all day (while the wind was rising and the air was wild with leaves) to bottom out, 23 hours and 37 degrees later.

All day, we had felt fate draw nearer and nearer as we snatched—handful by green handful—life from the jaws of darkness. With every degree the temperature dropped, we worked harder and harder, sneaking out from under the Reaper's nose all the green bell peppers and hot peppers, all the tomatoes and green tomatoes, all the eggplants and beans (including the intensely flavored yard-long asparagus beans, both red and green), all of the summer squash and cucumbers, and some of the tenderer greens, such as the sorrel, chard, New Zealand spinach, dill, cilantro, lettuce, and, of course, the basil.

The basil had already begun to turn black and tough in places because of previous nights in the thirties, but on Wednesday, we made the last 230 bunches of the year as it got colder and colder, windier and windier. It had to be done despite the wind and cold because neither time nor tide waits for any man ... nor does the Reaper.

On Wednesday night, Courtney and Mike made us a meal of corn meal and thyme-encrusted fried green tomatoes, from some of the just-rescued fruits.

After dinner, I had a call from my sister Jill, who asked if I could do some last-minute house and animal-sitting. So early the next morning, I drove the 80 miles due east to Danforth, and settled in at my grandparents' farmstead to do the chores while Jill, Will, and their four girls were away.

Courtney's Fried Green Tomatoes with Corn Meal and Thyme

1 tablespoon vegetable oil or bacon drippings

3–4 medium-size green tomatoes, washed, cored, and sliced (do not peel)

Corn meal, seasoned to taste with salt and pepper

1 teaspoon thyme

1 egg

1 cup milk

Grease a skillet with the vegetable oil and heat over medium heat.

Spread a thin layer of corn meal on a baking sheet or plate.

Beat the egg into the milk. Pour the mixture into a shallow bowl.

Dip each tomato in the milk–egg mixture and then into the corn meal.

Place the battered tomato slices in the preheated skillet. Brown each slice on one side, and then turn it to brown the other side. Serve hot.

Here in Grandma's kitchen, I feel my hands becoming her hands as I put a pot of water on the stove for tea. I feel my blue eyes becoming her blue eyes, and follow her gaze out the east window to the big red barn, built in 1912, and out the south window to watch the trucks zooming by on Interstate 57, which cut a corner off the farm when it was built in the 1960s. After my cup of tea, I go out to do the morning chores and feel my legs and knees becoming hers. Every morning and evening, I unlatch the top and bottom doors of the barn, and lift the pump handle just inside the door to fill up two five-gallon buckets with water. One in each hand, I slosh awkwardly through the narrow barn passageways, trying to tap into the genetic muscle memory of my grandmother, knowing she could walk this barn in her sleep, could navigate it with any load of water or hay or grain, and could work with any animal.

My chores consist of feeding and watering the cats, dogs, chickens, ducks, guineas, and the half-dozen female goats and their kids.

The goat population had exploded in the spring with one goat having four kids, another three, and the remainder two. No matter their age, goats are troublemakers—cunning and devious, always on the lookout for grain, and always jumping walls, butting open gates, and knocking you over to get at it. I was nearly run down the first morning I brought their grain out, so now I prefill the six grain pans and bring them out in a stack to distribute around the field before I let the goats out of the barn.

Although Grandma is nearly 102 and mostly unknowing in the Prairieview Lutheran Home, I feel her inhabiting these bones and muscles of mine, even these thoughts of mine. I was up at 5:30, and it's 8:30 already, and I can hear her scold, "Time's a-wastin'!"

By this time in the morning, when she was a working farm wife and I was a young child, she would have finished the chores and fixed the family a multicourse breakfast of stewed prunes and biscuits, bacon and eggs, and toast slathered with bacon drippings and Karo syrup. (I heard from a cousin that one morning when he came down for breakfast, there were stewed raisins instead of stewed prunes. "Aunt Henrietta, what happened?" he said, pointing at them. "The prunes had babies," she said, without missing a beat.)

Once breakfast was cleared away and the dishes were washed and dried and put away, she would start in on the laundry and the baking—honey–wheat bread, whole-wheat rolls, or her famous sugar cookies. Finally, she'd sit down to do some mending or make more quilts for Lutheran Worldwide Relief, the squares made from discarded clothing and stuffed with old pantyhose. All I have to show for my morning's work are happy cats, ducks, chickens, and goats.

In the evening, I wait for the sun to set so the chickens, ducks, and guineas will go into their shed, and I can lock them up safely for the night. The evenings are much shorter now, but I go out early and walk along the road, waiting for darkness to fall. Did my forebears take this walk, too, I wonder? Did they nod appreciatively as they listened to the corn leaves rustle companionably in the breeze? If they did, I am sure they did so without the slightest inkling of a day when their kind of farming would be called "organic."

I head over to the old sheep shed Grandpa built, where Jill and her oldest girl, Halley, now keep dozens of chickens, ducks, and guineas. The girls show them for their 4-H projects, so there are many different breeds and ages of birds, each in its own place within the shed. All are easy to take care of, except the guineas. Being not quite fully domesticated, they won't go into their coops until the last hundredth of a foot candle of light has disappeared from the sky. Just as that is about to happen, the full moon rises. It's hard to convince a guinea to go inside if moonlight begins as soon as sunlight ends, so I chase the wild ones around the shed a time or two before they finally decide to call it a night. Then I close and latch each of the small cutout doors the fowl use to enter and exit their various apartments, and finally close up the additional defensive perimeter of fencing meant to discourage the varmints (weasels, raccoons, foxes, coyotes, skunks, and others) from seeking out a chicken, guinea, or duck dinner.

We load a hayrack with pumpkins, kabocha, butternut, delicata, acorn, and more, and invite our annual Potluck and Tour guests to take some home.

As I turn back toward the old farmhouse, the waxing moon, arbiter of tides, pulls my eyes and my whole being skyward. I raise my arms, take a deep breath, and feel her cool beam of calmness pass through me.

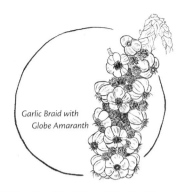

Garlic Braid with Globe Amaranth

XII. HARVEST MOON

WEEK 49. **Ozark Gold Comfort**

THE DAY DAWNED PURPLE AND PINK, AND THEN BRIGHT white and yellow. Everyone was already down in the field working on various tasks when, an hour later, God lowered a big lid on the pot. The sky darkened, and the wind ripped leaves prematurely from the trees. Clouds rolled in from the west, and just before they completely covered everything, a flash of eastern light hit the maples, red on their peaks, then orange, then green lower down. The leaves tossed and shook against the lavender gray sky in a colorful shudder before the breeze turned suddenly icy, the sky returned to predawn, and the birds went back to sleep. The owls started to call, tentatively, when the phone rang.

We let the Indian corn, cornmeal corn, and popcorn dry down in the field, sometimes waiting until late October to pick it.

It was my sister Beth calling from the nursing home in Danforth to chokingly tell me that Grandma Henrietta had passed away, just two months shy of her 102nd birthday.

There are deaths that you expect to happen for so long that when they finally do, you're as surprised as if it were completely unexpected. For nearly my whole life, each time we visited Grandma and Grandpa, Grandma would say, "Well, I may not be here the next time you come ..." as she gave us our goodbye kisses. Even after she moved to the nursing home, even through Grandpa's death and her own mini-strokes and diabetic crises, even then, it seemed her strong mind and body would never give out. When it did, we were all a little shaken.

But there was no time to indulge in feelings of shakiness. There were decisions to be made. People to be contacted. A visitation (two, as it turned out) and a funeral to organize. Our father was at his weekly appointment with the local doctor, and still so fragile that I told the nursing-home folks and the funeral-home folks not to bother him—that my sisters and I would take care of everything. Beth and I had already decided on no embalming and no open casket, although that is the local funeral culture. We knew that friends and relatives and neighbors would miss the traditional procession past the casket where everyone murmurs how wonderful the deceased looks, how youthful, how lifelike.

But this was one physical body we wanted to return to earth unimpeded by poisons. Of Grandma's many gifts to others during her long life, this final one, the giving back of water, minerals, salts, proteins, would be to the earth.

It reminded me of a story I had heard—I don't remember where—of a man who died and was buried under a small tree. Many years later, the area around the tree was disturbed, and people saw that a tree root had found the man's foot, followed it, turned at the heel, traced along the tibia, turned at the knee, followed the femur, wrapped once around the hips, then traced the backbone all the way to the skull, where it sent out smaller roots to capture all the rich minerals of the man's body, a poor man who had richly given back to the earth and now lived on in the towering tree above him.

We thought the owner of the local funeral home might object to our decision, seeing as embalming is one of the main things he does, and he is proud of his skills. But not only did he agree, he let us know there was no rush, that Grandma could be kept in cold storage until we let all the family members know and they had time to travel here for the visitations and funeral.

Since Teresa and Henry were busy on their farms, and Beth and Jill were busy at the nursing home and funeral home in Danforth, it fell to me to wait for Dad and Mom to return from the doctor. As soon as Dad came in and took his jacket off, glancing first at the phone to see if a message was waiting, I told him his mother had died. As I put my arms around him, I felt a shudder, and then a softening, as the years and years of weekly visits to his weaker and weaker mother fell away.

I told him that Beth had been next to Grandma all night long and all morning. That she had held her bony hands and gently rubbed the tissue-paper-thin skin on her forehead, and kept telling her it was okay to go. After helping her through the last hours, the last breaths, Beth told Grandma that now she was going straight to the farm to find the biggest Ozark Gold apple from the huge tree west of the farmhouse and eat it for her. And she did.

Almost immediately, food started appearing at the old farmhouse Grandma went to live in as a young wife and then kept shipshape for more than 60 years. Nothing spreads quite so fast in rural areas as news, particularly news of death. The intelligence is immediately transmuted into food, which arrives mysteriously on the doorstep. First, a big tray of yeasty homemade cinnamon rolls, still warm from an unknown oven, appeared at the back porch. They were quickly followed by a tray of pumpkin bars with cream-cheese frosting, something Grandma always had frozen and ready for quick thawing and serving if a visitor should drop by or someone should die.

The stream of hot dishes, cold dishes, covered dishes, and desserts did not stop for five days. Teresa said it brought to mind a passage in Howard Fast's novel, *April Morning*, about a boy growing up during the battles of Lexington and Concord on the eve of the Revolutionary

Grandma Henrietta's Pumpkin–Raisin Bars

For the Bars

2 cups all-purpose flour

2 cups sugar

1 tablespoon ground cinnamon

2 teaspoons baking powder

1 teaspoon baking soda

1 teaspoon salt

½ teaspoon ground nutmeg

½ teaspoon ground cloves

1¾ cup cooked pumpkin

4 large eggs

¾ cup vegetable oil

1 cup raisins

For the Frosting

6 ounces cream cheese, room temperature

1 cup powdered sugar

⅓ cup butter, room temperature

Beat the cream cheese, powdered sugar, and butter in a medium bowl until thoroughly blended. Spread the frosting over the cake in a thin layer. Cut the cake into bars. Eat some now, and freeze some for later.

Preheat the oven to 350°F.

Grease a 15½ × 10½ × 1-inch baking sheet. Stir together the flour, sugar, cinnamon, baking powder, baking soda, salt, nutmeg, and cloves in a large bowl until blended.

Add the pumpkin, eggs, and oil, and beat until blended. Mix in the raisins.

Spread the batter into the prepared pan. Bake at 350°F for about 25 minutes. Cool in the pan on a rack.

War. When his father is killed, many neighbors come to visit and prepare food. The young man, Adam, says he has a new appreciation for why so much food is cooked for the recently bereaved: "It is a tribute to the living, who are in need of it at the time." He also notes that his mother, who formerly made references to his excessive appetite, now seems to be worried that he might starve.

None of the living were going to starve at Grandma's funeral. When Teresa made apple muffins to bring, she automatically chose Ozark Gold apples for them, from the huge tree that Beth had gone to, that Grandpa had pruned, that Grandma made applesauce from for more than four decades, and that is still bearing fruit for us today.

The night after Grandma's funeral, I fell into a grateful sleep to the fading chorus of fall crickets and tree frogs. But coyote calls pushed through my slumber in the wee hours. Coyotes are demonized by most of the local farmers, who accuse them of the intent (if not the practice) of killing calves and lambs. In fact, stomach-content analyses show they dine mainly on fruits, berries, rabbits, field mice, and other small animals. If they are near humans, they supplement this diet with scavenged pet food and table scraps.

Soon after I moved back to Congerville, I was talking with one of our neighbors, who kept relating stories that featured "dem yodees." I was too embarrassed to reveal my citified ignorance of something she was so familiar with, referring to it in the same breath as chickens and sheep.

And it was not until the next morning that the pieces fell together in my brain and I realized that "dem yodees" were actually "them coyotes." Since then, I've also heard them referred to as "kai-oats," as it's said west of the Mississippi, with west–central Illinois close enough for linguistic mingling.

If the coyote is wily, it is perhaps because humans have made her that way. The hatred and fear she often inspires remind me of the monster Caliban, the disfigured and savage child of the dead witch, Sycorax, in Shakespeare's *The Tempest*. The civilized Prospero attempts to enslave Caliban, but he remains wild and untamable. Prospero finally comes to terms with Caliban at the end of the play, and says, "This thing of darkness I acknowledge mine."

Students and critics have conjectured endlessly on whether Prospero is speaking solely of Caliban, or of his own divided soul and inner tempests. The one thing that is certain is that Caliban is the true heir to the island, as the coyote is true heir to this continent. We humans are the interlopers.

As we were finishing up a long harvest day a few years back, Henry and I saw a lone coyote at dusk. He seemed to float in from the forest to stand in the center of the lane, solid and unafraid—almost human in his insolence.

"You think *you* are the top of the food pyramid," he seemed to say, with the demeanor of a creature who is supremely confident of his status: predator, not prey. None of us moved. His yellow eyes fixed us for a long moment. It is rare these days for us humans to ever be challenged by another life form. We are so used to everything scurrying away from us. This coyote did not scurry. We began to redefine ourselves: prey, not predator.

After an epoch seemed to pass, we acknowledged each other with something verging on respect. Then he slowly turned and sauntered into the woods as if he owned the place, which, in fact, he did.

As I listened to "dem yodees" and their wild midnight yips and howls, I wished them long life and increase.

WEEK 50. Resurgent Greens

THE LAST WARM WIND OF AUTUMN AWAKENED ME AS IT CAME through the window, making a low, damp roar in the distance and a light, dry sizzle up close. It flows through the dry leaves in slow rolls, building up and then subsiding into momentary silence. It is exactly the same mesmerizing sound and rhythm as waves on a pebbly beach. With each swelling breeze, my chest swells with something that seems very much like love—for the sight of glowing trees and shimmering sky, for the sound of wind and rain returning leaves to earth, for the sweet smell of decay rising up with morning mist.

After a hard frost, we always get a burst of lovely warm, even hot, weather. In some other world, this warm breeze and bright sun would resurrect the blackened basil and blasted tomatoes. But not in this one. The consolation is that, although we've reached the end of the road for basil and okra, summer squash and beans, cucumbers and the nonhoophouse tomatoes (the heirlooms in their hoophouse are still bearing), the cooler air has sweetened the greens and fall roots and killed their insect pests, and so they are growing ever more lush and tasty.

Although last month provided, in many ways, the best of both worlds—a plethora of summer as well as autumn crops—this is the month of final abundance. Not only is there a sudden profusion of fall cooking greens—bok choi, tah tsai, mei qing choi, gailan, broccoli rabe, turnip greens, mustard greens, kale, collards, and Henry's favorite stir-fry green, komatsuna—there are the salad greens—lettuces with their leaves growing thicker and tastier with the cool weather, fancy pizzo, ruby streaks, golden frill mustards, and the incomparable fall arugula.

We are also entering the heavy root season, extracting loads of celery root, parsnips, turnips, daikon, roseheart radish, Jerusalem artichokes, potatoes, sweet potatoes, burdock, and more. On top of that, there is the full complement of winter squash and pumpkins—including old favorites like acorn and butternut, and new favorites like red kuri and kabocha, delicata and sugar loaf, plus pie pumpkins, cheese pumpkins, and the lovely bronze Kickapoo. And now is the time to start making the garlic braids to grace kitchens all over Chicagoland and to provide that special boost that only garlic gives.

All of this work becomes urgent in October, the month most still know as the month of the Harvest Moon. The very words drip with the honey of nostalgia. They bathe and soothe in the soft glow of old-timey love songs that implore the moon to "shine on, shine on ..." not for work in the fields, but for "me and my gal."

Notwithstanding the pleasures of moonlit love, the Harvest Moon was named not for dallying, but for the hard work of harvesting. And this is what we do throughout all the shortening days of this month. Although there is less total work to be done now, there is so much less time to do it in that we are still busy for every minute of daylight. It is as if a large heavy door were slowly, relentlessly, sliding shut. And there is still so much to do, so much to get out of the fields—food for man and beast—before the cold clamps down, before the door slams shut.

For the farmer, the Harvest Moon is less a dreamy notion and more a simple fact: the full moon nearest the autumnal equinox. It rises early in the evening, eliminating any dark interval between sunset and moonrise, which meant in years past that harvesting could continue by moonlight. Although it may seem romantic to work by moonlight, it is easier and more practical to work in the barn under electric lights both before dawn, usually cleaning and braiding garlic, and after dark, usually washing vegetables.

During the hours when our spinning planet faces the sun, there are cover crops to sow, dry beans and dry corn to harvest and process, sweet potatoes to dig and cure, dozens and dozens of 50-pound crates of other roots to dig up and wash, and winter squash and pumpkins to pick out of the field and load on hayracks. The loaded hayracks are wheeled out of the barn each sunny morning and wheeled back each night, as if they were patients in a sanatorium being wheeled out to take the cure of fresh air and sunlight. Which, in a sense, they are—their skins hardening in the sunshine so they will last for months without rotting.

As the season winds down, the rack of winter squashes gets sparser and sparser until only a few jack-o-lantern pumpkins and swan-neck gourds are left to cast their long shadows.

Not only are the fields once again verdant and flourishing, but our dad, too, has turned a corner and is taking daily walks down the country roads, slowly regaining his strength. For the first month after returning home, Beth and Mom badgered and cajoled him to take even one step out onto the porch, but to no avail. Then slowly, slowly, as mind and body healed, he began to reenter the world.

We measured his progress, quite literally, in steps. First, just two steps to sit out on the deck. Then, to walk to the edge of the porch, some five steps from the door. Each day, he went one step further down the walk. Over a period of nine days, he went from stepping out the front door to getting to the end of the walk. Then it was another 10 or 11 days before he progressed from the end of the walk to the end of the lane. The next day, he got all the way down the lane and a few steps onto the road. Then, each day, further out onto the road, until he made it all the way to the pasture and partway down the lane to the fields. Now he is walking all the way down to our neighbor's fruit orchard and back, and we are grateful for what seems a small miracle but is perhaps no more or less than the natural resilience of life.

The fields, too, are rejuvenated. Many of our guests at the annual Farm Tour and Potluck were surprised to see the field so green, and especially to see the delicate-looking lettuces completely unfazed by the frost. Some marketgoers shake their heads with wonder at the profusion of greens each fall. And they are a wonder, having been planted during the hottest, driest time of year. With a lot of care and a little luck, they survive their seedling stage under the brutal sun and finally thrive once the autumn rains come.

In addition to the huge array of salad and Asian greens, this is also the season for the full, rich flavors of collard greens, brussels sprouts, kale, and rapini, also known as broccoli rabe, and for the enlivening tastes and aromas of herbs, both annual and perennial. Almost all of the herbs, except for the tender basil, grow lush in the cooler air until the harder freezes of late fall begin to do them in. Henry is now generous in the size of his bunches of parsley, dill, and cilantro at the market, and at home we are profligate in their use—not a pinch here and there, but great bunches of them ground up into full-blown pestos made with parsley, sage, dill, and even young mustard greens.

Sweet Dressing for Spicy Autumn Salad

This is the time of year when the bags of mesclun get bigger and spicier, full of not only the full-flavored lettuces but also spicy and pungent greens like arugula, red mustard greens, golden frill, ruby streaks, and mizuna. Henry supplied these to Kendall Culinary College for its special "Slow Food" dinner with Alice Waters a few years ago. The chefs there tossed the greens with a light vinaigrette, which is really all they need.

> **1 cup olive oil**
>
> **⅔ cup sugar**
>
> **⅓ cup distilled white vinegar**
>
> **¼ small onion, finely diced**
>
> **1 teaspoon salt**
>
> **4–6 cups fall greens of your choice**

Whisk together the oil, sugar, vinegar, onion, and salt until emulsified. Toss with greens. Serve.

Now that most of the summer annual flowers are gone, Teresa creates gorgeous fall bouquets with wheat and dried flowers. But my favorite bouquets are those she makes with her fall herbs. She brought one over to my house, where it sat on the kitchen counter for weeks—a source of such quiet joy and sensory delight that I got lost in it each time I walked by and got caught in the intoxicating aromas, seduced by the subtly varying shades of green in the wild mint, chocolate mint, rosemary, sage, and soft purple spikes of lavender with their felt buds. I can't help but steal a leaf each time I passed by, rubbing it and bringing it to my nose for a deep inhale and a relaxing exhale.

WEEK 51. Sweet Potatoes Cure

WHILE THE GREENS ARE STILL THRIVING, WE KNOW THAT, sooner or later, they too will succumb to ever-colder temperatures. But until that day comes, the CSA shares and the market stand are bursting with greens, and we encourage everyone to use them before they lose them. And we don't just mean use them for this week's meals, but to freeze some for winter. Some say we humans are the animal that is able to imagine the future and plan for it. Yet, looking around, I often think the squirrels have us beat on that one.

The other day, as we were accompanying Dad on his afternoon walk, Mom and I looked for nuts on the butternut trees my Dad had planted years ago at the edge of the pasture. Also known as white walnuts or oilnuts, butternuts look like walnuts but have a richer, sweeter flavor. Because the nuts grow slowly and have thick shells, and the trees do not live as long as other nut trees, butternuts have never been cultivated on a wide scale.

Yet they were an important source of food and drink for centuries, with the nuts cooked into breads and cakes, the sap made into a syrup, and the bark brewed into a beer. But we could not find one butternut, either on the tree or under it. That means the squirrels have been hard at work doing what they do so well: squirreling things away for winter.

We can take a lesson from them and squirrel away fall greens for winter. It's not hard to take a half-dozen bunches of greens—say, a couple of bunches of turnip greens, a couple of komatsuna, and a couple of kale—and put a big pot of salted water on to boil. While it's heating up, wash your greens, and chop them if you like. Then when the water is at a rolling boil, throw in the greens for just a minute or two. They will turn a gorgeous bright green (they do not turn lighter, even though this process is called "blanching") and then you simply take them out, put them in a colander and chill them under cold water. Squeeze them lightly, put them in ziplock plastic bags, and freeze them, and you will have serving after serving of fresh-frozen fall greens all winter long.

Another way we prepare for winter is by "curing" various crops. We air-cure the garlic by hanging it from the barn rafters all summer and into the fall. We sun-cure the winter squash and pumpkins by putting them out in the sunshine and fresh air in the fall. We heat-cure the sweet potatoes.

After the first hard frost in years when the frost comes early, or before the soil temperature falls below 50 when the frost comes late, Henry calls all hands to come help dig up the sweet potatoes. Sweet potatoes are warm-season plants, native to the tropics, and so they are very sensitive to cold temperatures. The greatest danger from delayed digging is the risk of cold, wet soil that will lead the tubers to swift decay. What staves off that decay and promotes the development of flavor is getting the potatoes out of the ground promptly, and then putting them in a room with a high temperature (85 to 90 degrees) and humidity (90 percent) for 7 to 14 days. This causes the periderm, the skin and layer underneath it, to thicken and re-form, healing any bruises or cuts and triggering the development of enzymes that convert some of the starch in the roots to sugar.

The sooner the potatoes are cured, the better. So immediately after they are dug up, before they are even washed, Henry takes over a room in the apprentices' trailer, spreads tarps all over the floor, and then puts the recently dug sweet potatoes out in a single layer on bread trays propped up off the floor to allow air to circulate underneath them as well. He then creates tropical conditions in the room by bringing in a small electric space heater and draping soaked towels and sheets from a clothesline suspended from the ceiling and walls to increase the humidity. For the next week or two, it is the trailer inhabitants' job to monitor the temperature and humidity closely, rewetting the towels and sheets twice or even three times daily, keeping the sweet potatoes in their sauna, so we and our customers will be able to enjoy them all winter long.

The apprentices don't mind having the sweet potatoes take over some of their territory, because the curing room is a great place to return to after a cold, rainy October day. It's also a nice place to warm up before going out on a frosty morning, and the sweet, earthy aroma emanating from the room warms the soul and promotes sweet dreams.

After curing, it's best to store sweet potatoes between 55 and 60 degrees. If they are refrigerated, they develop a hard center and are liable to rot. Under ideal temperature conditions, with 85 percent humidity and sufficient airflow, however, they will last up to six months. Some years, we've had perfect sweet potatoes clear into May—bringing us full circle to when the new slips are in the hoophouse getting ready to be transplanted for the next season. Storing actually improves the sweet potatoes, as it further develops the sugars and maltose–creating

enzyme. This same enzyme kicks in when you cook the potatoes, developing even more sweetness.

Sweet potatoes are indeed sweet, but they are neither potatoes nor yams, being rather a member of the *Convolvulus,* or morning glory, family. The confusion began when Europeans first encountered sweet potatoes in Haiti in 1492. The fleshy tuber was known by various names, but the one that stuck was the Haitian one, *batata*. Later, this name was inadvertently applied to the ordinary potato—another New World crop.

Meanwhile, at about the same time, but on the other side of the world, Portuguese slave traders watching Africans digging up a large root asked what it was. The Africans replied to what seemed an inane question by stating the obvious, that it was "something to eat"—*nyami* in a language of Guinea. So "yam" became an alternate term for sweet potato in British and Portuguese colonies. True yams, however, are very large, starchy roots of the *Dioscorea* genus.

To confuse matters further, when soft, orange-fleshed sweet potatoes were introduced in the U.S. in the mid-twentieth century, producers and

Empty crates are stacked in the field to receive the sweet potato treasure. Sweet potatoes continue to grow until a hard frost kills the vines, but must be dug immediately afterwards or they will begin to decay.

shippers wanted to distinguish them from the lighter colored, drier varieties. To do so, they used the word yam. But yams in the U.S. are actually just sweet potatoes with moist texture and orange flesh.

Henry grows many varieties of sweet potatoes, including the classic orange, moist yam varieties, such as the Beauregard and Georgia Jet. He also grows Japanese and Korean sweet potatoes, which generally have a purplish skin and a yellow or cream-colored flesh. This flesh is much drier, sweeter, and more flavorful than the yam varieties.

Henry and Hiroko's favorite way to cook any kind of sweet potato is in the ash pan of the wood stove. The heat from the wood coals chars the outside and makes the insides sweet and delicious. Every time I eat one of the Japanese sweet potatoes Henry and Hiroko make this way, I hear the song of the Japanese *yaki-imo* (roasted sweet potato) man—a plaintive, more or less monotone, "*Yaaaaaa-kkiiiii-moooo, oiiiiiishiiiiii yaaaa-kiii-mooooooo.*"

The *yaki-imo* man comes out in neighborhoods all over Japan at this time of year. He has a wood fire burning merrily in a barbecue pit–style box mounted in the back of his little pickup truck or pushcart. Inside, he is roasting the sweet potatoes, which he sells and puts in a paper bag for you. When I was in Japan, the sweet smoky smell emanating from a *yaki-imo* truck could make me turn around in my tracks. As wonderful as the slightly charred sweet potatoes were, an additional benefit was that they made fabulous edible handwarmers as the weather got colder.

It turns out that George Washington Carver, director of the Tuskegee Institute, was also a fan of sweet potatoes roasted in wood coals—although I doubt he ever heard the song or tasted the wares of the *yaki-imo* man. In November 1936, he published a bulletin entitled "How the Farmer Can Save His Sweet Potatoes, and Ways of Preparing Them for the Table." Here he describes his method, which is very similar to that used by Henry and Hiroko. If you don't have a fire handy, simply roast the potatoes in a heavy roasting pan at 375 degrees until forkable.

Before I leave my house to go help with more afternoon sweet potato digging, I watch a hairy woodpecker work away at the already large holes he's made in the dead tree off the north side of the house. They are two or three inches in diameter—big enough that he can perch

Sweet Potatoes No. 3, Baked in Ashes
By George Washington Carver

In this method, the sweetness and piquancy of the potato is brought out in a manner hardly obtainable in any other way.

Select the same kind of potatoes for baking (large and uniform).

Cover them with warm ashes to a depth of 4 inches. On top of the ashes, place live coals and hot cinders; let bake slowly for at least 2 hours.

Remove the ashes with a soft brush and serve while hot, with butter.

---

on the rim and tip his whole fat little body up and over the edge and into the hole to find some delicious grub. Mostly, though, he is patient and quiet and unmoving, waiting for the bug to make the first move, then levering himself in for the kill. When I pick up the binoculars, he seems to glance over his shoulder at me—one large eye fearlessly piercing my two assisted ones. Then he turns back to his waiting, and I to my watching.

He is harvesting too, using these last warm days of the Harvest Moon to stock up on food for the winter, just the same as we are, although he packs it on as body fat while we pack it in our freezers, cupboards, basements, and storage pit.

WEEK 52. Garlic in the Dark

UNTIL THIS WEEK, OCTOBER SEEMED, STILL, THE HIGH, FAMiliar endless summer. But now, there is a glint of silver in the chill evenings, and the cupped hands of milkweed husks stand emptied of their silken parachutes. The tall stalks lean over their own slanting shadows, ready for the fall.

Although it's been a month of mostly brilliant Indian summer days, we're edging inevitably into winter as the mercury descends further each night. All that is left in the field is frost-tolerant—kales, turnip greens, mustard greens, Asian greens, and even the lettuces, which can survive down to the low twenties. And all of the roots, except the sweet potatoes, do quite well even after the frost, insulated as they are in their blankets of earth.

With the days growing ever shorter, Henry and his workers start the days in darkness. The apprentices walk down the hill from the mobile home, across the stream, and up the hill to the barn, drawn to the lights under which Henry is already busy cutting down long strands of garlic from the rafters where they've been air-curing for the past few months.

Everyone sits on hay bales or upturned crates and cleans the soft-neck garlic for Henry to fashion into 12- and 18-head braids, some decorated with colorful dried flowers or hot Thai peppers. When the light creeps up over the trees, we put the garlic aside until tomorrow and head down to the fields to work. Walking down the back hill, the woods seem lit from inside, and I remember something Henry wrote 10 years ago, in one of the very earliest *Food & Farm Notes*, back when he had time to write.

> A section of the woods thick with young sugar maple trees is now a golden haven. The forest floor is blanketed with yellow leaves. The sunlight filtering down through the leaves tinges everything with a honey-eyed hue.
>
> "Have you ever seen yellow rain?" I ask Kazami, our four-year-old son.
>
> I grab a sapling next to him and shake it. For one long, two long limpid seconds he looks at me, waiting. Then leaves begin to float down into view.
>
> He looks up and laughs, raising his arms to the sky as the leaves flow down like great, graceful ships with billowing yellow sails and crash lightly against his upturned face and arms.
>
> We continue along the path, making it rain sugar maple leaves. Kazami shakes and shakes the limber saplings long after they have dropped their last leaf, and their bare black branches rattle.

Kazami is no longer a little boy, but he still shakes and climbs trees. Before the last October market, he and I worked together to pick the big Gold Rush apples, the late-ripening variety Henry planted years ago up near the house. It was the very end of a very long day that had started at 4:30 a.m., when my cat woke me as she was terrorizing a young mouse. This is her job, and I often wish she would do it better, but I wish she would not insist on doing it in the wee hours. The mouse was out exploring the world, or perhaps moving into a warm spot for the winter. In either case, he was not yet cat-savvy and had paid the ultimate price.

Since I was awake anyway, I got up and cut up some of the "for-us" winter squash, carving out the soft spots and putting the good parts into the heavy roasting pan to bake, so I could then freeze it for winter. My ulterior motive was to have the oven take the chill off the house as well. While it was cooking, I put away greens that had come back from the market and made some arugula pesto to freeze for winter. As the sky was just barely turning light, I headed over to the barn to work on garlic, and the day began. And before I knew it, it was ending.

Henry dispatched teams to the Asian pear trees and the Gold Rush apple trees. As I picked the low-hanging fruit, Kazami scampered up into the branches to pluck the biggest, ripest, most sun-kissed apples, which are always at the very top of the tree. He would call to me when he had some ready to toss down, and I'd catch them and place them gently in the crate. Looking up into the darkening sky, seeing large red-blushed yellow fruit outlined by branches and sky, stretching, reaching—from legs, through rib cage, armpit, arm, wrist and hands—then fingers wrapping around and plucking a hanging fruit, or catching a falling one ... this, I thought, is a genetic memory of ancient *Homo sapiens*, this is what we were meant to do. Look up, reach up, and pluck down fruit. How differently most people come by their fruit, I thought, and how sad that is—looking down at a shelf rather than up into a tree-framed sky.

It's almost dark, and Henry is satisfied we've picked all we can. He looks up at the stars starting to prick the cloudless sky, wondering if the soil will dry out enough to start planting garlic when he returns from the market. I hear him say, "This might be the first year we won't get the garlic in."

I leave Kazami high up in the tree, snacking on one last apple, as

Sugar maple saplings are filling in where the great oaks fall.

I head over to water Dad's cows, feed them some bad apples, and give the heifers some hay. Then I stop in to see Mom and Dad and tell them about our day.

I immediately see that something has changed. Life has returned to Dad's light blue eyes. It is an amazing thing to witness, a spirit reinhabiting its body.

Leaving their house for mine, I saw a crashing wave in the sky to the southwest—a sky-wide stretch of low, flat, gray clouds that rose up in a brilliant white froth in the west, illuminated for just a moment by a sun that was already below the horizon.

Soon, the garlic in the barn will return to the earth. Grandma is already there, while Dad still strolls along the country roads. Henry is sleeping a few hours before waking up again at 1:30 a.m. to drive to Evanston, and our sister Beth left today to drive herself and her dogs back down to her home in Mexico. It's a signal as clear as the big Vs of Canada geese in the sky: winter's coming soon.

The chill air is flowing in already, but I am cuddled in my padded jacket watching the gray mist descend. They say it will go down to 24 tonight. I am looking forward to building the first fire in my wood stove and sitting in front of it, book in my lap, feet on the footstool. I am 50—half my life is over. Only half, if I'm lucky. But my eyes are already turned toward that far hillside, far ahead of the road we have begun. So, as Rilke writes, "We are grasped by what we cannot grasp."

There is no sound tonight but the rushing wind through the drying leaves. But if you strain to hear, you can still catch the faint whirr of evening insects, slowed down from the frenetic sawing of summer to these last slow breaths, and then eternal rest.

INDEX

A

Against the Grain (Lappe and Bailey), 75–76
Akhmatova, Anna, 28
Alliums, 134–135
Angelus, The (Millet), 195
Animal husbandry, crop-growing and, 30–32
Apples
    Cox's Orange Pippins, 266–267
    flavors of seasonal, 94–95
    picking, 299
    Teresa's Priceless Apple Crisp, 87
    Traditional Winter Apple Wassail, 96
April, 149–166
    bees, 159–162
    chicken eggs, 155–158
    ducks, 162–166
    transplanting, 149–155
Aronia, 238–244
    Teresa's Aronia Juice, 242
Asparagus, 167, 171–175
    Roasted Asparagus with Olive Oil and
      Balsamic Vinegar, 174
August, 231–264
    aronia, 238–244
    corn, 231–238
    greens, 251–258
    harvesting and sorting, 258–264
    summer heat and melons, 245–251

B

Bailey, Britt, 75–76
Basil, 85, 279
    harvesting, 251–252, 257–258

Beans
    harvesting, 227–230
    Joel's Italian Flat Beans with Sweet
      Onion, Garlic, and Maple-Glazed
      Ham, 229
    in top 10 crops, 83–84
Bees, 159–162
Beetles, Japanese, 220–222
Beets, 84
Berries, 185–190
Berry, Wendell, 114
Biggers, Greg, 107
Biodegradable plastic bags, 89–94
Bio-Piracy (Shiva), 75
Brassica
    direct-seeding, 134
    transplanting, 153–155
Brennan, Patricia, 164
Broccoli, 123–124
Brockman, Asa, 27, 53, 182
    burdock and, 270
    market preparation, 175–176
    potato planting, 192
    separating bull from herd, 59–61
    truck space and, 256–257
Brockman, Beth, 82, 300
    aronia juice, 240
    dogs and, 275–276
    father's illness and, 243, 268, 269, 270,
      291
    Frosty and, 147
    Henrietta's death and, 284–285
Brockman, Fred (brother), 82, 205

Brockman, Fred (grandfather), 56, 78, 102–103, 122

Brockman, Henrietta
  death of, 284–287
  life on farm, 55–57, 78, 102–103, 108–109, 170, 266–267, 280–281
  sayings and stories of, 39–40, 57, 264

Brockman, Henry
  burdock and, 271
  cattle and, 58–59
  children of, 53
  cover crops and, 212–214
  garlic and, 21, 210–212
  harvesting of greens, 251–258
  hoophouse and, 123–128
  non-farm work of, 39
  November harvest and, 43, 45, 46–47, 48
  placing orders for next season, 67–71
  potatoes and, 191–194
  reading habits, 75–76
  record keeping, 67–71, 82–85, 247
  separating bull from herd, 59–61
  wood gathering and, 121
  workday of, 141
  writes about fall, 298

Brockman, Herman, 18, 49, 53, 70, 121
  aronia and, 240–241
  asparagus and, 171
  health of, 27–28, 71–72, 81, 145–147, 178, 220
  Henrietta's death and, 285
  Lucky Tom turkey and, 35–36
  purchase of Henry's Farm, 73–74
  return home and recovery, 268–270, 291, 300
  surgeries, 81, 224–225, 256
  writes about Brockman Centennial Farm, 78–79, 87

writes about fencing pail, 225–226
writes about peas, 206, 209
writes about tomato-sorting, 260–261

Brockman, Kazami, 27, 53, 223
  apple picking, 298–299
  August harvests, 263
  market preparation, 176
  planting, 151
  separating bull from herd, 59–61
  watermelon picking and, 250, 251
  weeding and, 180, 182

Brockman, Maria Zachgo, 78

Brockman, Marlene, 53, 69, 81, 82
  Herman's health and, 220, 268, 270, 291, 300
  mesclun-sorting and, 256
  peas and, 206–208
  purchase of Henry's Farm, 73–74
  tomato-sorting and, 260–261

Brockman, Zoe, 27, 53
  August harvest, 263
  market preparation, 176
  separating bull from herd, 59–61
  writes about harvesting, 215–216, 249–250
  writes about weeding, 180–183
  writes poem about grandparents, 81–82

Brockman Centennial Farm, 77–79, 87, 102

Bromfield, Louis, 255

Burdock, 270–274
  Mrs. Takayasu's Kimpira Gobo (Stir-Fried Burdock and Carrots), 274

Butchering, 107–114
  duck, 164–166
  hog, 110–114

Butternuts, 293

Butz, Earl, 31

C

Carrots
> harvesting, 45–46
> Mrs. Takayasu's Kimpira Gobo (Stir-Fried Burdock and Carrots), 274
> in top 10 crops, 84

Carver, George Washington, 296–297

Cattle
> birth of calf, 144–147
> Frosty, 58–59, 147
> separating bull from herd, 57–61

Chemical-based agriculture, 79–80

Chickens
> death in summer heat, 201–202
> eggs from, 155–158

Chico (dog), 201, 275–278

Chinese broccoli, Gailan Miracle recipe, 52

Chives, 196–198
> Asian Chive Pancakes, 197

Chokeberry, 238–244

Colwin, Laurie, 162–163

Community-supported agriculture (CSA), 29–30, 40

Confined animal feeding operation (CAFO), 110, 122

"Coon Tree" (White), 203

Corn
> fertilization, 231–234
> fungus on, 234–235
> Green Corn with Marjoram Butter, 236
> harvesting, 236–238

Cover crops, 141–143, 212–214, 290

Cox's Orange Pippins, 266–267

Coyotes, 287–288

Cream of Saskatchewan melons, 250–251

Crop-growing, animal husbandry and, 30–32

Cummings, Halley, 282

Cummings, Jill Brockman, 60, 279, 282

Henrietta's death and, 285
> living on Brockman Centennial Farm, 77, 102

Cummings, Tess, 249

D

Dahl, Roald, 265–266

Danny the Champion of the World (Dahl), 265–266

Davison, Bill, 112, 118

December, 63–88
> garlic mulching, 63–67
> land ethic, 75–80
> seed catalogs, 67–71
> time and life changes, 71–75
> top 10 vegetables grown, 81–88

Direct-seeding, 132–137, 154

Divers, George, 204

Dogs, on farm, 144–145, 201, 275–278

Donne, John, 55

Ducks
> Pan-Fried Duck Cracklings, 166
> sexual behavior of drakes, 162–166

E

Eggs
> of chickens, 155–158
> of ducks, 162–163
> Eggs a la Nabocoque, 158

Eliot, T. S., 219

Ericson, Matt
> August harvest, 263
> garlic and, 64–66, 215
> hoophouse and, 127
> May harvest, 178
> November harvest and, 24–25, 28, 41, 45–46, 49
> separating bull from herd, 59–61

transplanting and, 151
Eureka Meat Locker, 61, 109–110
Euripides, 114
Evanston Market, 50, 90, 137, 188, 246–247

F

February, 107–128
    butchering, 107–114
    hoophouse, 123–128
    mushrooms and fungi, 115–119
    wood, 120–123
Fencing pail, 223–227
Field pennycress, 142
Food & Farm Notes, 18–19, 92, 206, 208,
    251–252, 266–267, 298
For-us-es, 216–217, 237, 246, 251, 261, 262
Free-range hens, 156–157
Frost, Robert, 169
Frosty, (cow), 58–59, 147
Fruit Moon (September), 265–282
Fruit trees, 265–270
Fungi, 115–119
Fungicides, 119
Fungus, on corn, 234–235

G

Gailan Miracle recipe, 52
García Márquez, Gabriel, 173
Garlic
    cleaning and braiding, 43–44, 298
    harvesting, 209–212, 215–216
    Joel's Italian Flat Beans with Sweet
        Onion, Garlic, and Maple-Glazed
        Ham, 229
    mulching, 63–67
    planting in fall, 21–29
    Pockets-Full-of-Garlic Soup, 26
    Smashed Garlic Potato Therapy, 213

tending in March, 144
in top 10 crops, 84
varieties, 214
Geotropism, 47
Gibbons, Euell, 138
"Goose Music" (Leopold), 86–87
Grapes, 187–188
Grass Moon (April), 149–166
Green Corn Moon (August), 231–264
Greens
    blanching and freezing, 293
    in fall, 288–292
    harvesting, 251–258
    Sweet Dressing for Spicy Autumn Salad,
        292
    tropism and, 47

H

Harvest Moon (October), 283–301
Harvesting
    in August, 258–264
    in May, 177–179
    in November, 37–53
    in October, 289–290
Heat, 201–202, 245–248
Hecuba (Euripides), 114
Hedge, 120–123
Heliotropism, 47
Henry's Farm
    location of, 17–18
    purchase of, 73–74
Hero Twins, 233–234
Hime (dog), 275
Hoophouse, 123–128
    direct-seeding in, 134–137, 154
    first harvest from, 177
    planting seeds in germination trays,
        129–132

transplanting seedlings, 132–134
Horvath, Tibor, 238
Howard, Clare, 25
Huitlacoche, 234–235
Hunter's Moon (November), 21–61

J

James, Henry, 99, 157
January, 89–105
    freezers and Wassail, 94–97
    grandfather's death, 101–105
    plastic bags, 89–94
    storage, 97–101
Japanese beetles, 220–222
Jefferson, Thomas, 204
Joy (dog), 275
July, 209–230
    beans, 227–230
    fencing pail, 223–227
    garlic, 209–216
    peaches, 216–222
June, 185–208
    berries, 185–190
    chives, 196–198
    heat and rain, 199–202
    peas, 203–208
    potatoes, 190–195

K

Kahan, Paul, 165–166
Kale, Frost-Sweetened with Garlic, recipe, 60
Kaolin clay spray, beetles and, 222
Kennedy, Mary Ellen, 266
Kieffer pear trees, 267–268
Kinoshita, Hiroko, 19, 25
    apples and, 299
    August harvest, 263

basil and, 258
children of, 53
eggs and, 156
meals of, 178, 256
non-farm work of, 39
rhubarb, 178
separating bull from herd, 59–61
sleep mantra of, 50–51
strawberries and, 188
sweet potatoes and, 296
tomato-sorting and, 261
Koetke, Chris, 111
Koko (dog), 144–145, 201
Krutch, Joseph Wood, 245

L

Land Connection, 29, 77
Land ethic, 75–80
Lappe, Marc, 75–76
Leopold, Aldo, 76–77, 79–80, 86–87
Lettuce, 42
Livingstone, David, 248
London, Jack, 75
Long Night Moon (December), 63–88
Love in the Time of Cholera (García Márquez), 173
Lucky Tom turkey, 34–37

M

Mahany, Barbara, 214
Malabar Farm, 254
Malabar spinach, 254–255
Manure, 30–32, 78, 127–128, 142–143, 178
March, 129–147
    calf born, 144–147
    cover crops and early tilling, 141–144
    direct-seeding, 132–137

ramps, 137–141

seed planting, 129–132

May, 167–184

asparagus, 167, 171–175

market preparation and first harvest, 175–179

spring planting, 167–171

weeding, 179–184

Mayan myth of Hero Twins, 233–234

Melons, 248–250

X-Melon Salad with Anise Hyssop, 251

Mesclun, 85, 256

Mestral, George de, 271

Millet, Jean-François, 195

More Home Cooking (Colwin), 162–163

Mulch, 64–67

Mushrooms, 115–119

Sautéed Shiitake Toasts, 117

shiitake spawn, 116–118

Mycelium Running: How Mushrooms Can Help Save the World (Stamets), 115

N

Nabokov, Vladimir, 157–158

New potatoes, 194

November, 21–61

garlic planting, 21–29

harvesting before frost, 37–53

turkeys and, 29–37

Wabi-Sabi season, 53–61

O

October, 283–301

death in family, 283–288

garlic and fruit, 297–301

greens, 288–292

sweet potatoes, 292–297

Okra, 262

Old Moon (January), 89–105

Onions, 151

Onward and Upward in the Garden (White), 67

Organic farming, 78–80

Osage Orange (hedge trees), 120–123

Oxygen radical absorbance capacity (ORAC), 239–240

P

Pandel, Chris, 107

Parsley, 253–254

Peaches

beetles on, 220–222

pesticides on, 219–220

ripeness of, 216–219

Teresa's Simplest Peach Melba, 219

Pears, 267–268, 299

Henry's Autumn Pear Salad, 269

Peas, 203–205

"Waste Not, Want Not" Pea Soup, 207

Pelargonidin, 187

Peppers, 85

Pesticides, on peaches, 219–220

Petrini, Carlo, 53

Pheromone traps, for beetles, 222

Phototropism, 47

Pigments, in plants, 223

Pigs

butchering, 110–114

Chris Pandel's Grandmother's Lazy Pierogies with Fresh Italian Sausage, 112–113

Joel's Italian Flat Beans with Sweet Onion, Garlic, and Honey-Glazed Ham, 229

Pissarro, Camille, 245

Planting Moon (May), 167–184

Plastic bags, 89–94

Potatoes

    Boiled Stolen Potatoes, 193

    harvesting, 44–45, 194–195

    planting, 151, 191–194

    in top 10 crops, 84

    varieties, 190–192

Proust, Marcel, 172–173

Pumpkins, Grandma Henrietta's Pumpkin–Raisin Bars recipe, 286

Purslane, 257

"Putting in the Seed" (Frost), 169

R

Rain, need for, 199–201

Rains Came, The (Bromfield), 255

Ramps, 137–141

    Ramp and Goat Cheese Pasta, 140

Recipes

    Asian Chive Pancakes, 197

    Boiled Stolen Potatoes, 193

    Chris Pandel's Grandmother's Lazy Pierogies with Fresh Italian Sausage, 112–113

    Courtney's Fried Green Tomatoes with Cornmeal and Thyme, 280

    Eggs a la Nabocoque, 158

    Frost Sweetened Kale with Garlic, 60

    Frozen Tomato Sauce, 264

    Frozen Tomatoes, 264

    Gailan Miracle, 52

    Grandma Henrietta's Pumpkin–Raisin Bars, 286

    Green Corn with Marjoram Butter, 236

    Henry's Autumn Pear Salad, 269

    Joel's Italian Flat Beans with Sweet Onion, Garlic, and Maple-Glazed Ham, 229

    Mrs. Takayasu's Kimpira Gobo (Stir-Fried Burdock and Carrots), 274

    Pan-Fried Duck Cracklings, 166

    Pockets-Full-of-Garlic Soup, 26

    Ramp and Goat Cheese Pasta, 140

    Roasted Asparagus with Olive Oil and Balsamic Vinegar, 174

    Roasted Root Vegetables, 100

    Sautéed Shiitake Toasts, 117

    Smashed Garlic Potato Therapy, 213

    Sweet Dressing for Spicy Autumn Salad, 292

    Sweet Potatoes No. 3, Baked in Ashes, 297

    Teresa's Aronia Juice, 242

    Teresa's Priceless Apple Crisp, 87

    Teresa's Simplest Peach Melba, 219

    Traditional Winter Apple Wassail, 96

    X-Melon Salad with Anise Hyssop, 251

    "Waste Not, Want Not" Pea Soup, 207

Rhubarb, 178–179

Rilke, Rainer Maria, 301

Root cellars, 97–99

Root vegetables

    cold and, 41

    Roasted Root Vegetables, 100

    winter storage of, 97–101

Rosaceae family, 185–187

Rose Moon (June), 185–208

S

Sand County Almanac, A (Leopold), 76–77

Santiago, Gabriela, 18, 220–222

Santiago, Teresa Brockman, 17, 29–30, 60, 194–195

    aronia and, 239–244

    bees and, 161–162

    herbs and, 292

Lucky Tom turkey and, 36

potatoes and, 195

quilting and, 183–184

strawberries and, 188–190

writes about apples, 266–267

Sap Moon (February), 107–128

Sauerkraut, 98

Seeds

    direct-seeding in hoophouse, 132–137, 154

    planting in germination trays in hoophouse, 129–132

    planting in spring, 167–171

    seed catalogs, 67–71

    transplanting seedlings, 132–134

September, 265–282

    burdock, 270–274

    farm dogs, 275–278

    fruit trees, 265–270

    passing of time, 279–282

Shakespeare, William, 37, 38, 39, 287–288

Shiitake spawn, 116–118

Shiva, Vandana, 75

Sleep mantra, 50–51

Smith, Joel, 60, 70, 107, 253–254

Solanine, 194

Spence Farm, 137–141

Spinach, 254–255

Stamets, Paul, 115

Storage

    in freezers, 94

    in outdoor pit, 99–101

    in root cellars, 97–99

Summer squashes, 259

Sun, earth's distance from, 209–210

Sweet potatoes, 292–297

    Sweet Potatoes No. 3, Baked in Ashes, 297

Swenson, John, 44, 139

T

Tempest, The (Shakespeare), 287–288

Thunder Moon (July), 209–230

Tilling, early, 142–143

Time, passage of on farm, 71–75, 279–282

"To Build a Fire" (London), 75

Tomatoes

    Courtney's Fried Green Tomatoes with Cornmeal and Thyme, 280

    Frozen Tomato Sauce, 264

    Frozen Tomatoes, 264

    harvesting and sorting of, 259–263

    in hoophouse, 136

    in top 10 crops, 82–83

    varieties, 71

Transplanting, in April, 149–155

Travis, Kris, 137, 139

Travis, Marty, 137–141

Tropisms, 47

Turkey vultures, 252

Turkeys, 29–37

Turnips, 40

V

Van Camp, Jared, 107, 111, 114

Vegetables

    taking to market, 50–53

    temperature and heartiness of, 37–50

    top 10 grown in year, 82–88

Vetch, 142

W

Wabi-Sabi season, 53–61

Wassail, 95–97

"Waste Not, Want Not" Pea Soup, 207

Watermelons, 248–250

    X-Melon Salad with Anise Hyssop, 251

Weeding, in spring, 179–184

Wettstein, Dennis and Emily, 33, 108,
111–114

Wettstein, Larry and Marilyn, 34

Wettstein Organic Farm, 111

White, E. B., 203

White, Katharine, 67

Windy Moon (March), 129–147

"Winnie the Pooh and the Blustery Day"
(Milne), 130

Woolf, Virginia, 75

Wrinkles (dog), 201, 275–277

Y

Yaki-imo man, 296

Yams, 295–296

Z

Zalaznik, David, 25

Zucchini, 259

ABOUT THE AUTHOR

Terra Brockman was raised in central Illinois, where five generations of her family have lived and farmed. She earned a BA in biology and BA and MA degrees in English at Illinois State University, then lived and worked as a teacher, writer, and editor in Japan and New York City for fifteen years, with time out to travel extensively, from Nepal to Eritrea to Morocco to the Baltics. In 2001, she founded The Land Connection, a nonprofit working to save farmland, train new organic farmers, and connect consumers with fresh local foods.

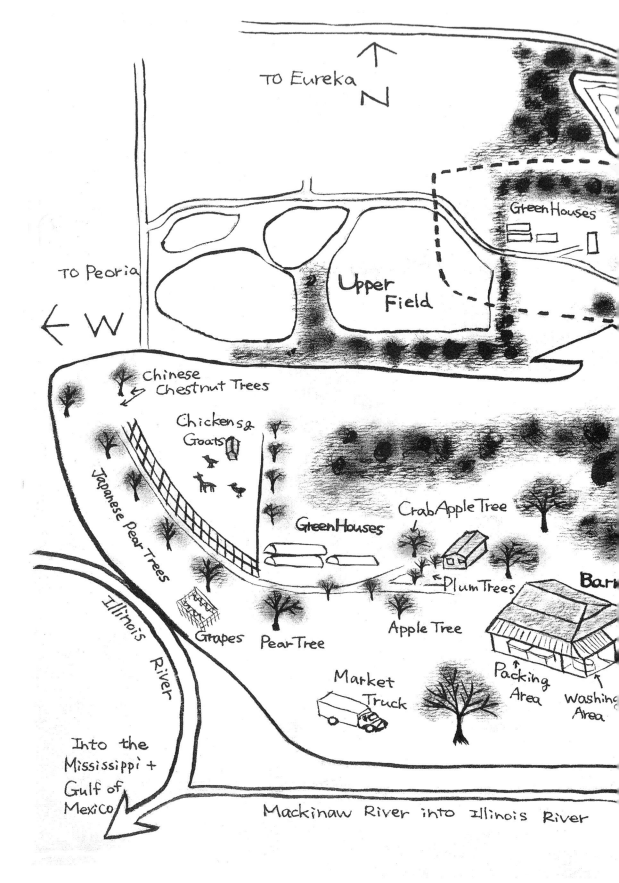

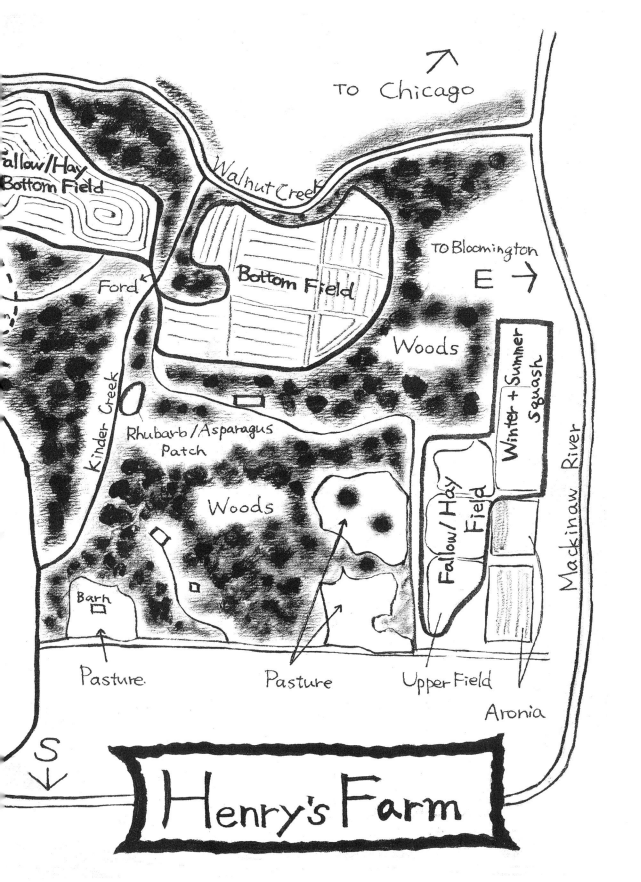